Secret Wisdom

The Occult Universe Explored

David Conway

JONATHAN CAPE
THIRTY-TWO BEDFORD SQUARE LONDON

First published 1985
Copyright © 1985 by David Conway
Jonathan Cape Ltd, 32 Bedford Square, London WC1B 3EL

British Library Cataloguing in Publication Data

Conway, David
Secret wisdom: the occult universe explored.
1. Occult sciences
I. Title
133   BF1411

ISBN 0-224-02992-4

Typeset by Gloucester Typesetting Services
Printed in Great Britain by R. J. Acford, Chichester, Sussex

FOR
E. C. J.

Diddan a fyddo'n dyddiau
Yn unol ddiddidol ddau

Only if we know that what truly matters is the infinite, can we avoid fixing our interests on futilities. In the final analysis we count for something only because of the essential we embody, and if we do not embody that, life is wasted.

C. G. JUNG

Contents

Introduction

The more we discover about the workings of the universe, the more we hesitate to make any statement about them. Nothing, it seems, may be taken for granted, when appearances disguise a reality which, upon closer investigation, turns out to be equally deceptive. No doubt our earliest ancestors found the universe every bit as puzzling and, like us, tried to understand it better, if only to feel a little more at home in it. And, until recently, few doubted that one day the immense puzzle would indeed be solved. Even as late as one hundred years ago, scientists felt confident, almost to the point of smugness, that the solution to the puzzle lay within their grasp. For them, confirming what Democritus had already postulated in 400 BC, the material world in all its rich diversity was ultimately reducible to invisible entities called atoms, often depicted as tiny billiard balls whose interaction proceeded according to certain fixed laws. Once these laws were fully catalogued, it was boasted, every event in the natural world could be predicted with complete accuracy. What had for so long been a puzzle would then reveal itself as a wonderfully intricate machine, its smooth functioning a source of welcome reassurance to those who observed it and were themselves part of its efficient operation.

Sadly, this comforting world view ceased to be tenable once Lord Rutherford demonstrated that the atom, far from being indivisible, was a composite entity whose constitution resembled less a simple billiard ball than an erratic game of sub-atomic snooker. To the smallest unit in this game the name 'elementary particle' was tentatively given, though it soon became evident that while an elementary particle behaved like a particle for some of the time, for the rest it transformed itself into a flow of energy, obliging scientists to speak of the 'complementarity' of its nature, part corpuscle, part wave. The study of this complementarity belongs to the field of wave mechanics where, in order to resolve the duality just mentioned, the particle aspect of elementary particles is said to manifest itself at specific points along the path of a wave. For us observers, however, these specific points are thoroughly unspecific, since, try as we might, we cannot identify them with any degree of certainty. As a result, scientists have concluded, not without reluctance, that a fundamental uncertainty characterises the entire behaviour of elementary particles, whose frequent contempt for law and order — even the law of cause and effect — means that, in the snooker game just referred to, it is the balls themselves that make up the rules.

The answer to the puzzle begins to look alarmingly like another puzzle even more perplexing than the first. Small wonder, then, that in frustration many people put aside their curiosity and resolutely get on with the day-to-day business of living, or that others substitute faith for imperfect knowledge and accept as revealed truth whatever comprehensive answers are provided by religion. There are still others, however, who find that the puzzle will not leave them alone, prompting them to ask the same age-old questions about the world and their part in it, questions which may be more urgent than ever now that we have at our disposal the means of destroying most, if not all, forms of life on our planet. The risk we currently face is not that the puzzle may cease to exist, but that no one will be left around to solve it.

The sense of urgency to which this gives rise may explain the recent spate of books on how, according to our present state of knowledge, the universe appears to function and how man, the 'naked ape' of popular anthropology, fits into the overall pattern. Faced with these disclosures, religion has, generally speaking, chosen to ignore them, even to make a defensive distinction between its own metaphysical concerns and the materialistic preoccupations of physics and biology. Any such distinction is, of course, artificial, given that our actual world is as much God's creation as the next one and that scientists investigating the nature of matter already trespass in the hallowed realm of metaphysics. It is true that a few churchmen, aware of this, have endeavoured to restate their doctrinal position in terms which do not conflict with the findings of science. The fact, however, that they have a doctrinal position to defend usually means that the 'how' proposed by science ends up discreetly tailored to fit the 'how' of theological dogma.

Strangely, in examining the 'how', nobody in either camp has addressed fully the question, 'why'. Yet this is the very question which the urgency of our times leads us to ask. Young people in particular desire to understand what the whole caboodle is about – not just how it works – and their search is one for meaning rather than mechanics. It is a search that has led many of them away from established religion, as well as from science and, not infrequently, reason itself. Many have turned to the East, if not for enlightenment then at least for peace of mind, while others, closer to home, paddle in muddy occult waters, later emerging wet-footed but not a jot wiser than when they began.

This is a pity, because occultism of an unmuddy sort, provided one can find it, does offer an explanation of both the universe and human life which covers the why no less than the how. Remarkably, the same explanation, though almost as old as humankind, anticipates much of what science now assures us to be true, and, moreover, invests it with a meaning whose validity we can judge for ourselves. The task I have set myself in writing this book is to present the occult view – its why and its how – as transparently as I can.

Three difficulties make the task especially daunting. The first is that occultism has no book in which its tenets are enshrined, though one of its best-known apologists, Mme Blavatsky, did claim access to an ancient volume ('The Stanzas of Dzyan') which, with others, formed part of a secret collection hidden away in the mountain fastness of Tibet. Instead, occultism is a diffuse and arcane tradition that has been passed down through generations of initiates in a kind of apostolic succession which the average person may find as hard to accept as Mme Blavatsky's hidden library beyond the Himalayas. That there have always existed beliefs which, being concealed from the profane, merit the adjective 'occult' is nevertheless a historical fact. All ancient civilisations had their Mysteries, those of Greece spring at once to mind, and, as any Freemason will tell you, the tendency has endured to this day. The exact content of the Mysteries is, appropriately enough, unknown to historians and scholars, though it may be partly inferred from hints given here and there or from the writings of the neo-Platonists and Gnostics. Towards the end of the nineteenth century many of these fragments were reassembled and made public by Mme Blavatsky, the value of her synthesis unaffected by the accusations of trickery and fraud which, as we shall see later, were levelled against her on other grounds. Blavatsky's successors, among them Rudolf Steiner (1861–1925), were to continue the trend set by her, and reference to their writings will be made from time to time. Even so, occult tradition, living up to its name, still stays largely secret and cannot be inspected at leisure in the various -isms, -ologies and -osophies that claim to represent it, most of them also claiming exclusive rights to its possession. It is, rather,

something to be learnt from one's own private experience, often by meeting, as happened in my case, an individual, as sane as the rest of us, who is
privy to its doctrines and, more important, is willing to divulge them. (On
this I shall have more to say later.) My first difficulty therefore is that in
presenting occult teachings, many of them for the first time, I am denied
the comfort of authoritative source material to which the reader may be
conveniently referred.

My second difficulty is that occultism, however popular, enjoys little
real respect in the contemporary world. Associated with fortune-telling,
claustrophobic seance rooms, black magic and even flying saucers, it is
taken seriously only by novelists and film-makers astute enough to realise
that nothing pleases the public more than to be scared out of its wits.
Neither have the many books written on the topic, nor, worse, the utter-
ances of whichever spoon-bender, witch-queen or extra-terrestrial voyager
happens to be in fashion, done much to help the occult case. Still less have
they helped promote the open-mindedness which is necessary if the views
expressed in this book are to receive the unprejudiced consideration I
believe they deserve.

I am profoundly convinced that in tackling the universal puzzle from
the occult point of view, its why and how, not to mention its whence and
whither, will begin to make sense, providing the explanation many people
are seeking. To show that this explanation merits serious attention and is
not just pie-in-the-sky, I shall, in the next few pages, first of all examine
what scientists, more informed in these matters than any occult theorist,
have to say about the origins of the phenomenal world and, since we
belong to it, also of ourselves. Drawing conclusions from this information,
I shall then trace the progress of humankind since its first beginnings to
the threshold of recorded history, seeing on the way whether the occult
version of events can be reconciled with the findings of the relevant
experts. Having demonstrated, I hope, that the theories of occultism are
not incompatible with those of science whenever both relate to a common
field of inquiry, I shall at last venture into fields that science has yet to
discover. In so doing, it is important not to lose sight of scientific method
or of common sense, though the certainties that await us may require us
to dispense with the first and adapt the latter to suit them. To bring us to
that point, to occultism proper, is my ultimate aim. To realise it is the
third and greatest of my difficulties.

I

Universe,
Matter
and Mind

There's something in a flying horse,
There's something in a huge balloon;

WORDSWORTH, *Peter Bell*, Prologue 1.1

We live in an expanding universe. On that scientists, observing the behaviour of galaxies, are able to agree. What they cannot agree upon is the cause of this expansion. According to some, it was a vast primordial explosion. The 'big bang' theory based on that view supposes that the galaxies now in recession were at some remote time compressed into a single dense unit, so infinitesimally small and compact that extremely high temperatures at its core provoked the explosion by which the universe came into being. Others suggest that the ubiquitous expansion now taking place occurs because matter itself is being continuously created throughout space, the universe thereby remaining in a steady state. The truth of this rival suggestion might be confirmed if it could be shown that the density of matter throughout the universe, in spite of the expansion, stays forever constant, but information so far acquired from the study of quasars tends on the whole to disprove this.

What radio-astronomy does reveal is that our universe may once have been far denser than it is now. That it also had a beginning is suggested by the general absence from space of heat and light, two commodities that would pervade the whole of interstellar space had the hot stars whose radiation generates both been active over an infinite period. That the universe may likewise have an end is suggested by the probability that gravitational forces prevail throughout space, unchecked by any opposing force of cosmic repulsion. From this it follows that if the amount of distributed matter were right, the current expansion would gradually decelerate and eventually come to a halt. (The process may be compared, at the risk of seeming flippant, with the inflation of a giant balloon which continues to grow until the person blowing into it runs out of breath.) Meanwhile, it should be borne in mind that this expansion involves space as well as matter, there being no question of matter expanding *into* pre-existing — and therefore extra-universal — space. The fact is that absolute space cannot exist on its own.

When the expansion of the universe finally comes to a halt, it is thought that an inverse process of contraction is likely to follow. This may involve either a sudden 'implosion', with everything that earlier flew outwards sucked back to its source at high speed, not unlike the violent formation of a boundless black hole, or else a more gradual process leading ultimately to the same result. If the second of these, then matter and space might contract at the speed they previously expanded, continuing over millions of years until such time as the original super-dense state had been recovered. Such a contraction is especially hard for us to imagine because the likelihood is that it would entail a reversal, as in a film played backwards, of the order to which we are accustomed: rivers would flow uphill, pudding be served before soup, and the child, literally, would be father of the man. To those experiencing a reverse order of this kind, such a sequence would doubtless seem quite normal, for their own thinking would similarly function in reverse, a notion not as far-fetched as it may sound since even today scientists working in the field of quantum physics have had to adjust their thinking to a sub-atomic world where time has a perverse habit of running backwards as well as forwards, practising, as it were, for the day when regression becomes the universal rule.

Whatever the conditions likely to accompany this eventual contraction — and it would be futile to speculate on them further — the clear implication is that our universe moves through successive periods of evolution and involution, obeying a law of periodicity inherent in its very constitution. Already, modern physics has admitted the same and, by means of the so-called ergodic theorem, demonstrated that whatever state the universe may occupy at a particular moment, it will subsequently pass in a given sequence through all other possible states before returning to its starting point. But even without theorems of this sort, our own experience enables us to confirm that a rhythmic law is in operation all round us, in the succession of day and night, in the passage of the seasons and in those recurring cycles through which all life, including our own, inevitably passes. On a far grander scale and over vast aeons of time, the universe itself oscillates between phases of expansion and contraction, as if slowly breathing out and breathing in like some awesome cosmic being. Such precisely is the image used in occult tradition to illustrate the centrifugal and centripetal phases the universe traverses, its source found in Hindu scripture where the name pravritti is given to the outward gust of breath that brings new worlds into being (sristi), and nivritti to the great inhalation that bears them all back to the quiescence, called pralaya, from which they emerged. On this matter science and occultism stand united, even if science took a great deal longer to get there.

This periodic oscillation in no way contradicts the theory, favoured by the majority of scientists, that the universe resulted from an initial big bang, but it does imply that the bang responsible for our present universe was only the latest in a series of bangs, each bringing into dynamic existence a new universe that developed up to a certain point and then retreated into itself. Strictly speaking, of course, none of the successive universes thus formed, except perhaps the first, if ever there was one, can be described as totally new, for it is clear that each shared the same antique fund of elementary particles with all of its predecessors. This being so, we may confidently assume that the appearance of our universe did not mark the beginning of time, as may once have been thought, but was itself an event that occurred within time, an event that compels us to suppose a cosmic prehistory which science, as yet, knows nothing whatever about.

At this point, with countless universes been and gone before us, and plenty of new ones ahead, we are bound to ask the question whether the whole process – and not, this time, our present universe alone – ever had a beginning. Upon our answer will depend whether we can take the universe for granted, a totality which was, is and will be always, and not worry further about where it came from, or whether, having endowed it with a commencement, we need to consider the possibility of an outside agent responsible for bringing it into being out of nothing. The first answer, because it assumes that the universe, like Topsy, just 'growed', is by far the easier one to live with. The second, in contrast, leads us straight to the problem of God.

For those who opt for the easier answer, God must seem a problem of our own foolish making. We have, they would urge, only to defer to the findings of science – and God is not among them – for the problem, denied sustenance, to disappear at once. To accept such advice, however, is to accept also that science, with its reliance on experimental proof, is the sole arbiter of what is and is not, what can and cannot be. This privilege may rightly belong to it in those areas of investigation that lie within its competence, as for instance when it identifies and measures the constituent parts of the universe so as to fit them within a manageable, if not always comprehensible, framework. But the problem of whether there exists a transcendental being, both external and prior to the raw material science deals with, is one that necessarily lies outside its scope. And that is not enough to make the problem go away.

Neither, to be frank, is reason much help to us in solving the problem, though pious minds have in the past appealed to it, arguing principally that our universe, being an effect, requires its own antecedent cause. Some have even argued that the notion of a supreme cause is itself sufficient proof that such a cause exists, while others have admiringly cited the design and purpose apparent throughout the universe as visible evidence of a wise and powerful creator. All of which is very comforting, were it not that reason turns out to be a fickle advocate and readily allows itself to be used to refute the selfsame arguments it earlier consented to sponsor.

It was Aristotle who argued that as each effect must have a cause, then there exists somewhere outside the universe a first cause – called the unmoved Prime Mover – which is God. It is, however, questionable whether the act of creation which brought the universe into being out of nothing is strictly comparable with the sequences of cause and effect observable in existing forms of matter. Moreover, the discovery from observing the behaviour of elementary particles that the law of cause and effect is not universally valid removes the whole basis of Aristotle's argument. Perhaps the philosopher Leibniz suspected as much – for Epicurus had predicted it nearly two thousand years earlier[1] – when towards the end of the seventeenth century he restated the argument in terms of contingency. Everything in the world, he maintained, is contingent upon something else, with nothing that exists containing sufficient reasons for its own independent existence: left to themselves things might just as easily not be, as be. Accordingly, the universe must have a reason external to itself on which it, too, is contingent. This reason Leibniz called God. It was Kant who demolished this argument a generation later by pointing out that the external reason advanced as an unavoidable proposition to account for the real existence of the universe was no more than a concept whose own existence depended only on reason, and not on direct and immediate experience.

Much the same objection might be made to the second argument put forward by reason to prove God's existence. Its basic premise, summed up

in the eleventh century by St Anselm, himself the most rational of theologians, is that God is 'that than which nothing greater can ever be thought
of', a premise later adopted by Descartes and Leibniz who like St Anselm
proceeded to argue that something which exists not only as a concept but
also outside the mind that holds it, has necessarily to be greater than something which exists in the mind alone. From this, they maintained, it could
not but follow that the existence of the concept of God was itself adequate
confirmation of God's real and objective existence. Again, the indefatigable
Kant soon made short work of this by pointing out that existence cannot
be treated as if it were a mere attribute like greatness or goodness. While
any concept may be legitimately invested with a variety of attributes, he
argued, these do not include the possibility of objective existence. It is
thus dishonest to seek to derive the reality of God's existence from the
proposition that God is the highest object of human thought.

The third argument which appeals to reason in support of the existence
of God, and which in fact is older than the previous two, is one that rests
its case on the design and purpose discernible in the natural world. It
enjoyed a revival in the eighteenth century when it was adopted by the
deists, who were fond of comparing the universe with a giant clock which a
divine clockmaker had wound up at the dawn of time and left to tick away
ever since. The same image was also popular among theists, except that
they insisted that the divine clockmaker ceaselessly attended to his creation, keeping it fully wound up and forever tinkering with the works. In
this case it was David Hume, the eighteenth-century founder of pheno-
menalism, who dismantled the clock and dismissed its putative maker,
showing how in reasoning backwards one should never credit a supposed
cause with any attributes not already present in the observed effect. Thus
although we might be tempted to credit a designer with the apparent
design in nature, nothing there allows us then to credit that designer with
omnipotence or even benevolence. On the contrary, the misery and suffering attendant on all forms of life suggest that neither term is appropriate.
What Hume could not know, though we now do, is that evolution involves
too many false starts and failures to suggest infallibility — even its successes
appear often to be only the products of chance.

Although it seems clear from all this that the problem of God cannot be
resolved by science or the exercise of reason, it would be rash to conclude,
as did Napoleon's astronomer, Laplace, after scanning the sky through a
telescope, that no God exists. The most we might venture to say is that
proof of his existence, of the kind we normally require to determine what
is real or true, is not at our disposal. We should bear in mind, however,

that the standards of proof familiar to us are proper only to the particular reality, set in time and space, of which we and all else within our common experience are part. God, as begetter of that reality, must consequently transcend it and, by so doing, transcend likewise all the knowledge we derive from it. By his nature therefore he remains unknowable, not least because human thought lacks the wherewithal to include, let alone comprehend, the sovereign wholeness of a higher, transcendent being.

Even the Catholic Church, despite its belief that God has revealed himself to humanity in a special way, acknowledges that he is essentially unknowable and beyond mortal understanding, an attribute formally recognised at the Fourth Lateran Council in 1215 and later confirmed in a text from the First Vatican Council (1869–70) which begins: 'There is one living God, Creator and Lord of Heaven and Earth, omnipotent, eternal, immense and incomprehensible, infinite in intellect and will and in every perfection.' Eastern thinkers would regard such a wordy definition as going too far, since for most of them the incomprehensibility of God allows of no other predicate, however lofty and fitting our private speculation considers it to be. The *Mandukya Upanishad*, for instance, bluntly states that God is 'unknowable and unthinkable' and leaves it at that. Elsewhere, the teachings of Vedanta refer to him briefly as 'That One' (Tat Ekam), a transcendent deity similar to that found in Plato's *Republic* or to the self-existent Absolute encountered in the musings of the neo-Platonists, conceivable only by way of the *via negativa*, that is, by describing what God is *not* ('immortal', 'infinite', 'boundless', etc.) rather than what he might be. Again it is the East, ever scrupulous, that shows most consistency in the matter by simply calling God 'Nothing', meaning by this that God, being featureless (nirguna), excludes all predicates, even negative ones such as non-existence, the whole summed up in the famous Upanishadic formula '*Neti, neti*' ('not this, not this').

This divine nothingness (ahava), it is as well to understand, does not imply an absolute nothing or the negation of everything (itself a pseudo-concept in that it assumes a positive ground) but instead an absence of *something*, as would happen for instance if we were to state that a particular object, let us say a British pillar box, is 'not red', but then neglect to state what other colour – blue, white, yellow, etc. – the pillar box really is. All we have maintained in a statement of this kind is that a given object lacks a certain attribute: redness (the correlate of non-redness) in the case of our pillar box; existence (the correlate, in so far as it may be considered an attribute, of non-existence) in the case of God. But the fact that non-existence can admit such a correlate and, as a result, be defined and particularised, at once makes it impossible to equate it with absolute nothingness. In denying existence to God, therefore, and calling him 'Nothing', the oriental thinker does not intend for one second to call into question the fact that God *is*. This same tendency, which often seems paradoxical to Western minds, is found in Buddhist, as well as Hindu, teaching, particularly in that of the Madhyamika school which variously speaks of God as neither 'is' nor 'is not', as 'both is and is not' and 'neither is nor is not', a technique developed further in Zen Buddhism whose disciples aspire to gain access to a realm of thought where such seeming contradictions, existing coincidentally, are happily resolved.

By now it may appear that God, the unknowable, is not unlike a hyper-cosmic version of the algebraic x that was meant to solve (but in my case never did) those troublesome equations encountered in our mathematics class at school. Indeed, some thinkers of the Upanishadic period, acknowledging the irresolvable nature of the problem, suggest that God's existence be given the benefit of the doubt simply because it provides a workable hypothesis to explain the origin of the universe. Interestingly enough, in Hinduism the begetter of that universe receives the name of Brahman (literally 'self-existent power'), which is derived from the Sanskrit root 'brh', meaning to expand – so at last we are back with the expanding universe we started from.

So lofty and sublime is speculation of this sort about a divine being – almost a state of permanent godness – outside the universe, uncontaminated by all mundane concepts, that we might wonder how something (or, to be more Eastern, nothing) so transcendent, undivided and incapable of change, could ever bring about the self-contained, heterogeneous and mutable universe we live in. The answer lies in that very completeness which is essential to the perfection of God and which means that self-existence is always accompanied by self-knowledge, the concomitant of consciousness. In other words, there obtains within God a mode of self-awareness, so absolutely and really identical with its own intrinsic being – in, of and by itself – that God remains unchanged because of it. From this self-awareness there emerges, according to the *Vedas*, an effulgence of cosmic light (Hiranyagarbha) which the neo-Platonists call Universal Mind (νοῦς). The original static and transcendent Oneness thus gave rise to a 'becoming' in which there flourished the duality which all discursive thought, made up of thesis and antithesis, necessarily contains. This duality, according to the neo-Platonists (who could never resist inventing sequences and hierarchies), manifests itself as a third hypostasis which they call the universal soul (ψυχή), by which Mind is able to give material expression to its thoughts in and through the universe, where – to use contemporary terms – it imposes 'form' (εἶδος) on elementary particles (ὕλη) which, left to themselves, would remain formless, indiscrete and undetermined, i.e. all wave and no particle. So, to sum up by reverting to the language of the *Vedas*, the action of infinite spirit (aditi) sets in motion the sensible world within the mode of time (kala). In this way it is the universal spirit, quintessence of multiple reality, that links all material things with their intelligible ground, its thoughts differentiating the whole, and themselves constituting the whole.

We have thus traced the progressive emergence of the universe from the self-awareness of the One, a self-awareness so directly related to its own subsistent, non-dualistic self that the 'twoness' resulting from it is consecutive to – and in no way constitutive of – the awareness thus acquired. Aristotle succinctly reconciled the identity of the One, as subject of thought, and the Universal Spirit, as its object, by stating that God, as pure act and immutable life, thinks himself, being thought of his own thought. All very well, some sceptical reader may protest, but the act of becoming which self-awareness produced, ending up with the world as we find it, must nevertheless have added something to God's nature, an 'accident' as the Scholastics would say, itself the carrier of such undivine attributes as contingency and finitude. This would certainly be the case, were the relationship between God and the world dependent on the reality of the world, thereby depriving God of his independence from all that is not himself. As we have noted, however, the universe is neither a presupposition of this relationship nor a real factor in its establishment, but the object of an act of self-awareness freely and purposefully exercised by its subject. Moreover, if freedom whether to know or not to know himself is one of God's intrinsic perfections, then no less perfect is the eternal exercise of that freedom in favour of knowledge, the result of which is the appearance of the universe, the outward and visible expression of the real.

A failure to think this through rigorously, caused perhaps by undue emphasis on the inviolable, immutable Oneness of God *despite* the 'becoming' which, resulting from his self-awareness, brought the universe into being, has led thinkers in the past to regard the derivative as inferior to its source. This tendency was noticeable among the neo-Platonists – and much regretted centuries later by Goethe, whose temperament was otherwise sympathetic to their ideas – and prompted Plotinus to describe matter as 'the primary evil', an antipathy shared by the Manicheans and others. Some have attempted to restore the God-created world to a proper state of grace by claiming, as do the Christian Scientist followers of Mrs

Baker Eddy, that evil is only imaginary; while in the East the idealists of the Vijnana-vada school of Mahayana Buddhism have always insisted that the world itself has no objective reality at all. More general throughout the East is the notion of maya or illusion which, at first sight, seems also to deny that the world is objectively real. Closer examination shows, however, that, like all illusion, the true source of maya lies in ourselves and not in what we observe: it is we who, seeing a woman's head sticking out from one end of a trunk and, across the stage, her feet sticking out from the other, believe that the conjuror's assistant has really been sawn in two. What maya really consists of is ignorance (avidya) of the ultimate reality to which the material world bears witness, a failure on our part to recognise the *relative* character of the world, as an element in Brahman: it is to see the lady sawn in half and forget about the conjuror. One of the practical aims of occult teaching is to encourage its followers to recognise maya in order to view the world correctly for what it is, a state of enlightenment which Hinduism calls jnana. In spite of maya, therefore, the world is not to be disdained, especially since having proceeded from the reality of God, it must, as the teaching of Bhartripapanca makes plain, partake of that reality, though manifesting it in a different way: as a product of God's self-awareness, it cannot but reflect a true image of its real subject, for anything less would be deception – and God would not deceive himself in the act of self-cognisance.

Frankly, it has to be admitted that although philosophical speculation – and occasional double-speak – on the nature of God and the emergence of the universe may afford a certain intellectual satisfaction to those who indulge in it, rarely does it produce in any of us an immediate, personal awareness of the reality it purports to describe. Earlier, I put forward the thesis that to know, let alone understand, what God is (perhaps to know *whether* he is) may lie beyond our limited human capacity, yet unless we 'experience' God, however imperfectly, all the philosophising in the world remains of academic interest only. Were that the case, we would have done better to opt from the outset for the easy answer mentioned on page 3, thus avoiding the problem of God altogether.

Fortunately, there is at hand evidence to suggest that direct experience of God may be available to us, since we have at our disposal not only the intellectual resources that animate science and reason but other faculties, among them feeling and intuition, which may be still better suited to the task. The Dutch philosopher Spinoza (1632–77), whose thinking was normally governed by reason alone, once admitted that in the search for the Absolute, such thinking was not sufficient but had to be illumined and reinforced by feeling. The same had been discovered centuries earlier by the Flemish mystic Jan van Ruysbroek (1293–1381), who declared that 'we must go forward towards God with our feeling, above reason', advice later echoed by St Bernard of Clairvaux, who distinguished between what he called 'consideration' and the 'contemplation' made possible by what others have called 'the eye of the heart'. None of these writers, it should be noted, pleaded for the abandonment of reason. Rather, each posited a state beyond acquired knowledge in which discursive thought might be transformed into a kind of immediate knowing, a fusion of reason and feeling which in the language of mysticism has been called the *amor intellectus Dei* and which enables the truth to be grasped unhesitatingly.

Confirmation, meanwhile, comes from the testimony, all of it remarkably consistent, of the numerous individuals who have enjoyed this experience in the past but who, that apart, seem no different from the rest of us. Transcending our everyday world of sense-impressions and of thinking, feeling and willing, these pioneers of the spirit have *lived* what others theorise about, have entered into that realm of ideas which Plato proclaims in his *Republic*, that 'intelligible world' (as the neo-Platonists call it) in which there shines a light that never changes. Their case, we have seen, rests not on logic but on life, a fact that, once realised, persuaded the great St Thomas Aquinas to lay down his pen and write nothing more. He, too, had discovered, beyond the limits of linear thought (Plato's διάνοιᾰ), a kind of creative contemplation, thanks to which the finite world may disclose to our mind's eye its true nature as the self-expression of the One or, as the unknown author of the *Cloud of Unknowing* more succinctly put it, thanks to which God 'may be gotten and holden'. For our present purpose, however, let us keep our unmystical feet firmly planted on the ground and, appropriately enough, proceed to examine what that ground consists of, an exercise to which science, not metaphysics, has the largest contribution to make. Its language, mercifully, will be rather less recondite as well!

We have seen that the material universe consists of agglomerations of elementary particles as variable in size and complexity as the requirement of stability enables them to be. Responsible for their loose cohesion are four types of force, all produced by primary agents known as 'gauge' particles and, at source, perhaps one and the same. The first of them, gravitational force, was discovered by Newton and later re-interpreted by Einstein as part of his general theory of relativity. It is believed to occur because the existence of matter causes space to curve, one result being that each particle of matter exerts a gravitational attraction on all the rest. Whole galaxies, it is thought, were formed because competing gravitational forces inside dense concentrations of matter caused individual stars to break off and hurtle into space, the same force later causing them to contract until a point was reached where other powerful forces, this time nuclear, awoke deep inside them. Two such nuclear forces have been identified, the one labelled strong, the other weak, and both collaborate in the subtle organisation of matter. To the strong kind falls the important task of binding together protons and neutrons – the so-called nucleons – which comprise an atomic nucleus. These nuclei, their complexity still not fully understood, are by disposition stable – which is why they become radioactive, shedding excess nucleons in an effort to maintain their equilibrium, whenever their stability is threatened, for example by the disruptive influence of a fourth force, known as the electromagnetic force. As its name suggests, this derives from the electrical charges, themselves a mystery to science, which operate, sometimes positively (giving rise to protons) and at others negatively (giving rise to electrons), inside every atom, their influence on the number and behaviour of its nucleons and electrons having an important role to play in the basic structure of the universe.

Research has shown that atomic nuclei produced by strong nuclear interaction are positively charged and, because of the rule that like charges repel and unlike attract, their constituent protons ensure that around them swarms a crowd of negatively charged electrons. It is when the opposing charges are exactly in balance that atoms are formed, though to survive intact they require cool conditions. Because such conditions are absent inside large dense bodies such as stars, where extremely high temperatures are found, so much jostling takes place among the close-packed nuclei that the attendant electrons are thrown into utter confusion. Before long all this activity provokes an explosion in which nuclei of all kinds and disorientated electrons are flung out into space, an event reminiscent of the primordial explosion – the big bang – which scientists credit with the formation of the universe. What then happens is that the dispersed nuclei and the homeless electrons encounter one another during their exile in space and, thanks to electro-magnetic forces, re-combine in these cooler surroundings to produce neutral atoms, which in turn react among themselves to form molecules. At that stage their own gravitational force attracts to them clusters of stray molecules and the lot of them later succumb to the gravitational field of a larger body – maybe a nearby star – around which they circle, eventually combining to form larger bodies which, as planets, orbit around the central star. This is one, though only one, of the ways in which the solar system, of which our Earth is a planet, may have been produced.

The scope for combination, diversification and growth available to the hundred or so atoms thus formed is limited only by their paramount need for stability, hence the wide variety of substances found on the surface of the earth. One of these, carbon, possesses an atomic structure far more complex than the rest, so much so that it is able to persuade carbonaceous molecules to form ever larger and more intricate structures without becoming unstable as a result. By this process, involving an exchange of properties between matter and energy, the organisation of matter is able to acquire a durability which, barring cosmic accidents like the collision of two stars, persists for long periods of time. It is to this end that matter may, literally, be said to direct its energies, its static appearance concealing a micro-structure which is a tireless whirr of frenetic activity. The temptation is strong to describe it as being alive, but the peculiar quality which, by common consent, betrays the presence of life is not yet manifest in it. Nevertheless, it would be to contradict the rules of evolution, according to which no new characteristic may emerge unless previously latent, were we not to concede that the activity intrinsic to matter is an indication of the life already dormant inside it.

So much – and it is a great deal – do we learn about matter from science. So much and no more. For once again science, which earlier disdained to concern itself with the source of the universe, becomes correspondingly reticent about the source of the energy flows and elementary particles that help to furnish space. Instead, science has busied itself observing a tiny fraction of the universal process, and from that deducing universal laws, without, of course, being able to guarantee that these laws are universally valid throughout space and time. Further than this it refuses to venture.

For although few scientists would nowadays admit it, they, like their nineteenth-century predecessors, still yearn for a universe that functions, however quirkily, like a great machine, the whole apparatus subject to laws which are of general application – the occasional exceptions doing no more than confirming the rule. This at once renders the world a more comfortable place in which to live, with knowledge removing from our environment the myriad uncertainties which, so anthropologists are fond of maintaining, led our primitive ancestors to invent the concept of God. But, as we have seen, the more scientists discover about the workings of matter, the more grounds for uncertainty there are. Elementary particles, for instance, are liable to mock the laws of causality and produce effects that precede their causes or else provoke causes without effects and vice-versa. So elusive is their behaviour that even their identity is hard to establish at any given time, while their past and their future are known only to themselves. To try to make sense of some of this, we are forced to rely on statistical probabilities, in the hope that a large enough sample of elementary particles will, on the basis of past observation, behave in such and such a way, though sudden rebellion can never be ruled out. At the end of the day, Einstein's famous equation $E = Mc^2$ may turn out to have been a gross over-simplification of the facts.

A true understanding of these facts, it now seems probable, may require a complete reappraisal by us of our current notions concerning space and time. Only then will it be possible to accommodate the observed properties of matter within the sort of conceptual framework science likes so much. Present evidence, meanwhile, suggests that the universe contains an indeterminacy – not quite a capriciousness, more a wilful independence – which can be adequately expressed only in terms of mentation. This may not provide a rational justification for the theological apologetics summarised in previous pages but, as stated there, in matters of this kind reason may not have the final word. Ironically, it is not a theologian but a physicist, Sir James Jeans, who said, 'The stream of knowledge is leading towards a non-mechanical reality; the universe begins to look more like a great thought than like a great machine.'[2] Today, a new generation of scientists would have no compunction about voicing their agreement, with those among them who believe the cosmos to be a closed system going on to argue that only the mentation which underlies matter – the great thought just mentioned – permits our universe to escape the heat death, leading to total entropy, to which the second law of thermo-dynamics would otherwise condemn it. Should we then silence common sense when it whispers to us that great thoughts come only from great thinkers? It would seem, alas, that science, far from sticking to the easy answer, has itself brought us back to the problem of God.

We need not stay with the problem for long, since science regains its confidence once it turns its attention to the emergence of life from inorganic matter. Here, after all, it can for the first time limit its investigation to our own small planet. It may be that life exists elsewhere in the universe – and the statistical probability, estimated (for the benefit of those to whom it makes sense) at between 10^7 and 10^{20},[3] is said to be in its favour– but, if it does, we know nothing about it.

What happened on Earth is that millions of years ago, certain chemical sequences, based on carbon, set about producing long chains – polymers–

which, thanks to cross linkages and other accidental relationships —
achieved a high degree of complexity. Among these were what we call
proteins, made up of carbonaceous derivatives of ammonia (amino-acids)
and capable of organising themselves in a vast number of ways. One such
combination, augmented by a group of substances called nucleic acids,
resulted in the formation of nucleo-proteins and these, we are reliably
informed, were the starting point of life.

At this point it is useful to consider what is meant by 'life'. What science
basically understands by the term is the power of self-replication. Thus at
a certain moment in the world's prehistory, there occurred a happy
conjunction of chemical conditions, both inside the nucleo-protein and in
its environment, the result being that it began for the first time to replicate
itself. And having once acquired the knack of doing so, it and its progeny
continued to reorganise themselves from their own resources, unlike
previously when new structures were due to the combination of disparate
elements. Admittedly, the transition from one method to the other is not
yet fully understood since the origin of the process by which the parent
cell transmits its characteristics to its offspring remains tantalisingly
unclear. On the other hand, it is now known that the actual mechanics
involve a genetic code preserved in deoxyribonucleic acid (DNA) which a
second acid (ribonucleic acid or RNA) delivers to each new generation of
cells. The only snag is that the production of DNA depends on proteins
which, for their part, depend on DNA for their own production, a chicken
and egg situation that recently prompted some scientists, including
Francis Crick, joint-discoverer of DNA, to suggest that the first germs of
life may not have originated on earth but have come here from outer space.
Another theory has also been put forward, based on the observation of a
process similar to the self-replication of nucleo-proteins that takes place
in inorganic matter, notably in the formation of crystals.[4] Until not long
ago, it was believed that the essential difference between the two processes
is that in every new generation, wherever located, each crystal was, like
its parent, a perfect replica of all other crystals, while the offspring of
nucleo-proteins are a very mixed bunch indeed. It is now claimed, however, that the uniformity of crystalline forms may not be the universal
rule, since certain clay crystals have been found to vary occasionally, with
slight differences or defects transmissible from one generation to the next.
From the chemical changes involved, both proteins and DNA may once
have emerged together, ready to undertake the co-operation needed to
ensure the self-replication of living cells. In other words, the life we earlier
supposed to be dormant in inorganic matter may already manifest itself

in a rudimentary form of organic chemistry which is the precursor to life as it is defined by science.

Even if this theory were true, however, one can talk glibly about the transition from nucleo-proteins to simple living cells (albeit consisting of millions of molecules) only by overlooking intermediate stages whose details remain undetected. And undetected they will doubtless stay for some time, given that conditions on and around the earth during its infancy no longer prevail. We may allow ourselves to speculate about the erstwhile composition of the earth's atmosphere or the effects of ultraviolet radiation on inorganic matter – we may even reproduce those conditions in the laboratory – but for the moment the secret of life hovers undiscovered on the frontier between physics and biology. Less of a secret is the subsequent development of the earliest cell forms, particularly the mechanism of their self-replication, called mitosis, and involving the separation of two entwined strands of chromosomes, a division of their common nucleus, and finally a splitting of the cell into two complete cells. Unlike inorganic matter which was primarily intent on increasing its molecular complexity, the tiny cell strives after stability and endurance, bearing inside it what scientists are obliged to call 'the will to survive'. There science stops short. It is left to us either to do the same or ask ourselves whether this will to survive does not confirm our earlier suspicion that all the processes hitherto described may have an *inner* motivation which determines the *outer* history with which science is exclusively concerned. The restless craving for additional complexity that is characteristic of matter and the cell's overweening concern to preserve its own identity are symptomatic of a universal purpose, the dynamic expression of a reality at once behind and beyond the objective phenomena which, as the Cambridge astronomer and physicist Sir Arthur Eddington (1882–1944) once put it, make up 'the world of shadows' investigated by science. From the reality behind these shadows flows the principle which assures the universe of its plurality, while preserving the fundamental unity of the many parts that comprise it.

Lest we start jumping to theological or, worse, occult conclusions, let us once again observe this principle at work. We have established that at the sub-molecular level, matter directs its activity towards achieving ever greater complexity. Each new and more complex unit thereupon displays properties not expressed in its separate parts – the word 'holism' is used to describe, if not fully explain, this phenomenon – and in the case of large carbon-based molecules the result has been still more complex units notable for their talent for self-replication and their survival-seeking behaviour. The next step was for these cells to adapt themselves appropriately by varying their stock of chromosomes, one of their techniques being to change their means of reproduction from the simple division of a single cell (mitosis) to a fusion of two separate cells with, as a result, the generation of a third, called a zygote, which carries within it, in equal measure, the chromosomes of both parents. This third cell later divides — again by mitosis — into male and female components that will eventually combine with new partners and so repeat the process. To the genetic mutation possible within each cell is now added a new factor for change, sexual reproduction, which serves to stir up the chromosomal cocktail even more.

At about the same time, while life was still composed of single cells, an important division took place among them, with some cells — the prototypes of plants — able to manufacture the carbonaceous molecules they needed for sustenance, mainly through a combination of sunshine and carbon dioxide (photosynthesis), and others, the proto-animals, unable to do so and having to find their nourishment by feeding on plants or other plant-eating animals. The theory is that because of this free-for-all among unicellular organisms, whether plant or animal, individual cells banded together into colonies (the sponge is an example) for their common protection, later uniting to form multi-cellular organisms in which groups of cells gradually developed specialist functions — future tissues, limbs and organs — while, true to the holistic principle already referred to, each organism, transcending the sum of talents contained in its parts, imposed on these an efficient co-ordination of function and effort, thus laying the foundation for what became the nervous system. From then on the joint efforts of sensory and motor nerves and, above all, the nerves of the brain and spinal column were to determine the course of animal evolution, a progressive enlargement of the size and complexity of the brain accompanying the transition from fish to animals and, finally, to the first human beings.

This rapid survey of the universe and its evolution has shown that modern science introduces us to, in place of a great machine, a dynamic system — the universe as process — which is characterised less by law than by *aliveness*. In it the formation of matter, the emergence of life and the developments leading to the appearance of human beings, far from being inevitable, seem to have resulted from the convergence of happy accidents which the participants, prodigiously active, have consistently turned to their advantage, using them to advance the overall process. Recognisable throughout are a spontaneity and a purposeful initiative, the unmistakable sign of something that is incalculable, unpredictable and, above all, supremely free. Observing these, we cannot help concluding that a collective force — what the Greeks called φύσις or nature — is active in and through matter, always seeking (sometimes by trial and error) new forms of expression and working ever outwards from within. For a long time science, blind to all but the surface of nature, attributed its workmanship to the operation of fundamental laws, thereby subjecting the universe to an inbuilt determinism that conveniently removed the need for any agency outside it. Nowadays, a closer knowledge of the inner workings has banished such complacency for good: what were once thought of as laws reveal themselves as no more than habits, liable at any time to change. (Whatever else modern scientists have done to Dame Nature, they have certainly freed her from the corsets into which their fathers tried to squeeze her.) In the end, it is science itself and not occult bias that ineluctably leads us to discern in the past, possibly infinite, process we have been considering, a cosmic life — for what else can it be? — transcending and including the innumerable fragments that constitute our universe, its varied and changing aspects bearing witness to a final reality which, greater than its parts, cannot be other than an all-inclusive Absolute. We may, if we wish, persist in calling this Absolute, bewildering yet inescapable, a cosmic version of the algebraic x, but it is very much easier just to call it God.

II

The Genesis
of
Humankind

'this little kingdom, Man'

SHAKESPEARE, *2 Henry IV*, IV. iii. 118

To look, or rather dig, for the earliest human being is likely to prove an unrewarding task, no matter how many bones are excavated from the ancient earth of Kenya, China or Java, the burial grounds of, respectively, Australopithecus africanus, Sinanthropus pekinensis and the big-jawed Meganthropus. The problem is that the physiological change that distinguished Adam from his pre-hominoid parents was probably so slight that it would pass quite unnoticed, even if his skeleton were ever discovered. The very nature of evolution, which advances not by leaps and bounds but by imperceptibly small steps, means that the beginnings of each innovation are impossible to trace, for by the time a change is seen to have happened, its starting point is lost to hindsight. The problem is the greater because innovations themselves are peculiarly fragile: initially few in number, structurally weak perhaps, they succumb all too easily to hostile forces around them, leaving little vestige of their frail and fleeting passage. It is for this reason that the fugitive 'missing link' between human being and monkey will doubtless continue to elude the palaeontologist's spade for several years yet.

On the basis of the earliest remains so far unearthed, the advent of human-like creatures is believed to have occurred near the start of the Quaternary period, some 3 million years ago, though there is a tendency to push this date progressively backwards. 'The time is past', we are told, 'when many palaeontologists placed the origin of the hominoids in the middle Miocene, 16 or 15 million years ago, or when some molecular biologists held that the entire hominoid radiation took place within the last ten million years, with the hominids diverging only a brief few million years ago. A tentative consensus would now place the radiation of all the great apes from an ancestral stock in the middle Miocene, with the hominids splitting from an African ape lineage in the late Miocene, perhaps eight or seven millions years ago.'[1] The setting for this development has been described in the following idyllic terms by Teilhard de Chardin:

A great calm seems to be reigning on the surface of the earth at this time. From South Africa to South America, across Europe and Asia, are fertile steppes and dense forests. And among this endless verdure are myriads of antelopes and zebras, a variety of proboscidians in herds, deer with every kind of antler, tigers, wolves, foxes and badgers, all similar to those we have today. In short, the landscape is not too dissimilar from that which we are today seeking to preserve in National Parks on the Zambesi, in the Congo, or in Arizona. Except for a few lingering archaic forms, so familiar is this scene that we have to make an effort to realise that *nowhere* is there so much as a wisp of smoke rising from camp or village.[2]

At this time, which in some places was less tranquil than here pictured – the Alps, for example, were squeezed upwards in the course of it – the distribution of anthropoid apes across the tropical and sub-tropical zones of our planet was wider than it is now and, to judge by the skeletons available, there flourished among them several whose appearance was more humanoid than that of any in existence today. It is among these advanced groups of primates that the transition from beast to human being supposedly took place. Certainly, by the Pleistocene epoch which began 2 million years ago, traces of human-like activity were being deposited in the soil of Africa and southern Asia. The fragmentary remains which date from this time suggest that their owners were cumbersome, unlovely creatures, having flat, elongated skulls and massive limbs, though it is far from clear whether they represent the direct ancestors of humanity or some defunct branch of the family which left behind it no modern descendants. In spite of their monstrous appearance, however, there is ample evidence that some of them, in Kenya, for example, as well as in China, chipped away at stones to make weapons and tools, and had also discovered the secret of fire, skills which earn for them from the experts the title of homo faber or homo habilis (meaning dexterous or tool-wielding man), though not yet homo sapiens.

With the subsequent arrival of the Lower Quaternary period, there followed an interval in which the earth, its surface still plastic in places, underwent more geological upheavals and we must advance to a time some 200,000 years ago before we encounter human remains, this time Neanderthaloid, other than the large-boned pre-hominoid sort. Not that the Neanderthalers were all that more prepossessing in appearance: short and stocky, they had long, thick-wedged brows, high, receding foreheads and no chin to speak of (nor, for that matter, much of a larynx to speak with). Even so, the standard depiction of them as slouched and shuffling creatures is now thought to be wrong, mistakenly conjectured from skeletal remains found in 1908 at La Chapelle-aux-Saints in the Dordogne, which exhibit deformities peculiar to their owner, a prehistoric victim of acute and crippling arthritis. Mostly cave-dwellers, these Neanderthalers are now reckoned to be the precursors, though not necessarily the ancestors, of more advanced creatures, classified as Cro-Magnon, whose sudden arrival is situated between the Palaeolithic and Mesolithic ages of the Quaternary period and who, without doubt, are human beings fully like ourselves. Proof of this comes not from the shape of their skull (whose cranial formation must nevertheless have housed a good-sized brain) but from the artefacts they left behind, none of them more remarkable than the exquisite wall paintings that decorate the caves and grottoes of northern Spain and south-western France. Seeing those at Lascaux – at least 15,000 years old – Picasso is said to have exclaimed, 'Nothing better has ever been done.' Like him, no one can stand before these pictures, at once naturalistic yet technically accomplished, without feeling for the artists a sympathy and kinship that set aside the several millennia that separate them from us. Here before us we have precious evidence of people who reflected on their surroundings and, more importantly, reflected on themselves; here we are in the company of homo sapiens who, gifted with reason and conscious of his own organisation, had become, as Erich Fromm put it in a passage that has often been quoted, 'life being aware of itself; he has awareness of himself, of his fellow men, of his past, and of the possibilities for his future'.[3] Moreover, not only was this new man aware of himself but, at the same time, he was aware of that awareness; not only did he know, but he knew that he knew. He was, in short, consciousness turned inwards and seized of itself. If, as a result of this new-found self-consciousness, man was free to act in accordance with his will – and this we shall need to examine later – then we may assert that with humanity's entry into history, the development of our planet ceased to be nothing more than the effect of an evolutionary impetus working through matter. Henceforth, human beings would influence and direct that development in a purposeful way.

Compared with the study of the universe, the macrocosm, the study of man, the microcosm, should be much easier since it requires us merely to study ourselves. Being not only a product of that reality, which is the ground of all things but, from our egocentric point of view, a measure also of its content, we have but to penetrate the mystery of our nature in order to solve the mystery of the whole. 'Know Thyself' (γνῶθι σεαυτόν) was the injunction given at Delphi where initiation obliged each neophyte to pass through a series of ordeals and trials, only to find himself at the end of them in a subterranean chamber on his own. In his solitude he was expected to realise that the world and even God resided inside him, just as everything inside ourselves exists – and always has done – in nature as well.

And it is by looking into ourselves that we are able to reaffirm our earlier statement that a coherent view of the world cannot be maintained unless we suppose that the life in us and in other organic forms is also to be found – as 'pre-life' perhaps – even in the first elementary particles and the energy forces which collaborated with them in the formation of matter. What is true of life must be no less true both of mind and, again being introspective, of consciousness as well, something Hobbes understood when he extended Descartes' famous *'cogito ergo sum'* (I think, therefore I am) to 'I think, therefore matter also thinks'. In similar vein the distinguished geneticist J. B. S. Haldane made the prescient comment some fifty years ago that because life and mind were not at once recognisable in inorganic matter, 'we naturally study them more easily when they are most completely manifested; but if the scientific view is correct, we shall eventually find them, at least in rudimentary form, all through the universe.'[4] That conclusion is inescapable since every phenomenon of general application, be it life, mind or anything else, must, by virtue of the fundamental unity from which all evolves, be omnipresent and, under one aspect or another, play its part in the universal drama. For that reason, any attempt by us to limit mind to, say, human beings or the higher animals would mean rigorously excluding it from the stream of evolution, making of it an alien intruder from nowhere, a kind of epiphenomenon divorced from all that went before it. Such an approach is completely indefensible: the plain truth is that the self-consciousness which rendered our Palaeolithic forebears so convincingly human, making them *persons* not brute individuals, was possible only because consciousness had always been implicit in·the totality of things.

Turning once more to this totality, we find – and science has confirmed it – that our universe probably passes through alternating phases of expansion and contraction, an aptitude that earlier encouraged us to confer on it a cosmic prehistory. This in turn encourages us to read into that history a cosmogenic development, of which the evolution occurring on earth is only a localised symptom, its manifestation adapted to present conditions. The odds are that these conditions differ hugely from those prevailing in earlier phases of activity, particularly since evolution, be it cosmic or local, means that what we now see in existence has unfolded out of what once was. Accordingly, if we are to seek clues to the content of our world's prehistory, our attention must rest not on the morphological changes wrought on matter – for matter belongs only to the here-and-now – but on those inner states whose outward appearance such changes represent. Here again, the most reliable point of departure is ourselves.

It was, you will remember, by acknowledging our own psychic life that we earlier felt entitled to suppose a vast psychic life enclosed within the world from the time of its inception. You will remember, too, that the universal character of evolution prevents us from detaching anything from the past and attributing to it qualities not already present in some anterior form. It is this same principle that now compels us to retrace the psychic life endemic among the elementary particles that make up our world to a stage that subsisted prior to what, overlooking their ambiguous materiality, we might call their initial concretion. It is there – for such is evolution – that the progression started which was to result in the appearance of intelligent beings in the Pleistocene epoch of our planet. To trace our human ancestry, therefore, we need to look beyond the troglodyte Cro-Magnons and their handsome artwork, beyond the simple nuclei of millions of years ago, swimming contentedly in cytoplasmic jelly, beyond the first encounter of nomadic protons and neutrons, beyond all these to a time when the 'big bang' that set our universe in motion still reverberated in the ears of God.

At this point, in the absence of historical record, it is to the occultists we must turn for information about everything that happened before the Earth became a solid body. No sensible reader need panic, however, since I shall endeavour to treat the information received from them with the scepticism owed to statements that cannot be corroborated. This cautious approach does not, of course, oblige us to reject such information out of hand since there are many things in our daily life we happily take on trust, despite the absence of corroboration, simply because they happen to make sense. We shall in no way compromise our intellectual probity if we now proceed, mindful always of what we have learned from science about subsequent events, to consider the occult record in order to see whether it, too, makes sense. While it cannot, admittedly, furnish us with adequate proof of its case, it may still persuade us to give it the benefit of what, inevitably, is a very large doubt.

Fundamental to the occult position is the belief — which we have already met and not been shocked by — that evolution is more than its observable effects, these being only the outward appearance at any given time of the inner life of the universe, the objective manifestation of a consciousness which is ceaselessly active beneath and within, and which is comparable to the subjectivity at work inside ourselves. Because of the premise that the universe results from the self-cognisance of God who, as it were, projects a reflection of himself into time, the ultimate starting point of evolution — and reference to a starting point is made only as an aid to comprehension — must be a spiritual condition from which there follows a descent into something else, that something, so far as concerns our world, being matter and space. Most modern occult writers, like the neo-Platonists whose successors they are, instinctively feel that what is spiritual has necessarily to be nobler than the non-spiritual, hence in discussing the 'descent' into matter, they turn up their metaphysical noses and describe it as a debasement or a 'fall'. Inevitably this prejudice shows itself later in their rather cheerless attitude towards the good things in life and even that most delightfully human of occultists Mme Blavatsky could never overcome an obstinate horror of the flesh, proclaiming, for instance, that the interior conflict in man 'will last till the inner and divine man adjusts his outer terrestrial self to his own spiritual nature' — which may be true enough — 'till then', she goes on to warn, 'the dark and fierce passions of the former will be at eternal feud with his master, the Divine man. But the *animal* will be tamed one day, because its nature will be changed, and harmony will reign once more between the two, as before the "Fall".'[5] It does not follow, of course, that we, products of a more liberated age, need to adopt the puritanical attitudes of Mme Blavatsky and other writers of her generation, attitudes all the more unreasonable when we recollect that what we are dealing with here is a process that is not only natural but, moreover, is said to stem from the Absolute, whose self-expression it purportedly is.

The concept of a reality which comprises the non-material (or 'spiritual') as well as the material is one that is no longer peculiar to theology or occultism. We have noted that physics is compelled to accept both, if it is to explain what goes on in the sub-atomic world with which it frequently deals. For the purpose of observing that world – or the larger one of which it forms part – we have at our disposal our five senses and the numerous scientific instruments invented to enhance their function, though even with the help of these there probably remains a great deal that escapes our notice. To argue otherwise would be to confine reality to whatever we may chance to have perceived, a presumption which is both vain and foolish. Only slightly less foolish is the presumption that total reality consists only of what is perceptible – i.e. capable of apprehension of our senses – for this would at once deny to the universe any components which, by their constitution, may not belong to the three-dimensional world of space and matter. Like both of these, such components may dwell 'inside' the universe but as their natural mode of manifestation is not quantifiable in terms of either, they defy empirical discovery. Later we shall have to consider whether knowledge of them, consistently withheld from our sense organs, may nevertheless be acquired, but for the moment we shall have to take them on trust, consoling ourselves with the thought that, though their existence is scientifically unprovable, it cannot be dismissed on those grounds alone.

The trust we have to marshal in this respect is, I fear, the greater because in talking about non-material existence, we lapse at once into language that cannot correctly describe it. For what are we to call the aspects of that existence? 'Things' they most certainly are not and 'forces', while sounding suitably non-material, are normally identifiable only because of the effect they have upon matter. The problem is that the language we commonly use, all of it derived from either sense experience or our consciousness of it, is unsuitable for describing conditions that owe nothing to either. Yet we have no alternative to it and, furthermore, no choice but to use it if we are to communicate, however imperfectly, what it is we are trying to say. In short, we find ourselves compelled to translate our meaning into words – and mundane concepts – with which they have nothing in common, a translation we may have unconsciously started inside our own head, for without it our thoughts might not be intelligible even to ourselves. (The psychological need to verbalise our thinking may explain why in many cosmologies the divine self-awareness which results in creation is described as an originating word, the eternal Logos, whose utterance brings the cosmos into fruitful being.) These preliminary caveats conceal a warning, therefore, that in now proceeding to examine what occultism has to say about the pre-prehistory of humanity, we shall find the message dressed in clothes which are at best ill-fitting, at worst a disguise. Without them, however, the message is doomed to stay unspoken.

Juggling her noughts like tennis balls, the dexterous Mme Blavatsky assures us that our universe has an active life of 311,040,000,000,000 years.[6] This impressive figure, known as a maha-kalpa or Century of Brahma, she obtained through multiplying by 360 'days' and 360 'nights' (or periods of quiescence) the 4,320,000,000 years which, according to the Hindu calendar, comprise a single Day of Brahma, and, having thus arrived at a Year of Brahma, she had then only to add a couple of noughts in order to complete the sum. Under the name of kalpa, derived from the Sanskrit for 'arrangement' or 'form', each Day of Brahma is held to be the time taken by a given planet to act as host to the life evolving on it, though the years said to comprise this and other divisions of time are not to be taken too literally, for much of planetary evolution takes place on non-physical levels of being and for that reason is clearly not reckonable in terms of earth years. Thus, for example, we learn that every planet has a lifetime composed of seven 'globes' through which evolving reality must seemingly travel no less than seven times before moving on to a new manvantara or planetary experience. (Seven, you will rapidly discover, is a favourite number among occultists.)

So important are these stages of planetary evolution that it is worth making an attempt, in spite of their complexity, at understanding precisely what they involve. To help us do this, occultists long ago divided manifested reality into four groups or classes, referring to these in ascending order of development as the mineral, plant, animal and human kingdoms. (Unlike science, they then went on to suppose six other groups called the elemental kingdoms, of which three were believed to precede and the remainder to succeed the manifested kingdoms.) For our immediate purpose, the four kingdoms are best thought of as the *type* of manifestation successively adopted by the dynamic reality that constitutes our evolving universe, its ubiquitous 'life-force' (for it is easier to conceive it as such) passing in turn through stones, plants, animals and, finally, human beings. Before we begin charting its passage, however, we need further to know that reality is subject also to several different *modes* of manifestation, these being the globes or conditions of being mentioned above.

Here again, alas, we have no choice but to take the occultists on trust. This time their contention is that reality, whatever its kind, functions on four manifested *planes* of existence, adapting its nature to whichever plane it finds itself upon in any particular period. The first of these, on the very rim of objective existence, is known as the 'archetypal world' and, not surprisingly, is the plane occupied by the first globe where reality is still without form or, to use a Sanskrit term, is 'arupic' (from rupa or 'form', the initial 'a' being privative). Scarcely more objective is the 'intellectual world' proper to the second globe and it is only when we arrive at the 'formative world' of the third globe that we may presume to talk of structures and shapes, though both, even here, are closer to the realm of ideation than to matter. Indeed, not until we reach the fourth globe do we enter the physical plane but once more we must guard against thinking that the forms manifesting there always do so in the solid, familiar terms of our own world. Nevertheless, with its entry into the material or quasi-material conditions of the fourth globe, the flow of evolving life has certainly reached the lowest point in its descent towards objective existence. Its falling curve may thus be said to have ended, and it has henceforth to start the journey back towards the 'archetypal' state from which it began, passing, as it does so, through the 'formative' and 'intellectual' conditions of the fifth and sixth globes until it returns at long last to the arupic conditions of the seventh and final globe, bringing with it, let it be noted, *all the experience it has gathered on the way*.

This circuit of seven globes, known in occult parlance as a Round, happens seven times during the lifetime of every planetary chain — the word 'chain' being preferable to 'planet' on its own since only with the fourth globe of the fourth Round does the planet assume the concrete form we are wont to associate with it. What, at least, should be clear from all this is that the succession of Rounds represents an *evolutionary spiral* which, thanks to the cumulative experience gained on each circuit, permits the life-stream inhabiting the separate kingdoms to progress until, with the completion of the seventh Round, most of it is ready to graduate into the next higher kingdom, a transition that occurs once a new planetary chain (again with seven Rounds of seven globes) reawakens into being.[7] By means of such a process, the 'life' imperceptibly evolving within, say, the mineral kingdom today will in due course be ready to occupy a plant-like condition on the planetary chain that succeeds our Earth, the latter by then withdrawn into the state of quiescence known to the Hindus as pralaya.

To avoid misunderstanding, it should at once be stressed that before its ascension to the human kingdom, the life-stream I have been discussing remains undifferentiated, in the sense that no *individual* consciousness illuminates the separate entities that populate the three subordinate kingdoms. None of us, therefore, is really entitled to claim that he or she was a pebble or an aspidistra or a donkey in some previous planetary lifetime. On the contrary, even the individual consciousness we now enjoy is but a recent acquisition, its beginnings to be found on our present globe which, for the benefit of readers concerned about their cosmic whereabouts, is the fourth of what is already the fourth Round: half-way through the Earth chain, we have by now passed the frontier beyond which our evolutionary progress, once dependent on a collective urge — which, as science has revealed, is at work inside the most primitive forms, including those judged inorganic — henceforth depends on our own self-induced efforts. Profiting from opportunities offered to us on this globe and on the three still to come (not to mention the twenty-one globes of the three remaining Rounds), we have, occultists assure us, the chance to aspire to a more exalted state than the human, a state which others, more senior to us, attained long ago on planetary chains far older than our own.

Up to now, in talking of Rounds and globes, I have dealt only with the biography of the planetary chain we call Earth. As already explained, however, our history (though, so to speak, 'pre-human') stretches back far beyond this to other planetary chains, all with their own Rounds and globes, and it is to Rudolf Steiner we must turn for more information about them. So far as concerns the last three chains preceding our Earth, Steiner calls these 'Saturn', 'Sun' and, our immediate predecessor, 'Moon', prefacing their names with the epithet 'old' so as to distinguish them from the heavenly bodies familiar to us, with which they no longer have a connection. (Some occultists suggest that the visible planets of our solar system are the fourth, physical, globe remnants of the seventh and final Round of past chains.) It is stated that a particular form of clairvoyance, which will be discussed later, enabled Steiner and others to perceive the conditions proper to these different planetary chains, it being further claimed that because each successive chain, Round, and even globe, begins by recapitulating, in its own terms, the characteristics of preceding ones, the conditions prevailing at the birth of our world may offer all of us, clairvoyant or not, a clue to what has gone on before.

On this basis, the earliest manifestation, 'old' Saturn, is not unexpectedly the hardest to describe, if only because, with one of the seven manifested kingdoms predominant in each planetary chain, its characteristics (those of the first elemental kingdom) are comparable only to the non-material or 'arupic' state which preceded the objective appearance of matter in our world. Steiner compares it with 'warmth', meaning only that contact with it, were its conditions reproduced today, might induce a warm feeling — and nothing more — inside us. In the beginning this Saturn state lay outside our spatio-temporal framework. In it were concentrated three types of spiritual energy, representing the ideas of warmth, light and being, which occultists allude to as the spirits of Movement (Dynamis), Wisdom

(Kyriotetes) and Will (Thrones). (Do not be put off by the quaintness of the terminology: occultism has yet to modernise the language it uses.) To the spirits of Movement Steiner attributes the role of 'containing' the chaos produced by this congress of forces, thereby making of Saturn a unity which the spirits of Wisdom were able to transfuse with 'warmth' or 'feeling'. By the action of other forces – described as Spirits of Form (Excusiae or Powers) – the soul-life of Saturn was differentiated, turning its collective 'soul' into a collection of diverse soul-units, each reflecting in the form of 'light' the life of the spiritual beings that sponsored their evolution.

Active among these were the Spirits of Personality (Archai or Principalities), each aware for the first time of its own uniqueness, and thus able to pass through a human stage on the later rounds of the Saturn chain. Somewhere, too, locked inside the Saturn equivalent of our mineral kingdom, there dwelt another, more primitive life-stream whose consciousness, quickened by the Spirits of Fire, was no more than a heavy dullness, similar to that which accompanies profound sleep, with 'a quivering, flickering glimmer or gleam that shone here and there for a moment and then sank into that darkness, in which the first beginnings of the germ of humanity developed'.[8] (Here, as you may have guessed, we meet for the first time the particular life-stream from which all of us, destined one day to become human on the Earth chain, originally sprang.) Meanwhile other spiritual forces, those of Love (Seraphim), Life (Angels) and Harmonies (Cherubim), had begun their activity. It was, for example, those of Life – the angels of western tradition, the pitris of Indian and, especially Puranic tradition – which, reacting to the 'taste' quality introduced into Saturn by the Seraphim (a 'taste' which became 'music' when transferred to a spatial environment), set about instigating a kind of insubstantial pan-metabolism which anticipated what, in our world, would become the biological processes of nutrition and excretion. These mundane analogies provide an important clue to the purpose of the Saturn stage, which was to lay the foundation of what, in the different conditions of our world, would eventually provide human beings with a physical body.

Moving on to 'old' Sun, we find that it began with a recapitulation of the conditions formerly met on Saturn, an essential prerequisite if the life-stream about to experience its human stage were to adapt to its new 'solar' environment. Thenceforth, with the passage of the first three Rounds, the warmth of Saturn began slowly to transform itself – as if by a process of condensation – into a gaseous state whose variable fluency and flux provided the differentiation which, in our world, form imparts to matter.

(These conditions, proper to the second elemental kingdom, can be compared, *mutatis mutandis*, with the semi-dense turmoil that attended the birth of our planet before its material consolidation took place.) In this gaseous, volatile atmosphere the energies previously encountered resumed one by one their productive work, notably the Spirits of Form which reproduced in mobile, evanescent shapes a prototype of the human entities due to reach maturity on 'old' Sun. Later, the Spirits of Wisdom, having themselves risen to a higher level of perfection than on Saturn (since they, like all spiritual beings, are also evolving) endowed these shapes and others belonging to the solar equivalents of our plant and animal kingdoms with a certain permanence, introducing into them a formative principle, at once supportive and cohesive, which occultists call the 'life body' or 'etheric body'. This development, the most important from our point of view, permitted the Spirits of Fire, then undergoing the human stage of their evolution, to work, as they had done in the previous chain, on what would later become our sensory system, while the Spirits of Love and Personality were left to elaborate our glandular chemistry. In addition there occurred in the Sun stage a division between those elements which adapted easily to the new conditions and those, still regretting the Saturn phase, which could not. Among other things, this division sowed the seed for the subsequent dichotomy in human nature, with its so-called 'lower' and 'higher' parts.

After a further 'sleep of worlds', or Prakritika Pralaya, the future Earth entity awakened to its 'old' Moon phase, first reliving, this time in 'lunar' terms, the previous Saturn and Sun phases so as to adapt its evolutionary heritage to conditions appropriate to the third elemental kingdom. These conditions, following the 'warmth' quality characteristic of Saturn and the 'air' of Sun, can best be described as liquescent since a further process of condensation resulted in a ubiquitous fluidity, permeated with air and warmth. Of primary relevance to our own development, both then and subsequently, was the bestowal by the Spirits of Personality of an astral body on the 'animal' and 'human' inhabitants of 'old' Moon, a body through which our desires and, since there is a connection between them, our feelings of pleasure and pain would much later operate on Earth. At the same time regressive tendencies, part Saturn and part Sun, continued to remain aloof from Moon evolution and these recalcitrants were to make their own special contribution to the psychological resources of future human beings. A picture of what this Moon phase, the immediate precursor of our Earth chain, was like, in its material (fourth Round and fourth globe) manifestation, has been given by Rudolf Steiner. Although he clearly does his best to describe the scene, one in which the higher beings we now call angels experienced the human condition, the result, it must be said, is far from happy. Speaking of the 'substance' of the Moon, Steiner calls it:

> ... a semi-live substance, which was in constant movement, sometimes sluggish, sometimes quick and lively. There is as yet no solid mineral mass like the rocks and other constituents of the Earth today. We might describe it as a kind of plant-mineral kingdom. Only we have to imagine the whole ground and body of the Moon consisting of this plant-mineral substance, just as the Earth today consists of rocks and stones, arable soil etc. As here and there rocks protrude from the Earth today, so in the lunar mass, harder portions also were embedded. These might be likened to forms made of hard wood or horn. Moreover, as plants today spring from the mineral soil, so was the ground of the Moon bedecked and also penetrated, by a second kingdom, consisting of a kind of plant-animal. The substance of this kingdom was softer on the ground and more mobile in itself. It spread over the lunar kingdom like a turgid sea.[9]

Before we get ourselves bogged down in this gooey selenic mess let us allow 'old' Moon to sink into a merciful quiescence, pending the arrival, after three recapitulative Rounds of seven globes each, of the more familiar world of matter that constitutes our planet Earth. Even when due allowance is made for the difficulties of language already mentioned, there is no denying that accounts like this stretch the credulity of even the most well-disposed mind. It can be argued, of course, that this has to be the case in any discussion concerning modes of manifestation totally outside our conceptual range. Similar difficulties would, for instance, arise in trying to explain to a congenitally blind person what a rainbow looks like. This may be why many occult writers prefer merely to acknowledge the existence of preparatory stages before the appearance of our world, without venturing to speculate in too much detail on their exact composition.

Confusing though these teachings about the pre-existence of our planet may seem, the clear message they contain is that the universal law of evolution applies to all being, whatever its present condition. This means that the creative impulse emanating from the Godhead has to pass down through every subordinate level of existence before it can begin, once past the human stage, its gradual, self-motivated ascent to what is both its source and final destination.

Corroboration of these ascending levels of evolutionary progress is to be had in the physical world – in the mineral, vegetable and animal kingdoms now before us – where, as was noted earlier, the evolving element is, as it were, 'lifted' to successively more complex states of manifestation. For an idea of its wider implications, we have only to turn to the history of our planet's material formation where we find, reproduced in terms relevant to itself (in this case those of the mineral kingdom), a memory not only of the states the Earth passed through on its descent through the first, second and third globes of our present Round but of the characteristics peculiar to the three planetary chains preceding its existence. Before venturing to examine these, however, we should note perhaps that still to happen is the passage of our Earth, as well as ourselves, through the last three globes of the current Round and, after that, the three further Rounds yet to come. There will then follow three more planetary chains, the names of which Steiner gives as Jupiter, Venus and Vulcan, though other names and a different sequence, no less valid, crop up elsewhere.[10]

Not unexpectedly, the first stage of the Earth's formation, thousands of millions of years ago, possessed the formless, arupic characteristics of 'old' Saturn, involving, as it did, a stormy courtship of the particles and waves whose eventual convergence would provide our world with the collective density it needed to gain admission into space and time. That event, you will be relieved to learn, brings us back at last to the micro-elements with which physics is nowadays concerned, but whose qualities, for all that, are hardly more conceivable than those of the non-material modes of manifestation previously described. In the wake of these early developments, there followed a gradual change from the Azoic period when life, as previously defined, was still absent from Earth, to the Archaeozoic period, when primitive life-forms emerged, 3,000 million years ago. This at once prepared the way for a second phase, its characteristics comparable with the 'aeriform' state of 'old' Sun, which began about 1,300 million years ago and reached fulfilment during the Proterozoic period, a time still within the Pre-Cambrian era (3,000 million to 600 million years ago) when the Earth lacked real stability and its atmosphere was a witches' brew of turbulent gases. Going back to 700 or 800 million years ago, to the start of a third stage, we arrive at a time, its characteristics comparable in earthly terms to those of Steiner's 'old' Moon, when water covered much of the Earth's surface, subsequently providing a home to all manner of strange fishes and amphibious reptiles. Occultists maintain, too, that the first lower animals now began to appear, though palaeontology transposes that event to a later period, estimated to be not earlier than 250 million years ago. Both concur, however, that by the succeeding period – the fourth and our present one – whose beginning is situated at about

100 million years ago, birds and mammals were certainly in existence, though the Earth's surface still remained susceptible to massive changes. It was still not uniformly settled as late as 18 to 15 million years ago when, following the fish, reptiles and animals, the earliest human-like beings 'came silently into the world'.[11]

In the sequence revealed by the evolution of living forms on our planet the emergence of human beings *followed* that of other, more primitive, creatures, enabling us, in retrospect, to regard humans as the 'crown of creation', the natural perfection of all that preceded their arrival. Yet, in the pedigree given to them by occult doctrine, we are led back to a planetary Round preceding our own, in the course of which the human body came into being, albeit – for such are the paradoxes of occultism – only in a quasi-physical, paradigmatic form. More junior to that body, having appeared only in the fourth globe conditions of the fourth Round, were the mineral, plant and animal structures which seemingly anticipate the advent of homo sapiens. We are thus left with the curious result that the physical body of man was the last to walk on to the Earth's stage, even though it had been waiting in the wings since long before the curtain first went up. What in fact happened is that when our present globe assumed concrete form, a prototype human being (the Adam Kadmon or Heavenly Man) had already been fashioned in the formative world, third of the four manifested planes. From then on, matter, as yet inchoate and unspecific, had to undergo a long process of evolution – almost a kind of 'catching-up' – before it was able to evolve to a point where, in general, the world had so arranged itself that its eco-system could accommodate human beings, and where, in particular, the cerebral organisation of certain primates, notably that part of the brain which permits self-awareness, was such as to allow the transition from hominid to man. By certain occultists this long wait is said to be reflected in the history of the human embryo, as well as in the time taken by human beings to pass from infancy to adulthood. Steiner's view on the subject appears nevertheless to differ somewhat from that just described, since for him, the materialisation of non-human forms occurred when units of life that were intended to animate human forms became impatient and incarnated too soon, one result being that instead of assuming human form (and the corresponding attributes), they occupied bodies consistent with the evolutionary stage reached by matter at that time.[12]

Understandably, those who look at evolution from the outside, studying only its effects, see nothing whatever of all this. To them we are descended from monkeys, who after the virgin forests of Africa became reduced in size were forced to do two things: either they had to cling on to what was left of their old homes, or, in an almost biblical sense, they had to face expulsion from the Garden. The ancestors of the chimpanzees, gorillas, gibbons and ourangs stayed put, and their numbers have been dwindling ever since. The ancestors of the only other surviving ape – the naked ape – struck out, left the forests, and threw themselves into competition with the already efficiently adapted ground-dwellers. It was a risky business, but in terms of evolutionary success it paid dividends.[13]

Meanwhile, down amidst the shrubs and lush grasses, these grounded monkeys, lacking anatomical specialisation, were forced to rely on their wits in order to survive, their brain (already relatively large) responding in Lamarckian fashion to the increased demands made upon it by growing even larger and more complex. It was not long before the cleverer among them, who in the mean time had learned to walk upright, grew bored with the society of their smaller-brained cousins and left these to grub around for berries, while they themselves marched off, 'like a brainy, weapon-toting wolf',[14] to conquer the world. For this purpose, they were much helped by other anatomical changes – again, presumably, in response to chance needs – such as the growth of vocal cords and a propitious dis-position of thumb and fingers which enabled them to fashion and manipu-late tools. The wonder, given man's urge to fly, is that they did not sprout wings as well, instead of waiting for the aeroplane to be belatedly invented!

To avoid misunderstanding, let me make plain at once that no self-respecting occultist would nowadays deny that man's physical body evolved, in its final stages, from ape to hominid and from hominid to man. The external view of evolution sees in this only the cumulative effect of a long series of gradual, perhaps accidental, mutations which results in a qualitative, as well as quantitative, change in the whole, the latter thereby becoming greater than the sum of its constituent parts. Occultists, on the other hand, would insist that evolution necessarily means that such quali-tative innovations are possible only because they are already implicit in the simple unity from which they have slowly evolved: thanks to evolution, the universe does not *become* greater than the sum of its elements, it merely expresses through them its own antecedent greatness. The more complex and numerous the material elements available to it at any time, the more it can reveal of itself, just as a thinker can better express his thoughts, the more comprehensive his vocabulary happens to be. The matter becomes somewhat clearer if, by way of analogy, we imagine an acorn and, at the same time, the entity 'oak tree' which lies concealed inside it but exists nowhere spatially. If conditions are right, our tiny acorn will later 'evolve' into an oak tree at whose appearance the entity may be said to have entered into space and time. To say that the entity did not exist until the oak tree appeared would, however, be to confuse appearance with being. Indeed, it would be more correct to say that the appearance of the oak tree was rendered possible only because the entity itself had previously existed. This in turn enables us to sum up the evolution from acorn to oak tree as being the entity's endeavour to mould the matter at its disposal into an objective realisation of itself. In like manner, according to occultism, have spiritual forces worked in and through matter so as to provide objective existence to those entities – that of the 'oak tree' among them – which at the dawn of our time were crowding the threshold to the physical world. First to exist yet last to appear were those entities destined to become the first human beings. Evolution was the means by which, at some point in the Quaternary era, if not before, the anatomy of certain hominids, particularly their brain size, but including details like the situation of their thumb, was such that it became the vehicle by which human beings could be realised and, being human, realise themselves. Henceforth, the history of the world would be the history of its human inhabitants.

It is difficult for us nowadays to put ourselves in the position of those primitive human beings who, in the paradisical setting described by Teilhard de Chardin, looked out upon the world intelligently for the very first time. No doubt other creatures, the simplest and smallest included, had all been aware to some extent of their surroundings – even single protons, perhaps, sensed the contiguity of others in the same energy field – and because of the effect these surroundings had on them, they became aware of their own existence. In the first human beings, however, there awoke a new capacity for self-awareness which distinguished them from the beasts, enabling our earliest ancestors to contemplate the world as a separate entity, totally distinct from themselves, with which they had nevertheless urgently to come to terms in order to survive. Part of the world, yet apart from it, they recognised a reality inside them – the only reality, say some philosophers, we dare take for granted – and, outside them, another reality from which they could not escape. All the more terrible must have been the impact of this exterior world, with its danger, excitement and perpetual challenge, because of the fact that no one of their own kind was available to educate them in its bewildering ways. Like small children curious to discover a world that is at once inviting and repelling, they had to do without the help and guidance parents and teachers normally provide. By continuous trial and error — the latter frequent and possibly fatal — they had slowly to acquire the rudiments of knowledge by their own unaided effort, adapting, inventing and, above all, thinking. How often must their thoughts have dwelt on their vulnerability, their helplessness before natural forces whose behaviour seemed perverse, if not downright malicious and hostile. It is small wonder that these fearful, novice human beings, conscious of their weakness, soon banded together in search not only of common protection, as certain animals do, but of company, of the society of others of their own kind, with whom to share the incommunicable feeling of isolation that is the penalty self-awareness imposes.

In vain do we search for a sign of these inhabitants of Eden. Here we are dealing with a relatively small number of people whose bare feet trod the Earth at a time when parts of its surface lacked the fixity and permanence familiar to us now. Volcanic disturbances, massive shifts of land and water, the unremitting wear and tear of the millennia, all these have conspired to make sure that our human origins stay forever lost. And there is something seemly about that. Such remains as have been found date from a later period, but even these, let it not be forgotten, are few and far between. Still fewer and more fragmentary are the hominoid remains of up to 3 million years ago. All that remains of our friend Meganthropus, the Java man, are his chin and three teeth. This shortage of evidence allows us to suppose that 'prehominid', meaning something that came before man, may be a name given too hastily to creatures that in reality were contemporary with human beings whose own remains have yet to come to light. Asked to set a date to the emergence of the first human beings, palaeontologists, as we have noted, are nowadays far less dogmatic than they used to be, and, with an insouciance worthy of Mme Blavatsky, think nothing of bestowing extra noughts on the estimates once current.

Quite simply, there exist no firm grounds for maintaining that the start of human history on Earth coincides with the age given to the earliest set of remains we happen to uncover. (And the margin of error in current methods of dating increases the farther back we go.) Equally unwarranted is the kind of speculation which, at the sight of a wisdom tooth or less, palaeontologists are encouraged to indulge in. So delighted are they by their discoveries that at once they begin to elaborate on the life-style and psychology of the person whose mortal remains lie before them. Seduced by the mistaken belief that the achievements of modern man are a valid yardstick by which to judge the capacities of his ancestors, many of them slip quietly into the error of thinking that human beings who worked only with stones and never knew of the wheel must have differed fundamentally from us, if not physically (since intervening changes have been slight), then at least mentally. On this basis one cannot help wondering whether philosophy would ever have been credited to the ancient Greeks, if all the archaeologists had to work on were a few bits of pottery and one of Plato's ribs.

To blame for this tendency is the fact that palaeontologists, consciously or not, are influenced by the common belief, an over-simplification of the truth, that human beings evolved from monkeys, and, were it not for the special formation of their brain, would in no time at all have lapsed into the extinction to which their physical weakness condemned them. Faced, therefore, with the crudeness of the artefacts left behind by primitive human beings – and, considering they started with nothing, their crudeness should cause no surprise – the palaeontologist is quick to assume that anyone living as far back as a million years ago had to be closer to the orang-outang than to him. This assumption then gives him a starting point from which he can trace in the subsequent history of humankind a straightforward linear progression from an early ape-like state to our present one, sometimes suggesting, since evolution provides a peg for all kinds of hats (even occult ones!), that this progression was accompanied by corresponding changes in the complexity of the human brain. No evidence of such changes is at hand. On the contrary, the earliest skulls so far disinterred suggest that their cerebral chamber was made to house a brain as big as, if not bigger than, our own. While it is true that the cortical area of our brain, often said to be the seat of reason, may have grown more complex over the thousands of years that separate us from our earliest forefathers, that period is probably too short to allow for the physiological changes that would be needed to convert monkey's minds into human ones.

To sum up, therefore, many palaeontologists mistake the original ignorance of our first ancestors for native dumbness. That early human beings were without the knowledge subsequent generations were gradually to acquire, together with the wisdom this knowledge affords, is something occultists are perfectly willing to accept. What they cannot accept is that the technological backwardness of ancient man is proof of mental deficiency. They know that, were they themselves – or any of us – to be transported back to that remote period, they would scarcely fare any better, even with the experience of past centuries in their DNA, than their primitive companions. What would cause them no astonishment, however, is the discovery that, though vastly better informed than the naked apes around them, their mind, as such, was scarcely different from theirs.

What our review of pre-material evolution has shown us up to now is that for occultists the first human beings came into the world 'trailing clouds of glory', an inheritance of the long preparation that preceded their initial appearance on Earth. To be more exact they came equipped with two bodies, one etheric, the other astral, in addition to the physical body bequeathed to them by some unidentified hominoid parent. Like the universe, therefore, they can be said to have carried inside them a prehistory which helped them to become what they now are.

To talk about 'bodies' other than the physical, however, carries so much risk of being misunderstood that we need to state quite plainly that an expression such as 'etheric body', popular in occult literature at the turn of the century, does not refer to some kind of doppelgänger which, like a phantom Siamese twin, stays at our side throughout life. Rather, it means a formative principle – or field of force, if we want to sound more scientific – which binds elementary particles into a coherent organisation. You may remember that in Rudolf Steiner's system this cohesive force came about during the Sun stage of ante-mundane history, a period when the solar antecedents of the current plant and animal kingdoms were successively established. As a result of it, form has since become a fundamental yet dynamic (since subject to evolution) attribute of the physical world, its relative stability assured because everything, our own bodies included, is interpenetrated by a subtler body, part of an etheric substratum whose presence saves matter from dissolving into chaos. Having said all that, we have also to remove a second source of potential misunderstanding, by explaining that the word 'etheric' was adopted by occultists at a time when physics believed space to be permeated by an all-pervading ether, a belief since abandoned but which, in its lifetime, seemed to provide a useful *physical* analogy with the notion occultists were striving to convey. However, because 'etheric body' has by now become the standard designation for something which, sadly, comprises neither body nor ether, we have no choice but to stick with it, especially as other names, like the Sanskrit lingasharira (causal principle or model body), while esoteric enough, are bound to seem precious.

If the etheric body is inaptly labelled, our other subtle body, the astral (with which the etheric is sometimes confused), is no less so. For a start it, too, is a body in name only, though this time we cannot render the idea more acceptable by suggesting that its existence, like that of the etheric body, can be inferred from the appearance of the physical world. The astral body, which came into existence, according to Steiner, during the Moon stage that immediately preceded our Earth, is the property of all animals, ourselves included. It is the repository of our feelings, a kind of individual energy field which is nourished by our sensations and through which our volitional life is translated into action. Because of it, every animal organism, each of which possesses an astral counterpart, becomes aware of its environment and, by so doing, achieves an awareness, albeit still contingent and derivative, of its own existence. Once again, the epithet qualifying this second accessory body is as misleading as etheric was in respect of the first, for there is nothing star-like about it whatever. The oriental name for what approximates to the astral body is kama-rupa but since the expression 'astral body' is sufficiently common to qualify for entry into the *Oxford Dictionary of Current English*, we need have few qualms about retaining it.

The multiple human being who, in addition to a physical body, the most ancient of all, having been planned on 'old' Saturn, is host also to etheric and astral bodies, plus a complex mentation which, more than anything else, is his hallmark, would rapidly have fallen victim to acute schizophrenia, were there not inside him yet another principle that co-ordinates the parts and makes each of us a complete human being. That principle, the heart of our self-centredness, is our 'I' or, in a non-Freudian sense, our ego, at once the essence of our individuality and the confirmation of our personal uniqueness. Thanks to the ego, we are able to get outside ourselves, so to speak, and contemplate the working model that is our own peculiar self. True, biologists may tell us that this precious self-awareness is the result of an electro-chemical process active inside our brain, but their explanation in no way deprives the ego of its overall responsibility for what is going on. It is the ego that allows us to pay attention to the process, even while it happens, being the means by which we can introspectively perceive whatever passes through our mind. (It matters little that this perception may at times be less than complete, preferring to overlook the lumber stored in the subconscious and unconscious basements of the brain.) Of primary importance, so far as concerns our practical life, is the ability our ego gives us to detach ourselves from our thoughts in order to examine their content and, where appropriate, judge their worth before acting upon them. To that extent, it is the guardian of what appears to be our free will.

Having insisted up to now that human beings are inextricably bound up with the evolving universe from which they emerged, it is not possible to separate the question of free will, the final uncertainty in our study of the little kingdom that is Man, from that larger kingdom of which he is a subject. Already we have seen how in our earthly life — and for most of us there is no other kind — we rely on our sense organs for all information concerning the outside world, one result being that a large part of our behaviour is simply an unthinking response to the various stimuli that affect our five senses. Even our thinking, it would seem, is ultimately decided by whatever information, its accuracy without any sort of guarantee, chances to be furnished by our senses, something that strengthens the scientific argument that physiological considerations, over which we have little independent control, go a long way in determining human behaviour: our actions may owe more to our cerebral chemistry or glandular secretions than to what we fondly think of as a rational evaluation of competing possibilities. When we take into account the extent to which heredity and environment are said to influence us, from the faulty potty training condemned by the Freudians to the Jungian concept of a collective unconscious, we are understandably left with grave doubts about the freedom we enjoy to direct our own lives.

Neither is the case for free will advanced very far, if, like some of its advocates, we point to the unpredictability that characterises so much of human behaviour. After all, as casinos know to their profit, the results of a game of roulette are just as unpredictable, yet the ball spinning around has no freedom to decide at which number it will finally come to a stop. On the contrary, its unpredictability is due not to any intrinsic indeterminism but only to our ignorance of the mathematical data, such as the strength of the croupier's wrist and the respective velocities of ball and wheel, which combine to determine how the game will end. Similarly, were we to have more exact information about the electro-chemical reactions that occur among neurons whenever we think, the unpredictability of our behaviour might also vanish at once. Even so it is to the elementary particles that make up those neurons we must turn, if we are to establish the possibility of free will.

Earlier we mentioned that Epicurus, who believed that every object was composed of infinitesimal atoms constantly in motion, believed also that individual atoms might on occasion swerve a little from the track laid down for them by nature, following, as it were, their own inclination rather than the prompting of external forces. His followers were to emphasise this idiosyncratic behaviour in order to argue that human beings, thanks to their own constituent atoms, were equally independent and free to exercise moral choice. Now that this idiosyncrasy has been confirmed by the anarchy observable among the sub-atomic constituents of matter, we can conclude, with a certainty denied to the Epicureans, that nature as a whole is not subject to an all-embracing determinism. Neither, therefore, are we. The only question then left is whether this apparent independence can be equated with free will.

The difficulty here is that the independent behaviour of certain particles, acknowledged by the quantum theory, is at first sight completely erratic, while the free will attributed to human beings supposes a purpose, being always directed to the attainment of specific ends. However, it is surely right to infer that the lack of purpose among elementary particles may be only apparent, due entirely to our failure to discern it. After all, we know already that the simplest evolving forms, even those dubbed inorganic, are adept at turning to their advantage any situation they find themselves in, pressing ever on towards more complex and durable structures. Confronted by such evidence of purpose, we have every reason to attribute it also to the stray particles which, to the consternation of physicists, seem cussedly determined to act as they please. To any unbiased observer, these offer satisfying proof that free will, however rudimentary, is inherent in matter. That proof is particularly satisfying since in the past science has tried to discredit free will by stressing that thinking is merely the passage of energy along the network of neurons built into our brain. We can now see, however, that if free will is an innate property of matter, this materialist argument serves only to reaffirm its existence. Not only that, but such emphasis on the indissolubility of matter and mind can in the long run help us to understand better, given the complex development of our brain, especially perhaps its cortical region, why the full exercise of free will which our ego permits is uniquely the privilege of human beings. Indeed, we might conclude that just as the prevalence of form in the physical world confirmed for us earlier the presence of an etheric substratum, so does our cerebral anatomy testify to the existence of our ego, that divine spark or monad whose individual and self-conscious manifestation is characteristic of all human beings.

This same divine spark is a product of the differentiation that followed when the primal unity of the Absolute became aware of itself, though the words 'became aware', implying, as they do, a beginning, can be justified only in relation to our own occupation of time. In reality, of course, there never existed an instant when the Absolute was *not* aware of itself and it was this eternal self-cognisance that was to fill the universe with consciously evolving life. In the world about us we can observe how, through the matter that entraps it, this ubiquitous consciousness strives to find collective self-expression. In the human ego, on the other hand, the same consciousness has developed further: individual and morally free, it can choose whether to collaborate or not in the evolutionary course available to it. Our fragile humanity now stands at the fourth and middle stage of the earth's history, with, behind us, a descent through the first, second and third planes of manifested existence and, before us, an ascent in reverse order through the same conditions. Viewed thus, evolution can be seen to have started from above, its downward progress accompanied by a gradual materialisation of forms until what Mme Blavatsky fastidiously calls 'a fixed ultimate of debasement is reached'.[15] But there remains grounds for optimism, for the ancient teaching goes on to reveal that:

> We have finished the descending arc and have begun our return to the Deity, both the globe and the human family on it. Exiles from God, prodigal sons in a far country, we have set out on our journey home.[16]

In the next chapter we shall see how early humankind began the long and weary pilgrimage that we, generations later, are still making today.

III

Lost Lands
and
Vanished Cultures

*Queequeg was a native of Kokovoko, an island
far away to the west and south. It is not on
any map; true places never are.*

HERMAN MELVILLE

By placing several human beings, all of them contemporaries, at the top of
mankind's family tree, the occult account of our origin repudiates the
biblical version, which, according to Pope Pius XII, in his encyclical
Humani Generis (1950), can admit of no other interpretation than that the
human race was descended from a single historical couple, the Adam and
Eve of the Old Testament. To him, it doubtless seemed that ecclesiastical
teaching required nothing less, if it were to explain how the original sin
committed by Adam, our common first parent, could be transmitted to
the whole of mankind, putting it collectively in need of the salvation
offered by the vicarious sacrifice of Jesus Christ. Even then, the Supreme
Pontiff did not completely close the door to further debate, with the result
that a new generation of theologians has found it possible, to their own
satisfaction at least, to reconcile the fact of polygenesis with a belief in
original sin. No such problem worries occultists, though several of them,
as already remarked, do regard man's descent into matter as a kind of
Fall in which all of us participate. To them, this Fall is not so much a
spiritual or moral contagion inherited at birth, but a general characteristic
of manifested existence, its chief symptom being the plurality inherent in
our human condition and the realisation of it that self-awareness brings.
This it was that provoked in men on 'the very day they tasted the fruit of

the Tree of Wisdom, a struggle between the spiritual and the psychic, the psychic and the physical'.[1] And, since all manifested reality has, in the course of its evolution, to pass through every level of being, the Fall is a universal, educative experience which the angels, no less than human beings, are required to undergo.

Having 'fallen', albeit unwittingly, our ancestors found themselves scattered over the segments of what had once been a single land mass but which subsequently divided into what are now Asia, Africa and South America, the westward drift of the latter resulting in the formation of the Atlantic Ocean. (It is probably unnecessary by now to repeat that in the period I am discussing, the geophysical arrangement of the Earth differed from what it is today and was still in the throes of massive restructuring.) Later the more adventurous of these emergent human beings were to establish themselves on another, horseshoe-shaped continent which, like India and Australia, had drifted slowly eastwards, having earlier detached itself from the African land mass. This continent formerly

> . . . covered all the area from the foot of the Himalayas, which separated it from the inland sea rolling its waves over what is now Tibet . . . From thence it stretched south across what is known to us as Southern India, Ceylon and Sumatra; then embracing on its way, as we go south, Madagascar on its right hand and Australia and Tasmania on its left, it ran down to within a few degrees of the Antarctic Circle, and from Australia, an inland region on the Mother Continent in those ages, it extended far into the Pacific Ocean, beyond Rap-nui (Teapy, or Easter Island).[2]

Such, at least, is the picture we are given, its geographical details less than reliable, of what existed during the Miocene epoch, up to 20 million years ago. By the time the earliest societies were consolidated on it, this continental land mass had already been reduced by volcanic and other violent upheavals to a smaller area. Its existence is hinted at in early Brahmanical literature and the name Lemuria was given to it in the middle of the last century, not by the occultists who nevertheless took it over with alacrity, but by an English zoologist, P. L. Sclater, who surmised its existence in order to explain the presence of lemurs and other small primates in both Africa and the Far East. (The explanation now favoured by contemporary zoologists, based on the drifting just mentioned, dispenses with any notion of a vanished land mass, though agreement persists among geologists that ocean levels were formerly low enough to join Borneo and

western Indonesia together, and to expose a tract of land connecting New
Guinea to northern Australia.)

Remote though these dates undoubtedly are, we have seen that they
are not incompatible with the probable existence of human beings. We are
dealing with a time at least two million years removed from our own, yet
the earliest humanoid remains date from a period still older than that. At
the start of his book describing human origins, Richard E. Leakey writes:

> Close to three million years ago, on a camp site near the east shore of
> Kenya's spectacular Lake Turkhana, formerly Lake Rudolf, a primitive
> human being picked up a water-smoothed stone, and with a few skilful
> strikes transformed it into an implement . . . It is a heart-quickening
> thought that we share the same genetic heritage with the hands that
> shaped the tool that we can now hold in our hands, and with the mind
> that decided to make the tool that our mind can now contemplate. [3]

While palaeontologists are reluctant to declare that this tool-making
hominid was yet homo sapiens, this does not mean, supposing the experts
to be right, that homo sapiens did not exist elsewhere at around the same
time, whether in fabled countries like Lemuria and Atlantis or in places
still above water today: after all, even in the last quarter of the twentieth
century, parts of our planet are still home to primitive people whose Stone
Age way of life remains untouched by civilisation. On the other hand, this
does nothing to support the view of some occultists, mainly the disciples of
Mme Blavatsky, that the Lemurian race was in reality the *third* root race
in human history, successor of two earlier ones known as Polar and
Hyperborean. [4] The first of these races, 18 million years ago, is said to have
inhabited an 'imperishable Sacred Land' and to have been 'self-born',
thanks to the tendency of matter to cluster around an etheric matrix. The
second race, its home Greenland and northern Europe (then conjoined and
blessed with a warm climate), is described as 'boneless' and 'sweat-born',
the latter term, borrowed from ancient cosmology, [5] meaning that asexual
means of reproduction still applied. Much the same was attempted by the
Chinese sage Lie-Tze when he described how the earliest human beings,
inhabitants of the legendary land of Hua-hsu, 'bestrode the air as though
treading on solid earth and moved about like gods'. We have, fortunately,
no need to take these descriptions too literally: they may be thought of as
an attempt to explain the primordial conditions through which humanity
has passed on its descent into matter at the start of the fourth globe of our
present fourth Round.

Credible information about Lemuria, all of it from occultist sources, is woefully scarce, while the more extravagant theories, though plentiful, are unworthy of serious attention. Most writers agree – and none of us should find it hard to accept – that the inhabitants had a consciousness vastly different from our own. Their mentation is commonly described as 'pictorial', meaning that impressions from the outside world were printed directly on their minds, as a series of pictures, without any of the ordering and analysis to which our sense impressions are nowadays subject. Because these impressions followed one another continuously, like changing reflections in a mirror, none left a memory trace behind it and, for a long time, the Lemurians had no power of recollection, experiencing only the here-and-now about them. (It is interesting that Plato, when talking about Atlantis, observed that its inhabitants similarly lacked a memory.) The virtual absence of intellectual activity among Lemurians meant also that for much of the time the pictorial impressions they enjoyed had about them a dream-like quality, the more so because, mixed with them, were impressions from those non-material worlds where for so long the Earth's archetype had been in preparation.

The proximity of early human beings to these formative worlds (which, of course, must not be thought of as occupying space) led to the result, so occultists claim, that when they began having 'thoughts' of their own, these were of a kind that could influence matter and accomplish in it changes corresponding to the thinker's will. However tempting it is to dismiss so far-fetched a claim, we should first recall perhaps that over the last few years a growing number of serious researchers have been prepared to admit that 'mind over matter' (manifested in phenomena like telekinesis and telepathy) is scientifically proven, while the psychosomatic origin of many diseases has convinced doctors everywhere of the influence our thoughts, conscious or not, have on our bodily processes. Is it so far-fetched, we might ask, to imagine that this activity is but a diminutive remnant of a power which, in the remote corner of antiquity with which we are dealing, continued to be widespread among human beings until such time as their maturing intellect rendered it obsolete and caused it to atrophy inside them? This possibility should at least be borne in mind when occultists describe how our Lemurian ancestors could will changes in, for example, their physical bodies, thereby producing deviant forms (eventually doomed to extinction) such as the giants who, as the Titans of Ancient Greece, the Idzubars of Babylon, the Jotunn of Scandinavia, the Danavas of India and the Anakim and Rephaim of the Jordan valley, survive in the myths and legends of popular tradition, but who may also have been the ancestors of those strange hominoid creatures, the Megan-thropus or Java man among them, whose giganticism is a puzzle to many palaeontologists. Truly, perhaps, 'there were giants in the earth in those days',[6] though it remains doubtful that reliable evidence of their activity is provided, as some authors claim, by the enormous spears, bows and other weapons, all too heavy for any but giants to carry, supposedly found at Agadir in North Africa, or, more dubious still, by the petrified footprints reputed to exist in North America, particularly in Texas and Nevada, and to date from a time when dinosaurs still roamed the earth, some 150 million years ago.[7] Not surprisingly, these same footprints have been a godsend to those wanting support for their view that in the far distant past our planet was a busy staging-post for extra-terrestrial travellers.

The end of Lemuria, the experts affirm, occurred over 700,000 years before that of Atlantis, the last remnant of which is estimated to have perished 12,000 years ago. Other experts (and there is no shortage of them) maintain that the destruction of Lemuria happened as late as 25,000 years ago, allegedly brought about by intense volcanic activity, possibly originating in what is now called St Paul's Ridge, which caused it eventually to disappear beneath the Indian Ocean, leaving behind only such vestiges as Madagascar in the West, and Australia, Java, Sri Lanka and Sumatra in the East. During its lifetime, a period of hundreds of thousands of years, Lemuria had provided a cradle for primitive mankind and a site for its earliest strivings towards civilisation. Of the latter, it is true, no reliable trace has been found but, all things considered, that is hardly unexpected. In the end, therefore, we are left with only the occultists to assure us that Lemuria ever existed – and, it must be said, the louder and more dogmatic they become (their habit whenever proof is in short supply) the less do their assurances carry conviction. Whether Lemuria was or was not is something each of us must decide independently. Fortunately it matters little, whatever we decide.

Up to this point, apart from our brief excursion to Lemuria, we have not wandered too far from the paths of scientific orthodoxy. True, the prior manifestations of our Earth described by Mme Blavatsky and, particu-larly, by Rudolf Steiner, may be hard for some readers to swallow, but not too hard perhaps, given the varied curiosities even modern science now comes up with. The existence of Atlantis, our next port of call, is a topic so beloved of occultists and cranks, however, that we need to examine at greater depth whether, in this matter at least, both are not birds of one feather. To that end, we had better start, as we could not in the case of Lemuria, by looking at what evidence there is for a sunken continent, once part of a bigger land mass which, occultists allege, detached itself millions of years ago from what is now South America as both drifted westwards together across the area now covered by the Atlantic Ocean.

The first specific reference to Atlantis in ancient literature is offered by Plato who, in his two books *Timaeus* and *Critias*, reports conversations which Socrates is supposed to have had in 421 BC — when Plato was six years old — with Timaeus, a Pythagorean philosopher from Locris in Italy, Hermocrates, a general from Syracuse, and Critias, said to have been Plato's uncle. Responding to a request from Socrates for a historical example of an ideal state, Critias begins to describe how his grandfather, also named Critias, inherited an account of Atlantis written by the Athenian poet and law-giver, Solon (c. 690–558 BC). This story, 'strange but perfectly true', was narrated to Solon, then visiting Egypt, by an elderly priest at Saïs, an ancient city on the Nile delta, who interpreted for him the hieroglyphic script on a pillar in the temple of Neïth. The visitor was told:

> There once existed beyond the strait you call the Pillars of Hercules an island, larger than Asia and Libya together, from where it was still possible at that time to sail to another island and from there to the continent beyond them which enclosed the sea named after it . . . on this island of Atlantis there existed a great and estimable kingdom, which had acquired dominion of the entire island, as well as of the other island part of the continent itself. [8]

Anticipating the rhapsodical excesses found in most subsequent descriptions of Atlantis, Plato extols the glories of its scenery and the beauty of its cities, emphasising by that the tragedy of the mysterious cataclysm that was later to dispatch all to the bottom of the sea.

The question arises whether Plato put together this tale with a mind to making his political theories more attractive for the reader. Were that so, he certainly went to great lengths to give his invention a spurious historicity, for instance by having Critias declare that he inherited Solon's written account from his grandfather, whose own father, Dropides, had received them from Solon himself. These papers, claims the narrator, 'were in my father's possession and are in my own to this very day'. Moreover, it would not be unknown to Plato that during the travels he undertook as a young merchant between 571 and 562 BC, Solon had indeed visited Egypt — mention of the journey is made by Plutarch in his *Parallel Lives* — calling at Heliopolis and Saïs, where the story of Atlantis was allegedly told him. Thus, although these authentic-seeming details lend an aura of truth to the story, the suspicion nevertheless remains that they are a literary device employed for that specific purpose. The suspicion is renewed later when the talkative Critias, completely forgetting about his family papers, admits to having lain awake all night struggling to recall details of the Atlantean epic he was about to resume for the benefit of the rest. To argue from this, however, that Plato invented the whole story is probably going too far: the legend of a great deluge and a sunken continent is too ancient and widespread for that. Without the legend, one feels, the account given by Plato would not have been sufficient to generate the belief in Atlantis that flourished after him and does so, more vigorously than ever, today.

A little support for the historical details furnished by Plato is provided by Herodotus (480–425 BC) who, as a young man, visited Saïs in Egypt and, like Solon a hundred years before, was given a guided tour by local priests. But Herodotus (called by Cicero 'the father of history') was a cautious man, the first historian to base his work on careful research, and seems to have lent little credence to the tall stories his priestly guides told him. Nevertheless his *History* – covering the period from Croesus to Xerxes, but enlivened by anecdotes not always relevant to the main story – does contain an intriguing reference to a tribe called the Atlantes, natives of Libya, who are said to have eaten nothing that lived and not to have been able to dream. More solid support comes from Theopompus of Chios, a Greek historian of the fourth century BC, who wrote two works, called *Hellenica* (a history of Greece) and a hefty opus called *Philippica* (a history of Philip of Macedon). Only fragments of these writings survive, having been preserved in the *Historical Miscellanies* (*c.* AD 200) of one Claudius Aelianus, but among them there is mention of a former large continent called Meropis, beyond the known world, graced with beautiful cities and abundantly provided with gold and silver. Unfortunately the great Aristotle, a contemporary of Theopompus and for twenty years a disciple of Plato, flatly rejected his master's claims for the historical reality of Atlantis. Scholars nowadays incline to the view that Plato's account, the model for so many others, was based on a widely-known tradition – again, traces of it can be found in Indian sacred writings – that may also have provided Homer with some of his ideas when composing the *Odyssey*: the islands of Calypso and Scheria, home of the Phaiaecians, are often cited as evidence of this common source, while Homer's description of the city of King Alcinous, before which Odysseus stood silent and awe-struck, is compared with the magnificent capital situated by Plato on his own island of Atlantis.

Further references to the vanished continent are elusive until we come across Strabo (*c.* 64 BC–AD 19), the Stoic author of a geographical work in which he pokes fun at Posidonius of Apamea, a fellow Stoic and geographer of the first century, well-known for his assertion, still quoted at the time of Columbus, that a man sailing west from Europe would eventually reach India. According to Strabo, the same gullible Posidonius believed not only in a North-West Passage but also in Atlantis. Another believer was the fifth-century neo-Platonist Proclus (the neo-Platonists were not, it must be admitted, the most sceptical of men) who, in a commentary on the *Timaeus*, recounts how one of Plato's disciples, Crantor, retraced the journey Solon had made to Saïs three hundred years earlier, and beheld for himself, within the temple precincts, the venerable column on which the hieroglyphic account of Atlantis was written. Elsewhere Proclus describes how the existence of Atlantis had been debated by the intellectual élite of Alexandria, by 200 BC the largest city in the world, with a majority of them, mostly neo-Platonists, arguing in its favour. Elsewhere, it is still being debated today.

The case for and, less often, against Atlantis is set out in the many books that deal with the subject, their number close to 2,000 even as far back as 1926, when the last serious count was made, and now estimated to be more than ten times that figure. Their authors, when not plundering the fruit of one another's researches, harvest their supporting data from the same fertile fields, three of them – those of geology, zoology and anthropology – being sufficient to show that the arguments in favour of Atlantis are not altogether implausible. The books listed at the end of this volume will permit a more thorough investigation by anyone with the stamina needed to embark on it.[9]

Taking – and plundering in our turn – the three types of evidence already mentioned, we find that the first argument levelled against those who support the existence of Atlantis – what might be called the Atlantophile case – concerns the geological unlikelihood of so big a land mass having ever sunk to the bottom of the sea. Cataclysms on that scale, it is claimed, do not happen and cannot be compared with similar, but less important, events such as the appearance or disappearance of small islands in mid-ocean or even huge volcanic eruptions like those of Thera (Santorini) which brought Minoan civilisation to an end in 1450 BC, or Rakata which in 1883 drowned the island of Krakatoa in the Sunda Strait between Java and Sumatra. It is these, so the argument goes, as well as the frequent subsidence of coastal regions, that have given rise to the many legends – an important part of Druidic teaching, according to the fourth-century

historian Ammianus Marcellinus – that tell of sunken lands, not only
Atlantis but also such Celtic favourites as St Brendan's Isle (the Island of
the Blest) off Ireland, Lyonnesse, birthplace of Tristam, Iseult's lover, off
Cornwall, the Breton city of Ker-Ys, and near my own home in Wales,
Cantre Gwaelod, the kingdom of Gwyddno, whose ancient tree-stumps
and causeways are still visible at low tide in Cardigan Bay. Those intent
on demythologising Atlantis refer also to the consensus among modern
experts, following Charles Lyell's *Principles of Geology* (1830), that
geophysical changes of any magnitude occur as a result of gradual processes and not, as the followers of the French palaeontologist Baron
Georges Cuvier (1769–1832) once believed, of sudden and gigantic
catastrophes. At this point the theory of continental drift is usually served
up to drive the lesson home.

According to this theory, elaborated in 1912 by the German geophysicist
Alfred Lothar Wegener (1880–1930) and essential to any consideration of
Atlantis (or of Lemuria), the Earth's crust consists of several layers. Of
these the lowest, silicate layer, called sima, is characterised by its mobile,
viscous texture, reminiscent of the 'sluggish . . . turgid sea' that Rudolf
Steiner once identified as the surface of 'old' Moon. Floating on this
glutinous bed of sima are the lighter, more solid platforms, usually called
tectonic plates, that make up the remaining layers. Wegener maintained
that about 200 million years ago, during the Mesozoic era, America,
Europe, Africa and Asia, hitherto a single homogeneous unit which he
named Pangaea, had splintered into massive sections that began from
then on to drift slowly apart, the westward-travelling portions, our future
North and South America, leaving in their wake the Atlantic Ocean.
Nowhere do Wegener and his followers suggest that either portion left
behind it another piece, possibly a segment of itself, that might have been
Atlantis. On the contrary, they are quick to reject any such possibility. [10]
Too quick, perhaps, for when cartographers take the trouble to reassemble
on a globe the parts that once formed Wegener's original Pangaea, pushing
the dispersed continents together again, and then project these on a flat
map, they are forced to admit that substantial pieces of the pattern are
missing. True, South America and the west coast of Africa nestle cosily
together but farther north the parts do not interlock so well, with an even
bigger gap in the oceanic area where Lemuria is held to have been. This
remains so, even when due allowance is made for subsidiary fragmentation
along the edge of the severed continents, leaving the jig-saw with spaces
which, arguably, might well betray the former existence of an intervening
land mass.

To be fair, however, the main geological argument against a missing continent is not that Atlantis could never have existed, but that, had it existed, it would still be there, given that cataclysms of the size needed to destroy it are discounted by the experts. Yet the phenomenon of continental drift may provide confirmation that while cataclysms are not the rule, they are nevertheless the exception that serves to prove it. In order to explain how the fragmentation of his original pan-continental land mass came about, Alfred Wegener was forced to posit something he called a pole-fleeing force. The role of such a force is open to question, especially as its influence, presumably subject to changes in the Earth's polarity, would probably be too slight to provoke the relentless drifting which has placed the continents where they are now. A more persuasive explanation is that the initial breaking up and subsequent drifting, following convection currents within the Earth's mantle, were the result of a major cataclysm — what Professor Hoyle blames on the 'nuclear engine within the earth itself'[11] — a possibility confirmed perhaps by the sudden acceleration (and slight shift of direction) which caused the American land mass to move farther westward close to the start of the Quaternary period, some 10 million years ago. Geologists are confident that had a second — cataclysmic — impetus not occurred at this time, the movement would have come to a halt sooner than it did. Nowadays, too, most of them, though still prepared to accept Wegener's theory of continental dispersion, tend nevertheless to reject his explanation for it, and, basing themselves on the latest palaeo-magnetic and oceanographic studies, argue that seismic obtrusions from inside the Earth's crust (with consequent expansion of the ocean floor) best account for it. We may speculate, therefore, whether the cataclysm that sank Atlantis may not similarly have been a massive seismic upheaval, violent enough to cause the Earth's lithosphere locally to sag and so bring down all that rested on it.[12]

Afterwards nothing was to remain above sea-level except the Greater and Lesser Antilles (which may even have been submerged with the rest before being pushed up again) and in the East, the Azores whose volcanoes, though by now mostly silent, bear eloquent witness to the fragility of the Earth's crust in that region. Still more striking testimony was to come from the sea-bed itself in 1896, when workers laying the transatlantic cable from Brest to Cape Cod, a thousand miles north of the Azores, brought up pieces of vitreous lava (trachyte) which were shown to have solidified in air, evidence, albeit not conclusive, that the whole region was once above water. Further analysis of volcanic ash from the same submarine area also disclosed that its submergence could not have happened before the end of the last glacial period less than 15,000 years ago, a reason, too, for the paucity of marine sediment, its thickness rarely more than $3\frac{1}{2}$ inches, lying on the oceanic bed rock, and, more relevant still, for the presence under it of a *fresh-water* plankton (diatom) of the same recent vintage, specimens of which reportedly have been dredged up by investigators from the Riks Museum of Stockholm. Alas, no ruins of Atlantis were found underneath this layer of sludge, though reports are at hand that in 1973 an expedition sponsored by the University of Pepperdine (California) did come across several mysterious and apparently man-made structures submerged in the Bay of Cadiz. In shape not unlike the Megalithic monuments found in Western Europe, these structures are comparable with others said to lie off the Bahamas on the opposite side of the ocean, several of which were photographed by the French underwater explorer Dimitri Rebikoff.[13] In view of the distance between them, it is unlikely that *both* sets of ruins, if such they be, represent the last architectural glories of Atlantis and, though tempting to think otherwise, it seems equally unlikely that any souvenirs of that missing land still await discovery 2,000 fathoms down. By now the fissure that caused Atlantis to collapse on its foundations has long since closed over its booty, leaving only the northern part of the Mid-Atlantic ridge to remind us of what the topography of the missing continent might once have been like, a huge mountain range, over 200 miles wide in places, whose loftiest peaks break water to form the Azores. To be honest, none of this allows us to proclaim that geological evidence is at hand to prove the existence of Atlantis – as a lecturer at the French Oceanographic Institute recklessly claimed in 1912[14] – but what evidence there is, does nothing to weaken the Atlantophile case.

That case is further strengthened, some of its advocates insist, by another natural phenomenon, the Gulf Stream. Visible from the air as a cheerful blue ribbon, hundreds of miles wide, the Gulf Stream runs through the grey waters of the Atlantic at latitudes of between 36° and 40°, pushed along by the trade winds which are a side-effect of the Earth's rotation. Nowadays, these warm tropical waters flow from the Florida straits, first along the eastern seaboard of North America and then eastwards across the North Atlantic to the coast of Europe where they temper the harshness of the climate. Palaeontological evidence shows, however, that after temperatures generally had begun to drop during the Cenozoic era, 70 million years ago, the climate of Europe gradually became far cooler than it is now, with intermittent ice ages every 10,000 years or so. Going back through the Bronze and Neolithic ages, when much of northern Europe was lushly clad in deciduous forests of oak, birch, beech and hazel, we come to a time when the landscape consisted only of pine slopes and tundra, of moorland areas still waterlogged after the melting of the ice that once held them fast. From here it is but one step back to a period when a coating of ice up to half a mile thick stretched cold and heavy down to a latitude of 50°N. Theories differ as to the cause of this widespread glaciation (which affected North America as well), the most popular supposing fluctuations in the sun's radiation and others, more earth-shaking, blaming changes in the orbit of our planet or in the Earth's elliptic. A less satisfactory explanation, offered by the defenders of Atlantis, is that until Europe thawed out after the last and most recent ice age some 10,000 years ago, the warmth of the Gulf Stream never reached its shores. In other words, throughout the Lower Quaternary period, when the Atlantic looked much the same as it does now, an obstacle located in the middle of it acted as a barrier, preventing the Gulf Stream from reaching Europe which, as a result, was left at the mercy of invading polar ice. Because the Gulf Stream, in its journey across the Atlantic, broadens to a width of 500 miles, it follows that the intervening land mass, for the barrier can have been nothing else, was every bit as big. It follows, too, that the supporters of Atlantis identify it as none other than the missing continent itself.

Returning now to the Azores, we have observed how these islands are alleged to be Atlantean mountain tops. It is not surprising, therefore, that they retain a certain importance when zoological evidence is marshalled on behalf of Atlantis. Evidence of this sort needs to be treated with extreme care – Mr Sclater's lemurs are a cautionary example – but, for the record, it includes the presence of rabbits on the islands prior to their discovery in 1432, and of sixty-five species of beetle (genus *Amphisbonidae*) that burrow unconcernedly away, not only there but also in America, Africa and southern Europe. Equal importance is attached to the ubiquity characteristic of a multifooted crustacean called the fresh-water decapod, possibly a type of crayfish, and some otherwise unnoteworthy molluscs, known as Oleacinidae. Since we can be fairly certain that America, Europe and Africa were still joined together close to the start of the Tertiary Period, I am not at all sure whether the wide distribution of these insects and shellfish really does much to prove the existence of Atlantis. I confess to much the same feeling about the suicidal behaviour of lemmings and of various sea-birds, both regular favourites among those sympathetic to the Atlantean case.[15] Rather more impressive, however, is the curious behaviour, almost as suicidal, of the European eel (*Anguilla*) whose life history, revealed by the Danish naturalist Johannes Schmidt in 1924, and retold, in support of Atlantis, by Otto Muck in his book *The Secret of Atlantis*,[16] certainly merits a further retelling.

The story begins in the seaweed-filled water of the Sargasso Sea, to the east of the West Indies, where adult eels mate and where, later, leaf-like larvae (*leptocephali*) hatch out. Obeying some primitive instinct, these young transparent larvae, no more than 4 cm. in length, struggle through the matted weed until they reach the Gulf Stream. Borne along by its current, those among them that manage to survive the perilous three-year voyage eventually arrive, by now changed into young fish, off the coast of Europe. Here, the males stay together out at sea while their female companions disband in search of the river mouths that will afford them access to fresh water, remaining upstream for two years. At the end of that time, they return as adult fish to the open sea where their male consorts are waiting. Together the eels then begin their journey back across the Atlantic, swimming along the deep, cold currents that flow westwards, until four to five months later — but five and a half years in all since their departure — they find themselves restored to their Sargassan home, there to mate and so renew the cycle their generation has just completed.

That young female eels should seek out streams and rivers is no longer the mystery it was to scientists from Aristotle onwards, it being known now that only in a fresh-water environment can the eels become sexually mature. The real mystery is why larvae on the eastern side of the Sargasso Sea, instead of joining their western neighbours and heading for the rivers of nearby islands or the American mainland, undertake instead the long and hazardous crossing that carries them to Europe. While the prospect of Europe's far-off rivers and their own biological needs may be enough to persuade female larvae to surrender themselves to the warm current of the Gulf Stream, no similar considerations are there to influence the males. Unless, that is, the instinct of both has always been to make for the closest land mass which, far back in time, was again none other than Atlantis. If so, their eastward journey might start to make sense, for the Gulf Stream would previously have conveyed the young fish to the estuaries on the west coast of Atlantis, allowing female eels to find there the fresh water they wanted. In those times, too, the Gulf Stream theoretically would have been deflected by Atlantis and so flowed back towards America, circling the Sargasso Sea and restoring the mature eels to the safety of their traditional breeding ground. The recollection of all this, indelibly registered in the group memory or, to be more scientific, the cerebral chemistry of fresh-water eels, has meant that while we, for our part, wonder if Atlantis ever was, they, poor things, have never learned it is no longer there.

The geological evidence so far adduced suggests that if Atlantis ever existed, it was still above water until well into the Quaternary period and sank less than 100,000 years ago. That human beings, in the full sense of the word, inhabited Europe by then is accepted by palaeontologists generally, with Neanderthaloid remains of twice that age having been discovered. Also discovered are Cro-Magnon remains, so named after the place in the Dordogne where the first bones were found, and it is with these Cro-Magnon people that modern men and women feel immediate affinity. All around the Bay of Biscay traces of this new type of man have come to light, a man frequently over six feet tall, with high cheek-bones and a thin nose, his appearance in many ways comparable to that of the North-American Indian – a comparison which assumed new significance after Cro-Magnon remains, less ancient though still more than 10,000 years old, were excavated in America, one specimen found in 1970 as far south as Tierra del Fuego at the tip of Argentina. In Europe, no less than in America, the Cro-Magnons appear to have led a Stone Age existence – as did many Europeans until as late as 2000 BC – but, for all that, were by no means uncivilised, living in settled communities (indicative of a knowledge of agriculture) and, to judge by their amulets, charms and funeral rites, possessing, as the Neanderthalers had done before them, their own religious and magical beliefs. In addition, the stone engravings and rock paintings they left behind, like those already mentioned at Lascaux and at Altamira in northern Spain, display an art so highly developed that it must even then have been ancient, though its origins can only be guessed at.

One guess, it need hardly be said, is that the sudden appearance at a time, if not contemporary with Atlantis, then at least close to its destruction, of a new race of human beings, more civilised and artistic than any of their predecessors, constitutes proof that the western seaboard of Europe was colonised by Atlantean settlers or refugees who brought to it their own more advanced culture. And it is undeniable that the arrival of the Cro-Magnons does introduce an entirely novel feature into the prehistory of Europe, one which, irrespective of its true antecedents, has nothing in common – beyond a technique found also in the Balkans, of making detachable axe-heads – with anything dating from that period in central and eastern Europe. Unable to bring themselves to consider Atlantis as a possible explanation, archaeologists are reduced to admitting that here we have a situation, unique in prehistory, when over 'an astonishingly brief period of 10,000 years were shaped the diversities and intricacies of civilization itself'.[17] Meanwhile, the discovery of similar human remains and their artefacts on the American continent, together with the tradition still prevalent — the Hopi Indians, in particular, lay great store by it[18] — that civilisation was brought there by immigrants from a land now lying under water in the East, have naturally given added comfort to the supporters of Atlantis. It would seem, too, that further study, particularly in Yucatán and Guatemala, of Mayan remains which, though much younger than Cro-Magnon, suggest a parallel derivation, will do nothing to deprive them of that comfort. Neither, given the quantity of evidence available, much of it involving similarities beyond the reach of coincidence, is this comfort lessened by the frequent claims that people from the Old World entered the New in palaeolithic times by crossing the Bering Straits when these were still dry. They may well have done so, but recent evidence found at Cross Creek, western Pennsylvania, by archaeologists from the University of Pittsburgh, shows that Archaic Indian settlements existed in North America more than 20,000 years ago. Moreover, some experts have challenged the claim that migration over the Bering land bridge explains how men and women first entered the Western hemisphere, arguing that such a route would have required them to undertake a long and, given their ignorance of their destination, apparently purposeless journey across the bleak and inhospitable wastes of north-east Siberia. (Interestingly enough, human remains of the period have yet to be found in this region north of a latitude of 60°, though some Stone Age tools recently discovered near Yakutsk, slightly farther north, are estimated to be more than a million years old.) Whatever its historical validity, the Bering theory is at least proof that while archaeologists are unlikely to call on Atlantis or Lemuria to explain the distribution of prehistoric mankind, they are nevertheless happy to refer to submerged tracts of land — and even invent them if necessary[19] — whenever their findings require it!

To sum up, then, we might say that the anthropological arguments marshalled in favour of Atlantis turn — at times precariously — on the question, still not totally resolved by scholars, of whether similarities in the culture of geographically disparate regions betray a common origin (called the Garden of Eden theory) or reflect characteristics common to mankind as a whole. Defenders of the latter view maintain that the symbols and architectural structures which, for example, Mexico shares with Egypt, are due to a universal fondness human beings have for the same shapes and forms. Supporters of Atlantis, on the other hand, prefer the Garden of Eden approach, making that lost continent responsible for such

things as the similarities between the Basque language and several
Amerindian languages or between the Atlantis legend and that surrounding Quetzalcoatl, divine king of the Toltecs – similarities identifiable also
in the *Popol Vuh*, the epic of the Quiché Mayas, and in certain inscriptions
found on a pyramid in Xochicako, Mexico. (That the native name for
Mexico was Atzlan does not go unremarked in most books on Atlantis!)
Yet in the end, anthropological arguments of this sort cannot help giving
the impression of being all things to all men, much as do the arguments
drawn from the various other fields I have briefly explored. None of them
is so persuasive that the case may be regarded as proven, if only because
the events in question happened so long ago and so much else has happened since. Fortunately for them, occultists do not depend on external
evidence alone for their knowledge of Atlantis.

Occultists claim to have at their disposal a specific kind of clairvoyance
that affords them access to a pictorial record of the past which can then
be re-run, like a piece of cosmic video tape, for the inspection of those
trained to read it. To this the name 'akashic record' has been given, being
derived from akasha, a Sanskrit word occurring in Hindu and Buddhist
literature which means 'space', one of the five elements or bhutas which
nature, as the manifestation of Brahman, is held to contain. (The others
are air or vayu, fire or agni, water or apas, and earth or prithivi.) Each
element is associated with one of the five senses, in the case of akasha with
sound (shabda). To understand akasha better, we have to think of it, not
as empty physical space but more in terms of the nineteenth-century
concept of ether, an all-pervading substance containing within it both
time and measurement. Interestingly enough, just such a substance has
been postulated by Professor H. H. Price, formerly Wykeham Professor
of Logic at the University of Oxford, to explain some of the findings of
psychical research: a substance which, in his opinion, lies between matter
and mind, and serves as the warehouse of our thoughts. In a way, akasha
may be thought of as the infinite and universal version of the etheric
substratum that determines corporeal form, not so much diffused ether,
the nineteenth-century idea, as the etheric constitution or 'body' of the
Universe as a historical entity. The so-called akashic record exists because
the formative influences of akasha function in time as well as in space,
adapting to the 'shape' of historical events just as they adapt to the
ideographic 'shape' appropriate to objects occurring in space. Perhaps
'vibrations' would be a more suitable word in this context than 'shape',
particularly in view of the traditional relationship between akasha and
sound, making it more correct to speak of clairaudience, which involves

hearing, rather than clairvoyance, when we speak of acquaintance with
the akashic record. On the other hand, those to whom the idea of
such a record is barely conceivable may well find such refinements
pedantic!

In order to reduce this conceptual difficulty, let us call to mind the more
familiar process, so familiar that we take it for granted, of memory. By
memory I do not mean cosmic or akashic memory, but that private
faculty, no less mysterious for being the product, we are assured, of
electro-chemical reactions, which for each of us can resurrect the past in
all its movement, colour and detail. When this happens and we relive a
past experience, the things we once again see, taste and touch are not
actually present, having long since been and gone, but their conservation
somewhere inside us means that they are available for instant recall. So
it is, on a far grander scale, with the world memory, with whatever happens
in time leaving its imprint upon it, just as, on the microcosmic level, the
energy content of our own experiences endows these with a phantom
existence no longer dependent on their real one. The collective unconscious
that Jung talked so much about may itself be part of that same cosmic
record. And, if the idea of seeing in our mind's eye events that happened
centuries ago seems totally divorced from reality, it is well to remember
that our eyes do exactly that when they observe galaxies out in space
which ceased to exist thousands upon thousands of years ago. What we
then are doing is looking backwards through time at clusters of
stars which have long become an insubstantial part of the universe's
past.

So much for the akashic record, but what about the clairvoyance needed
to read it? The term clairvoyance, all too reminiscent of pier-head sibyls
behind bead curtains, is by now part of the shop-soiled vocabulary
occultism uses, but, while we cannot dispense with it altogether we might
at least take the trouble to try to smarten it up. Earlier, we had occasion
to challenge the view, implicit in a great deal of our modern thinking, that
what is inaccessible to our senses cannot exist. That view is a consoling
one, since it protects those who hold it from ever being proved wrong: we
have simply to believe that our sense organs are our only source of knowledge, for our mind, duly conditioned, to see to it that none other reveals
itself to us. Ancient thinkers were aware of this danger and it worried
them, for they believed that the acquisition of knowledge depends to a
large extent on the disposition of the knower, requiring him to adapt to
the type of information available to him. His 'adequacy' (*adaequatio rei et
intellectus*) was the term they used to describe this process and, though

doubtless ready to admit that our sense organs are more or less adequate to acquaint us with physical reality, they realised too, that other types of reality might lie beyond their reach. It was important therefore that the *possibility* of these should never be rejected. As Heraclitus put it: if we do not expect the unexpected, we shall be sure not to find it.

All this does mean, of course, that the existence of other non-physical kinds of reality has first to be assumed in order to be known, implying that faith precedes knowledge – *credo ut intelligam* – but, were we to pause to think of it, we would see that we routinely put the same amount of trust in much of our sense experience. That human beings possess an organ suited to this kind of knowledge was something ancient thinkers never doubted. Already convinced that insight is born of understanding, not the mere accumulation of sense data, the boldest of them used that faculty, not to reflect on knowledge already acquired, but to acquire new knowledge, seeking contact with those higher realities which their faith – or optimism – had made them believe in. Although intuition and imagination had a part to play in this mental exercise, it was conducted in full consciousness and under the control of the will, unlike the ecstasies that accompany certain lower forms of mysticism or the self-induced trances of spiritualistic mediums. Those who doubt whether such clairvoyant states are anything other than subjective or, who, unlike modern science, find it hard to accept a reality other than the physical, will become assured of the contrary only as a result of personal experience. The ways in which that experience may be gained will be examined later. For the moment, let us suspend our disbelief and see what the akashic chronicle reveals about Atlantis and the post-Lemurian history of mankind.

The most advanced among our human ancestors had managed to survive the destruction of Lemuria by crossing over into Africa. Of their compatriots who stayed behind, not all were to perish in the flood, since those living in outlying parts of the drowned continent were able to find refuge in mountainous areas which were high enough to stay above water. The aboriginal natives who now inhabit these regions, among them Java, Sumatra and other islands, can thus claim descent from post-diluvian Lemurians, as can their counterparts in Australia, with memories of the deluge enshrined in their myths, ritual practices and legends. Easter Island, too, was inhabited by Polynesian people of ancient Lemurian stock, their centuries-old isolation continuing undisturbed until 1722 when the Dutch seaman Jacob Roggeveen landed among them, soon to be followed by Peruvian marauders who deported their king, Matura, and all the priestly scholars of his court. With their departure, many of the ancient traditions of the islanders were allowed to fall into oblivion, though the few that survived tell how the first inhabitants, led by their religious leader (ariki henua), left their home (Hiva) in the West after it sank beneath the sea. Moreover, the few remaining inscriptions – the so-called talking boards – of the Easter Islanders have been found to resemble closely the rock markings of Australian Aborigines, as well as others, thousands of years old, found in the Indus Valley.

On the continent of Africa, meanwhile, there began one of those mass migrations which, however incredible they seem to us now, are vouched for by archaeologists and historians. According to these, 'the state of flux and shifting populations . . . was a reality in the ancient barbarian world'.[20] Just as 3,000 and more years ago entire populations, among them the Sea Peoples and the Celts, were to move from one side of Europe to the other, so the Lemurians years earlier commenced the long trek that was to take them westwards across Africa to the Gulf of Guinea. Evidence of their passage, it is claimed, can still be found in the distinctive culture of those natives who today live in the regions the Lemurians traversed hundreds of thousands of years ago. Ethiopia is often mentioned in this connection, though in reality we know next to nothing of Ethiopian culture prior to the arrival of the Sabaeans in 1000 BC. More interesting, perhaps, are the alien influences discernible in the whole area embracing the Gulf of Guinea,[21] where the Lemurians briefly halted before they set sail for Atlantis. Thus the first great chief of the Benin tribe is said to have been an olive-skinned man with blue eyes, while non-African features charac-terise many of the oldest bronze statues found there, as well as the faces of some of the population. The same is true of the Yoruba area, north-west of the city of Benin, where large settlements of more than 100,000 people flourished long before the arrival of the first European colonisers. Among Yoruba beliefs said to be inherited from Lemuria (and found also among Australian Aborigines) is a matter-of-fact acceptance of reincarnation which leads tribesmen to call children born shortly after the death of a grandparent Babatunde ('Father has returned') or Yetunde ('Mother has returned'). Finally, it should be added that the particular nature of these beliefs and of native culture generally in this region does nothing to suggest indebtedness to Moslem influences which may have travelled southwards at a time when Timbuktu was still an important centre of Islamic learning. On the contrary, local tradition, such as that of the Kagoro folk of south Kaduna, still preserves the memory of far older migrations, its details suggestive of a palaeolithic culture, involving a race whose home had once been in the East.

Abandoning their temporary settlement on the Gulf of Guinea, our refugees from Lemuria ventured across the narrow stretch of water that then separated north-west Africa from the southern shores of Atlantis — no small achievement when one remembers that navigation was still in its infancy and that early man had a prudent distrust of the sea. Once safely across, some settled in the south while others proceeded northwards to an area opposite mainland Spain where the climate was cooler, despite temperatures significantly higher than those currently found at these latitudes. (In the early Tertiary period this warm weather had also been enjoyed by Northern Europe and Greenland, then part of the Hyperborean region, to which nostalgic reference is frequently made in occult literature, as well as in Greek legend.) Henceforth climatic conditions very different from the equatorial ones of Lemuria were to influence the physical and mental development of the Atlanteans, their effect reinforced by cosmic forces emanating from outer space.

Tempting though it is to relegate the notion of such forces to the fantasy world of science-fiction, evidence of their activity has been available since the beginning of the century when the Austrian-born scientist Viktor Hess demonstrated their existence. Since then, researchers have confirmed that the Earth is relentlessly bombarded by energy streams consisting of atomic nuclei and electrons, and caused by explosions taking place on distant stars or by the formation of supernovae out of burning stellar debris. While some of these cosmic rays emanate from or, at least, traverse the constellations that make up the zodiac, their true source is hard to determine because of the intervening magnetic fields that deflect them from their course. No less hard to determine is their effect on the Earth and on ourselves. That they do produce an effect is, however, suggested by the demonstrable influence which the Moon and the Sun (in particular sun spot activity) have on our metabolism and our behaviour, possibly, in the case of the Sun, by influencing the production of melatonin, a hormone that governs our moods.[22] A similar influence may be exerted upon us by the five planets nearest to our own.[23] It is part of occult lore that in Atlantean times the effect of these cosmic rays was stronger than it is now and, moreover, that human beings were more susceptible to it.

Not only was the effect of cosmic rays stronger thousands of years ago (when the atmosphere surrounding our Earth was doubtless other than it is now) but it varied — as it may still do to a lesser extent — according to the rhythm of the so-called Platonic Year. The latter, consisting of 25,868 calendar years, is known to us from the discovery, attributed sometimes to the Babylonian astronomer Kidenas, at other times to the Greek mathematician Hipparchus, that the spring equinox is not permanently located in Aries, the first sign of the zodiac, but is slowly moving backwards through the twelve constellations along the ecliptic at the rate of approximately one sign every 2,000 years. Henceforth it was to be its position at given periods that would determine the intensity with which these cosmic forces, each with its own characteristics, influenced the development of Atlantean civilisation.

The susceptibility of the Atlanteans, like their Lemurian forebears, to such cosmic influences was all the greater because their astral body had yet to co-ordinate its activity with that of their physical organism or, to put it another way, the astral body's descent into matter was still incomplete. Here, we have again to think of the astral body only in psychological terms, seeing in its lack of co-ordination a symptom of early man's difficulty in adapting his ego or selfhood to the material conditions in which it had from then on to function. The extent to which human beings succeeded in making this adaptation decided in its turn to what extent their impressions of the physical world crowded out the subtler impressions they received directly from non-material levels of reality. On this basis, several authorities, among them Rudolf Steiner, have divided Atlantean humanity into four categories according to whichever set of impressions was predominant among them. At the two extremes stand, firstly, the Taurus type, whose feet stayed firmly planted in the world of dense matter, and, secondly, the Eagle type, for whom the world was but a window to 'the glory and the dream' which lay beyond it. A third category, the Leo type, found themselves torn between these two competing realities, at one moment opting for the one, at the next for the other, without ever being on thoroughly good terms with either. By contrast, a fourth category, called the Aquarian, had succeeded in reconciling both, deriving from them the distinctive advantages each had to offer.

This psychological differentiation was followed by gradual, but unrelated, changes in the physical appearance of the Atlanteans, bringing with them early signs of those variations in hair and skin colour that still characterise their modern descendants in different parts of the world. In the hotter, southern areas, lived swarthy, dark-haired people, some of whom began from an early date to cross over to America. Prominent among them were the early forebears of the Toltecs, many of the Eagle type, who later became the ancestors of pre-Mayan and other early Central or South American people like the Olmecs, the Pipils and the Nicaraos. Still more emigrants from southern Atlantis landed in Florida, rapidly spreading all over the eastern part of North America where, possibly, they later interbred with the Mongolian tribesmen who are alleged to have travelled south after crossing the Bering Straits while this low-lying area was still above water. (Several authorities have commented on the mixture of Mongolian and Red Indian (i.e. Atlantean!) features in the Cro-Magnon remains discovered in America, where, incidentally, the 'Eagle' influence is alleged by some writers to be detectable in the feathered headdresses and decorations of the Indians in the North and the Aztecs, Incas and Mayans farther south.)[24] Meanwhile, paler skinned people dwelling in the northern part of Atlantis had also chosen to emigrate, in their case to western parts of Europe where they soon set about re-establishing their native traditions and culture.

Needless to say, the Atlanteans were not the only human beings inhabiting – and already colonising – the world at this early time. What distinguishes them from their contemporaries, however, no less than it had done the Lemurians before them, is that they, more advanced than the rest, blazed a trail which others might follow in due course. The term 'root race', often applied by occultism to Lemurians and Atlanteans, must be understood in this limited sense, for the progress achieved by a root race or, as happened in practice, by the seven sub-races into which it was divided,[25] would later be of benefit to more dilatory races as well. With each root race, moreover, was associated a charismatic leader, in touch with the forces that sponsor human progress, to whom the oriental name, manu, is commonly given. (History has always been shaped as much by individuals as by governments and nations.) It was thanks to such a leader that the timely exodus from Lemuria and the long journey that followed to Atlantis had been successfully accomplished, just as years later a new manu, known to tradition as Vaivasvata, would lead a group of his compatriots to a destination half a world away from their doomed mid-Atlantic homeland.[26]

By the time this came about, Atlantean civilisation had already passed through seven stages. In the first three its inhabitants adjusted with growing ease to their environment and slowly learned to exploit it in their common interest. By the fourth and fifth, their civilisation had attained a degree of sophistication which, after the deluge was past, successive generations would strive in vain to recover. Even so, it would be unwise to exaggerate the material accomplishments of the Atlanteans, as many of their defenders, owing more to Jules Verne than the akashic record, so often do. And while it is just possible that metal was worked in Atlantis, it is unlikely that the great temple mentioned by Plato was covered in finest silver or its roof made of ivory and its decorations clad in gold. Not as hard to believe, however, is the tradition that the Atlanteans had a thorough and exact knowledge of astronomy, one which, we now know, was shared (inherited according to occult tradition) by the men who, shortly after the sinking of Atlantis, built the great Megalithic monuments that still stand guard along the western coast of Europe.[27] How the Atlanteans acquired this knowledge remains a mystery. Some authorities suggest that their natural clairvoyance or that of their leaders made up for shortcomings in their methods of observation, a suggestion that prompted Mme Blavatsky solemnly to declare that 'Atlantean zodiacal records cannot err, as they were compiled under the guidance of those who first taught astronomy (among other things) to mankind.'[28]

What is more important to us, for we are heirs to it, is the success the Atlanteans had in coming to terms with themselves and with one another. It is true that among individual Lemurians there had already existed a self-awareness of sorts but the distinction between it and external realities, be they physical or not, was more blurred. Absent, too, from their social life were the ordered structures which the Atlanteans later imposed on their own, an absence brought about because the folk identity of the Lemurians overwhelmed that of the individuals who shared in it. By contrast, among the Atlanteans a more active ego, replete with new-found confidence, ensured that men collaborated freely in a society which, presaging Rousseau's 'social contract', promoted the happiness of one as well as that of all. Indeed, remnants of this primitive social organisation in hitherto unexplored regions of the world were to lend substance to the myth of the noble savage in which Rousseau and most eighteenth-century reformers fervently believed.

Having adjusted to their own self-awareness and to their awareness of the outside world, bringing under their control the information received about both, the Atlanteans began next to impose upon their notions of time an order similar to the one they had already imposed upon their impressions of space. This they did by making an innovatory distinction between what had been, what was, and what had yet to be. Borrowing concepts from their experience of three-dimensional space, they now began — starting, it is said, with the females — to consign certain events to a past situated 'behind' them, and others to a future that lay ahead, reserving for the present those events that stood precariously in the immediate here and now. Once this linear time sequence had been fully grasped, the faculty of memory, its activity no more than sporadic up to then, commenced at last to function. Interestingly enough, the Hopi Indians, descendants of an Atlantean migration that coincided with this stage of human development, still have no words in their language for past, present and future: for them the only temporal distinction that exists is between manifested or objective reality on the one hand, and its unmanifested, subjective equivalent on the other, the first corresponding to what is past, the second to what still lies in the future.

From all of this we can see that if Lemuria was indeed the cradle of mankind, Atlantis became its schoolroom. Thanks to the experiences they underwent there, these early representatives of humanity were made to feel at home in the spatio-temporal world which lay outside them but of which they nevertheless knew themselves to be an integral part. It is this – and not all the nonsense we read about it – that constitutes the real significance of Atlantis.

For a long time the Atlanteans retained, alongside their growing familiarity with the physical world, a congenital awareness of spiritual realities, but as their civilisation, setting a pattern others were later to copy, entered its final, decadent phase, these realities increasingly expressed themselves in symbolic form. At once there began an insidious process by which the symbols themselves gradually replaced the sublime realities they were meant to represent, thereby giving rise to all manner of mumbo-jumbo and wretched superstition. Even the priesthood was not immune from this terrible contagion and allowed magical practices of an ignoble, shamanistic kind to invade the religious sanctuaries and usurp the sacred mysteries that were meant to be celebrated there. Only in a few isolated centres, most of them dedicated to the Sun, viewed as a token of spiritual fecundity, was this degeneracy resisted, though occultists maintain, sometimes amid harrowing tales of bestiality, civil war and bloody sacrifice, that in the end black magic triumphed everywhere, its wanton abuse of cosmic forces – Mme Blavatsky specifies a sidereal force called Mash-Mak, identical, she claims, with one called 'vril' in Lord Lytton's fantastic novel *The Coming Race*[29] – helping to provoke the catastrophe that eventually destroyed Atlantis.

Underlying this explanation is the premise that when the cosmic forces strike our planet, the 'muons' that comprise them penetrate its surface, something physics now confirms, and thereupon follow natural channels set up by the Earth's own electro-magnetic currents. According to authorities, the paths these currents take were once known to early man and are indicated by the ley-lines or straight-track alignments that purportedly cross large expanses of countryside, linking up ancient sites and monuments.[30] Some occultists maintain that a similar network of forces was marked out over 2,000 years ago near Nazca in southern Peru, though there are many different theories to account for this spectacular artefact.

(Maria Reiche, who spent over thirty years studying the Nazca markings, maintains that they in fact represent a vast astronomical calendar, though others, less expert, have argued that they are the remains of a prehistoric airport for inter-planetary spacecraft.) If, as seems likely, these subterranean energy flows were known to the Atlanteans it is not altogether improbable that in the ultimate phase of their civilisation, some of the more irresponsible inhabitants managed to divert them from their natural conduits so that, left to run wild, they provoked the submarine earthquakes that eventually plunged land and people to the bottom of the sea.

Since that calamity came about, assuming it did, the question of whether Atlantis existed or not has defied all attempts at providing a definitive answer. That the question continues to be asked is in the end perhaps the best evidence that neither sceptics nor believers have at their disposal the facts each side really needs to destroy the other's case and, by so doing, vindicate its own. Atlantis, however, is of importance to occultism – and this should be carefully noted – only because it forms so conspicuous a part of the doctrines made public by Mme Blavatsky at the end of the last century, her revelations on the subject echoed, and often embellished, by every supporter thereafter. Their enthusiasm and that of their listeners is, of course, understandable, given the dream so many people nurture of an earthly paradise that has long ago been lost: a sunken continent, out of sight but never out of mind, promises to show that once upon a time this precious dream was true, for as Oscar Wilde has said about another ideal country: 'A map of the world that does not include Utopia is not worth even glancing at.'

On the other hand, none of this can be expected to carry much weight with those who are impatient with promises of a sentimental kind or, worse, unwilling to dream. For them Atlantis has never existed. Of that they remain as convinced as they are (in this case quite rightly!) that the Moon is not made of green cheese. Fortunately, this conviction does not mean that those of little faith are left with no choice but to abandon occultism without further ado. The truth is that, despite the nostalgic attention Atlantis receives in contemporary occult writings, it is not an essential ingredient of occultism itself: without it there are slightly fewer currants in the cake but otherwise the cake remains the same. Since that is also true of the occult version of what happened in the world *after* Atlantis had vanished under the sea, we can proceed now to examine this post-Atlantean chronicle in the comforting knowledge that readers unable to believe in it are free to set it aside.

Tradition has it that with the disappearance of Atlantis another root race took up the vanguard of civilisation. Its home this time was not some dubious, long-drowned continent but a remote corner of central Asia, on the western edge of the Gobi Desert, an area identified as east of the Takla Makan basin whose borders are defined by high mountain ranges, those of Tien Shan in the north, Kunlun Shan in the south and, in the west, the Pamirs. Significantly, perhaps, its situation at a longitude of 90°E is the polar opposite to that of Guatemala and Yucatán (90°W), where pre-Toltec settlers from Atlantis are believed to have laid the foundations of the ancient Mayan culture that archaeologists have since discovered there. Significantly, too, its latitude of 38°–40°N is exactly level with that of the Azores, whose connection with Atlantis has already been remarked upon.

Whether this new civilisation sprang up spontaneously among the indigenous population or was conveyed there by refugees from Atlantis is still debated among occultists. Most of them, with a feeling for historical continuity and, so they claim, a peep into the akashic record, assert that before Atlantis sank, there emerged a new manu who, sensing that the corruption we have mentioned would soon become universal, led a group of righteous citizens all the way to central Asia, passing between the Altai and Tien Shan mountains into the Gobi Desert, before turning back towards the Tarim river. There, or at least in the vicinity – some suggest a more westerly settlement in what were once Bactria and Sogdiana, while Hindu pandits favour the area surrounding Lake Manasarowar in Tibet – by now weary and, presumably, footsore, they came at last to a halt.

That no evidence of this expedition is available to us is in itself not reason enough to say that it never took place. It may seem *unlikely*, but, mindful of the vast migrations that were common in times to which history and archaeology have access, we cannot dismiss it as impossible. Neither should we be surprised if evidence of the kind we normally expect in other cases is, in this case, denied us: we are, after all, dealing with a relatively small group of people – perhaps a hundred thousand at the most – whose arduous progress from one side of the world to the other, whatever their route, has left no trace behind it. Not that any serious attempt to look for its traces has ever been undertaken. Possibly, therefore, some are still to be found, unrecognised by anthropologists among the megalithic monuments of northern Europe or in the beliefs and traditions of certain tribes in central Africa, where indications given earlier in connection with the westward migration of the Lemurians may just as properly apply to the return journey accomplished by the Atlanteans. A further indication of this sort is the age-old mythology of the Dogon tribe in what today is the Republic of Mali, much of it bound up with the nature and elliptical orbit of an invisible satellite belonging to Sirius, a star eight and a half light years away from our Earth.[31] This satellite, known to us as Sirius B and to the Dogons as Po-Tolo, was unsuspected by astronomers until the last century and only in 1848 did telescopic observations confirm its existence. According to occultists, the Dogons (whose monotheism is something of a rarity among the native religions of Africa) have inherited their knowledge of Sirius B either from Atlantean star-watchers who passed through their territory on the way to Arabia and thence to central Asia, or, the other explanation currently on offer, from extra-terrestrial visitors.[32] Until a third explanation comes along, my money stays on the Atlanteans!

When these Atlanteans set up home there, the Tarim Valley was a pleasanter, more hospitable place than it is today. At that time the Takla Makan basin, by now consisting almost entirely of desert, was irrigated by rivers flowing from the Kunlun mountains, many of them tributaries of the Tarim, and all, except a small number, long since lost beneath layers of restless, windswept sand. Only occasional shrubs and sparse clusters of poplar and willow nowadays remind the visitor of the lush vegetation that previously grew there. And the only signs of the successive civilisations that have flourished in the area are the relics, among them Buddhist and Nestorian–Christian writings, dug up by archaeologists, several of whom have even gone so far as to identify Takla Makan as the birthplace of oriental culture. Confirmation of this may lie in the oldest Chinese tradition that speaks of a mysterious country, the source of massive emigration and the home of those 'men of perfect virtue' whose qualities were extolled by such venerable authorities as Chuang-Tze and Lâo-Tsze, supposed author of the celebrated *Tao-teh-Ching*. The lives and deeds of these ancient people, Chuang-Tze regretfully observes, have 'left no trace, and there is no record of their affairs'![33] Memories of the same civilisation may also account for the many legends that still exist of vanished cities lying underneath the Gobi Desert or of a time still earlier when the area was a huge inland sea on which there floated an island paradise, its wonders not unlike those attributed to Atlantis.

While Atlantis still prospered there had occurred among its inhabitants the beginnings of a racial differentiation whose effect survives to this day, itself evidence of how far man's physical body had evolved since its transition from a uniform hominoid phase. This was accompanied by the further development of memory and a more ready adjustment to physical conditions, trends that were now to continue in Asia, considerably helped by the fact that human beings had at their disposal a growing fund of experience, which enabled them to learn from the successes and failures of their past. Slowly, too, their knowledge became illumined by *understanding*, encouraging them to have greater confidence in themselves and in their capacity for rational judgment. As a result they set about extending their dominion over their surroundings, and, self-reliant and increasingly self-assured, felt no longer in need of the comfort which their supersensory awareness of spiritual realities had formerly brought them. Soon there came a day when that awareness, already dimmed in Atlantean times and by now irrelevant to their everyday concerns, had all but disappeared among the mass of the people. No blame can be attached to them for this change which, if anything, was unavoidable if men were to stand on their own two feet in the world and so enjoy the moral independence without which free-will is deprived of all meaning. Only in this way, occultism teaches, could the spiritual monad inside man pass through the human stage of its evolution.

Even so, the human race, however complete its integration in the material world, was not to be completely cut off from that spiritual world to which it essentially belonged. To a small number of individuals who, not without effort, had retained the spiritual awareness once universal, there fell the important task of reminding their fellows of what had been lost, as well as providing them with the wise guidance they would require at turning points in the history of our race. Reference to the earliest such teachers is especially to be had in the Hindu *Puranas* which speak, for instance, of holy sages or Rishis, part of whose teaching is preserved in the *Mahabharata* (of which the *Bhagavad-Gita* forms part), though the miscellany that now bears this name was not committed to writing until a much later date. (Here, incidentally, we see the beginnings of that esoteric knowledge to which occultism persistently lays claim.) As for the loss of supersensory awareness, this event is commemorated in the tradition of a third eye (the Eye of Shiva) which, located in the centre of the forehead, symbolises the long-lost organ of spiritual vision: variously depicted as a lotus flower, a snake, a star, the sun or, literally, a third eye, it is found in paintings and on statues all over the world. To the period that has followed its disappearance the name kali-yuga or 'Dark Age' has been given by Hindu tradition, its starting point, some 5,000 years ago, said to date from Krishna's death in 3102 BC.[34] Needless to say, this loss of spiritual vision affected not only the inhabitants of the Tarim Valley but, more slowly though no less surely, the remainder of humanity as well.

During the Atlantean period, the migrations that occurred had involved separate proto-ethnic groups (it would be premature to speak here of 'races') whose culture differed but little from one group to the next. Only in the central Asian evolution centre did a real cultural divergence begin, its different forms, albeit derived from one source, characterising the various groups that emigrated from there. Among the first to leave was one that travelled through Kashmir into north-west India and along the Ganges Valley, coming into contact, the more so as it moved south, with a backward population composed of early Dravidian settlers and aboriginal tribes like the Nisadas, whose ancestors were largely descended from Lemurians who had never made the journey to Atlantis. The meeting of these different peoples, some more backward than the rest, was not in the end unfruitful, a development which explains why, over the next 2,000 years, successive waves of Aryan invaders from the North (the earliest of them led, claim occultists,[35] by Rama, the avatara whose conquests are described in the epic *Ramayana*) would frequently encounter tribesmen with a culture higher than their own. Not that this discouraged the invaders, most of them tall and light-skinned, from feeling superior to the indigenous Dasyus (wild or 'dark-skinned' folk) and other tribes they came across: all of them, with the passage of time, destined to be transformed by legend into ghouls and demons known as Rakshasas. These feelings of superiority were to survive in early Hindu literature where the Aryans of the priestly and warrior classes (kshastra) are extolled above the ignoble remainder of society (anarya), thereby laying the foundations of what has since become the caste system. Because this new civilisation prospered at a time – the Platonic Year (8000–6000 BC) was governed by Cancer – when human beings still remembered, though no longer possessed, the spiritual awareness they had once enjoyed, it also bequeathed to Indian thought its somewhat ambivalent attitude towards the physical world, fostering in generations to come those exaggerated notions of maya or illusion which persist to this day.

As the Platonic Year regressed, dispatching the spring equinox into Gemini, a second migration, led by a sage whom tradition calls Zoroaster (not to be confused with the historical figure who lived around 600 BC) moved into what is now Iran. In very little time there established itself in this area a Persian civilisation which lasted from 5000 to 3000 BC. Not unexpectedly, the religion of the inhabitants was in many ways similar to that of the people who had earlier migrated to India. Evidence of this similarity, though dating from a much later period, is apparent in the most ancient sacred books of both countries, the *Gathas*, in the case of Iran, and, in the case of India, the *Vedas*, particularly the earliest of them, the *Rigveda*. Even the names of the gods and demigods are often the same, as, for instance, in a treaty concluded in 1380 BC between the Hittite emperor and one of the Mitanni kings. There we come across, among others, Mitra, Indra and Viruna, as well as other features similar to those found in early Indian mythology, features whose reappearance in Greek and even Nordic mythology offer still further evidence of their common origin. Meanwhile back in Persia, an enduring memory of the primitive Zoroaster, first leader of the nation, was for centuries to bestow a legendary reputation on the outstanding religious reformer known to history by the same name: to the Greeks, the historical Zoroaster grew into the wisest of mortals who, well-versed in mathematics and astrology, became the tutor of Pythagoras, while to the Jews and Christians, more narrow-minded, he remained the blackest of all black magicians. For once, occult tradition stays refreshingly down-to-earth, claiming only that the first Zoroaster taught husbandry and agriculture to the people under his care, his influence reflected in the teachings of his later homonym which divide the world into two hostile camps: in the first stand herdsmen and farmers whose loyalty is to Ormudz (Ahura-Mazda) and the forces of light, in the second loiter robbers and nomads, the servants of Ahriman, lord of falsehood and lies.

From here on, the history of further migrations from the Tarim basin becomes difficult to chart with any exactitude, since people who had never lived there were quick to copy the beliefs and habits of those who had, disseminating these over an area far beyond that occupied by genuine émigrés from Takla Makan. This demographic uncertainty means that we cannot say much about the claim, so often made by occultists, that priestly refugees from central Asia brought their advanced knowledge with them into Hamitic Egypt, sowing there the seeds of the great civilisation that later came to flower under the Platonic sign of Taurus, and witnessed the building of the Pyramids between 3000 and 2200 BC. Even more confused are the influences that forged together the glittering civilisations which sprang up along the valleys of the Tigris and the Euphrates though, here again, the Atlantean and post-Atlantean contribution, particularly in the field of astronomy, is indubitably large. The same is also true in the case of the Sumerians who, though noted for their concern with statesmanship and politics, are above all famous as the inventors of writing. Using clay tablets for their purpose, they supplemented pictographic forms with ideograms and, more important still, invented different cuneiform signs to denote different letters. So readily did their Middle Eastern neighbours copy their invention that by 3000 BC the art of writing was known throughout the region, the next big advance following a thousand years later when, in the reign of Hammurabis, cuneiform characters were simplified by the Babylonians and their number reduced to twenty-nine. Still more simplification, in this case by the Phoenicians, themselves descended from the Aryanised Panis of India, was to result in a series of twenty-two consonants, but no vowel signs, which, after being adapted for transcription on to papyrus, finally led to the elaboration of our modern alphabet.[36]

This delay in the invention of writing – speech, for the most part agglutinative, had existed as far back as Atlantis – assumes a special meaning once it is remembered that until it happened, human beings were forced to depend on their memory for the preservation of knowledge, a situation not without its benefits at a time when memory, still young and untried, needed all the practice it could get. The fruits of this practice become apparent when one recalls that for centuries the epics, myths and sagas of nations all over the world survived only as part of an oral, often sung, tradition, and were not written down until much later. As for the speed with which writing spread throughout the Near East after its invention in Sumeria, this was due in large part to the similarity of the languages spoken in the region, something that has led philologists, from Greek and Roman times onwards, to suppose a common parent of what is now known as the Indo-European family of languages. This parent, as the occult record shows, is none other than the language formerly spoken by the descendants of Atlantean settlers on the banks of the Tarim river. Transmitted by those among them who migrated to India and Iran, it was soon carried in one form or another so far afield that by 5000 BC its derivatives had spread to Kurgan on the southern steppes of Russia and, long before our present era started, had arrived as far west as Ireland and the Iberian peninsula. By then, too it had developed into Sanskrit (the name, meaning 'polished' or 'perfected', itself indicative of a more primitive source) and would soon become mature enough to put into words the most sublime elements in the metaphysical thought of old India – though not at first into writing, since all the evidence points to an *oral* transmission of the sacred Vedic teachings before they came to be written down between 1500 and 800 BC.

With the invention of writing, the human record ceases in every sense to be an occult one. No longer in the pursuit of information about the course of human affairs do we have to rely exclusively on broken bones, chipped pottery and, for our specialist purpose, the mating habits of sea-fish or the murky revelations of the akashic chronicle. Up to now that pursuit has carried us, dry and unscathed, from one marine catastrophe, Lemuria, to another, Atlantis, and then back again across the forests and wastes of Africa into the barren highlands of central Asia. As the people whose footsteps we have sedulously followed must more than once have thought, there finally comes a point at which it is better to stop. The threshold of history is just such a point: history is best left to the historians.

IV

Ancient Wisdom
and the
Esoteric Tradition

*All souls do not easily recall the things of the
other world. Few are they who keep an
adequate remembrance of them.*

PLATO

Because occult knowledge is by definition hidden and secret, even the most
zealous historians are of little help to us when we begin the attempt to
trace its origins and development. For instance, we have no choice but to
accept on trust the claim that its beginnings coincided with the extinction
of supersensory awareness, formerly the property of all, in the majority of
human beings. Or that, once this happened, the knowledge such awareness
had provided became confined to a minority of individuals whose ability
to acquire it remained unimpaired. Some of these, realising its worth, then
chose a few others to whom to impart it, selecting for that purpose people
whom they judged capable not only of understanding its secrets but, after
rigorous training, of themselves gaining access to its source.

   From the outset, it is important to realise that, though derived from an
acquaintance with transcendental realities, the information on which
occult tradition rests is every bit as reliable as the information that is
furnished by our senses in the course of our everyday life. More so, perhaps,
for even when our senses agree not to deceive us, the evidence they offer
has to undergo a complicated process, one dangerously susceptible to
error, before it finally reaches the conscious levels of our mind. In contrast,
the immediacy peculiar to supersensory impressions serves to ensure
that the latter stay always faithful to their subject. Naturally, the

interpretation given to such impressions may sometimes err, as may the recollection of them or the conclusions they induce, but these are risks we have necessarily to run, if we are to remain free and independent human beings. Not for one instant do these risks alter the fact that supersensory impressions, unique among those available to us, are never less than perfect copies of the reality they claim to represent. It is this quality that allows us to understand better why the knowledge thus obtained became – and stayed – esoteric, its treasures jealously guarded by those entrusted with their safe-keeping. Moreover, because one of its noblest concerns was our relationship to a universe which, as the product of God's self-awareness, is intrinsically divine, occult tradition soon acquired a sacred character which, for those acquainted with it, strengthened the need to hold back its contents from profane eyes and ears. Herein, too, lies the basis for a further claim made by occultists that these arcane teachings contain the essence of the world's great religions and so represent the denominator common to them all, whatever superficial differences happen to divide them. 'What we desire to prove', writes Mme Blavatsky in her *Isis Unveiled,* 'is that underlying every ancient popular religion was the same wisdom-doctrine, one and identical, professed and practised by the initiates of every country, who alone were aware of its existence and importance.'[1]

Although most people had become shut off from spiritual levels of reality by post-Atlantean times, their yearning for the numinous never left them, exacerbated by their memory of what they had lost. Refused direct access to these sublime realities, they endeavoured now to reach them *through* the material world with which they felt themselves increasingly bound up. In some primitive, often matriarchal societies, particularly those still without a settled way of life, this took the form of a special devotion to an earth goddess, a supernal mother whose recurring fruitfulness was looked upon with awe and affection by her grateful human children. Others, having learned that good crops depended as much on agricultural planning as on fertile soil, directed their gaze to the sky, seeing there a divine father who, as lord of the weather, could bless or ruin the season's crops according to his mood. Some of them, not satisfied with just one God, then went on to establish a whole pantheon containing gods and goddesses of earth, sky and sea, as well as subordinate deities linked with natural phenomena of every kind.

Together, these developments expressed, in terms relevant to the societies concerned, the irrepressible feeling human beings have of their own transcendence and were symptoms of a dynamism towards the Absolute, as ground of all being, which was inherent in everyone. This becomes clear when we consider three Latin verbs from which, according to some philologists, the word religion (*religio*) may derive: *rĕlĕgĕre, rĕlĭgari* and *relĭgĕre*, meaning, respectively, 'to turn back towards something', 'to be bound once more to something' and 'to choose something again'. What early men and women turned their minds to were the spiritual levels of reality they no longer saw but still half-remembered. To these they renewed their personal commitment and, by so doing, chose to give to what alone is true and permanent the priority it merited above the transitory world in which they found themselves exiled. Theirs was a natural religion, the validity of which even the Church, normally intolerant of competition, has felt bound to recognise, for it testifies uniquely to the durability of the primordial awareness the human race has of that supreme One which in its absolute and total wholeness unites the multiplicity of all that exists.

Alas, psychologists and anthropologists sense nothing of this. To the former, the worship of Mother Earth is little more than a sexual obsession on a macrocosmic scale, with — they rarely mention women — man a kind of Oedipus figure whose father, Laios, becomes an envious sky god, lurking bitter and resentful in the clouds.[2] As their contribution to the same topic, anthropologists point to the stressful anxiety that must have afflicted early human beings as they tried to hold their own against the menacing forces around them, their situation so unbearable that they were driven to invent a divine power whose favour they hoped to earn by means of sacrifice and prayer, with a little magic thrown in when persuasion yielded no results. The same power, they go on to say, offered to our ancestors the promise of a happier world beyond this present vale of tears, with admission to it their reward for the miseries they had patiently endured in their lifetime. What these theories seek finally to prove is that religion was a response by early human beings to needs and wishes alive inside themselves, a kind of escapist therapy or, as Marx said, the opium of the people.

The error in this type of thinking lies in the belief that early men and women invested their environment with divine or spiritual meaning so as to make it less incomprehensible and frightening to live in. The reality is, however, that instead of finding a divine *presence* in the world, our forebears were aware only of a divine *absence*, albeit one more apparent than real since it was the vision of God, not God himself, which had been withheld from their experience. Unable to renew this vision now that their third eye had closed, human beings looked for signs of God's activity in the natural phenomena around them, inferring from these God's own ulterior existence. At that point, adapting to their spiritual needs the methods they successfully used in their dealings with the physical world, they began to fit their religious speculation into a system like those their intellect had constructed to accommodate their growing knowledge of temporal things. It then required very little time before popular piety rendered the system – and God himself – more personal by introducing into it a number of rituals and devotional practices, or before theologians began elaborating the first moral codes, taking care, while doing so, to keep one worldly eye cocked on the social needs of the community they lived in. The rest belongs to the history of religion.

Alongside these religious systems there persisted, often within the priesthood itself, a body of esoteric teaching which was derived from and intermittently nourished by, direct acquaintance with the spiritual truths it revealed to its disciples. Admittedly, this teaching soon adapted its imagery to whatever society its advocates found themselves in, its characteristics determined by the ethnic and cultural background of the people it addressed, but for all that, its substance stayed unchanged. As a result occult tradition, often to the surprise of those meeting it for the first time, is still, even today, much the same all over the world, regardless of the local colour it chooses to wear.

Such, for instance, is the case in India where the gupta-vidiya or secret doctrine found its way into the *Vedas* and, later, the *Aranyakas* and other material destined to make up the fourteen classical *Upanishads*, while to the north in Tibet, it stood concealed behind the shamanistic excesses of the old Bön religion, its preoccupation with a primal spiritual reality so close to Manicheism that scholars, ignoring their common source, once believed that it was carried to the roof of the world by third-century missionaries from Samarkand. (With the arrival there four hundred years later of Buddhism – which assimilated rather than replaced the Bön – the same tradition was to help produce the Tibetan refinement of Buddhism known as the Diamond Vehicle or Vajrayana.) Next door in China, occult tradition directed its secret influence on the mystical content of Taoism, causing particular emphasis to be placed on the reconciliation between the individual (yin) and the universe (yang) which is ultimately achievable through the cultivation of wu wei (inactivity). Turning back to the West, we find it again in Central America, possibly brought there by pre-Toltec migrants from Atlantis before it passed to the Mayans, though our information, dependent on a few pictographic records and the biased writings of Conquistadores, permits of only the most tentative speculation. More helpful by far, because more plentiful, are the signs of its development in Europe.

That such signs are plentiful in Europe does not, of course, mean that occult tradition simply ceased to exist elsewhere in the world. It is true that in some places the streams which had hitherto fed it slowly dried up, producing a stagnation that fostered in due course many of the deviant and superstitious practices that still give occultism such a bad name. However, in other places it stayed fresh and vital, its contents enriched and, when appropriate, corrected by those individuals who retained a primitive ability to look directly into its source. This was certainly the case in the East where adepts familiar with its teachings dedicated their lives to the contemplation of the transcendental realities with which it was concerned, letting the rest of the world pass them by unnoticed. Their approach, however understandable, typifies the indifference to our earthly surroundings that was to infect much of Asia and deprive its inhabitants of that adventurous curiosity which, in the West, did so much to further the advancement of knowledge. In its turn, this knowledge, though related to mundane affairs, demanded that in the West even occultists take its findings into account when forming a view of the total reality, seen and unseen, to which we all belong, and it is largely thanks to their refusal to shun the phenomenal world where modern men and women feel so much at home, that the development of occultism in Europe is particularly relevant to our human condition today.

This development may be said to have begun with the Sumerians, whose practical notions of statesmanship and civic responsibility, a novelty in the post-Atlantean world, were permeated by a religious awareness which owed its existence to esoteric tradition. Every New Year the priest-king (In-gal) and his royal consort re-enacted a sacred marriage that symbolised the optimal fusion of the material and spiritual levels of being, though most of the spectators saw in this only the ritual coupling of the god Dumuzzi and his queen Inanna (Ishtar), two of the 360 gods and goddesses adopted by the exoteric form of the Sumerian religion to represent the unseen forces at work throughout nature. Later the same occult tradition, inherited from the Akkadians, was upheld by Babylonian priests who, during the lifetime of the first empire (1700–1600 BC) revived the art of astrology as it had once been practised in Atlantis. Their researches in this field were taken over by their Assyrian conquerors who, under the all-powerful Adad-Nirari (809–782 BC), built a magnificent temple in honour of Nabu, the Babylonian god of astrology, at Calah, now Nimrud, where the great astrological libraries of Sargon II, Sennacherib and Assurbanipal, were stored until their removal to Nineveh. With the fall of that city in 612 BC, this important knowledge reverted to Babylonian custody. (Berosus, a Babylonian priest of Bel, would later translate these astrological texts into Greek — fragments of his work are known to us — afterwards retiring to the island of Kos, where he taught occultism to a select group of disciples until his death in 280 BC.)

Particularly noticeable about the Assyrian empire, despite its wealth and might, is the desperate sadness its inhabitants felt about their loss of spiritual vision. Nowhere is this situation more movingly described than in the epic of *Gilgamesh*, a work rich in occult significance, whose hero searches in vain for the vanished immortality which he feels to be his birthright. A similar feeling, its source the same tradition, had already tormented the Hittites whose own predominance in Asia Minor lasted from 1900–1200 BC: holding themselves entirely to blame for their separation from the spiritual world, the Hittites bequeathed to their successors an oppressive sense of personal failure and sin.

Related feelings of human frailty seem also to have existed among the Egyptians, with signs of it easily discernible in their funeral rites and in the religious texts associated with them, foremost among these being the various passages that make up the famous *Book of the Dead*, many of them written down around 1800 BC but containing elements that are considerably older. While the *Book of the Dead* is ostensibly concerned with the journey a deceased person's soul undertakes into the next world, its covert message relates to the voyage every spiritual monad must make to regain its true home among the Shining Ones (𓄿𓏤 𓈖𓃀) in the realm of spirit. In the text we are introduced to two guides, both aspects of ourselves, the first, foolish one who keeps his head turned back towards the world of matter, the second, wise one who stands in the bows of life's ship and looks confidently into the darkness ahead, knowing that the light of the Absolute, sum total of all things (𓏤𓊪𓏏) awaits him. So much a part of everyday life were the mysteries in ancient Egypt that the Greek historian Herodotus made a point of observing that its inhabitants were the most religious people in the world. For the moment, however, I am concerned less with the exoteric form religion took there, involving, for example, the worship of the reigning Pharaoh as an incarnation of the Sun god, Horus, than with its esoteric meaning, the latter inseparable from the name of Hermes Trismegistus or Hermes 'Thrice Greatest'.

The title Hermes Trismegistus is a Graeco-Latin version of the Egyptian Thot or Tehuti, the name of the divine law-giver who, ibis-headed and linked with the Moon, was held to be the divider of time and reckoner of the stars. In this role Thot was of great practical importance to the

Egyptians since lunar movements, calculated in advance, enabled them to anticipate certain natural events: a full Moon in the constellation of Aquarius, when that rose in July, meant that the Nile would soon start to flood, its waters receding only when the Moon waxed among the stars of Taurus (in October); full in Scorpio, when that constellation rose in the evening during April, the Moon heralded the dreaded Khamsin or fifty days' wind.

In the sixty-fourth chapter of the *Book of the Dead*, Hermes is described as both a wise physician and a worker of magic and although his efforts are in this case directed to an individual's post-mortem welfare, the reference betrays a lingering memory of the historical persons on whom the legendary figure came later to be based. Occultists are undecided about how many such persons existed, though most agree that there were at least two, the second reinvigorating the esoteric tradition which the first, many dynasties before, had helped introduce in the kingdoms of the Nile.[3] There is an account, too, that this first Hermes, himself a Pharaoh, wrote a book containing magical secrets that was stolen by Prince Ptahneferku, one of many writings either attributed to him or said to contain his teaching. Much later, Iamblichus, the neo-Platonist, was to claim in his book *On the Egyptian Mysteries* that their number totalled 36,525, a figure (first mentioned by the Egyptian historian Manetho) which led Clement of Alexandria to state that 30,000 works by Hermes were stored in the library of Osymandias (Rameses II). Plato was to refer several times in his work to Hermes, sometimes under the name of Theut, and these references in due course encouraged his followers to turn the legendary Egyptian into their version of a god-man, bearer of the eternal Logos and earthly agent of the Creator. In addition, the renown Hermes enjoyed as Ra's mouthpiece prompted the Roman poet Ovid to make him the inventor of speech,[4] while his mastery of measure and number led Plutarch to praise him for having added five days to the 360 which up till then had made up a calendar year. As for the 'hermetic' philosophy to which he also lent his name, this was a late development belonging to the period that followed Alexander's conquest of Egypt in the third century BC, though as the particular expression of an age-old occult tradition, its only real novelty lies, of course, in its name.

The astrological researches of the Egyptians offer further testimony to the discreet but unrelenting influence of that same tradition. Here, we learn, for instance, that the stars — gods, according to exoteric religion — were privately regarded as the source of different cosmic forces involved in the pre-earthly evolution of humanity. Considerations of this sort have to be borne in mind if we are to understand fully such antique star-calendars as those of Esneh and Denderah or the Theban ephemeris of the Ramessid kings (20th Dynasty, *c.* 1150 BC). At the same time, it cannot be denied that many writers have exaggerated the mysterious side of ancient Egypt, the more enthusiastic going so far as to find occult significance in virtually every brick used to build the Pyramids at Giza – which at least explains why there is a smile on the face of the Sphinx. The temptation to do this is the greater because until the 18th Dynasty, mystery-mongering of a kind commonly, though mistakenly, identified with occultism, and based largely on superstition, was notoriously widespread throughout the whole of Egypt, a situation not so very different from that found in certain places even today.

Egyptian influences, mixed with others from Asia Minor, were brought westwards in 900 BC when Etruscan settlers began to arrive in north-west Italy, their civilisation reaching its zenith some 300 years later. Such was Etruscan involvement in the mysteries that the Romans sent their novice priests there to learn magic and prophecy, while Etruscan piety was so widely admired and commented on by classical authors that the early Christians resentfully dismissed Etruria as the begetter and mother of all superstition (*genetrix et mater superstitionis*). Among the pagan practices offensive to them had been the important role assigned by the Etruscans to the goddess Uni (the Roman Juno) who, in her munificent fruitfulness, was identical to Cybele, the Phrygian *magna mater*, herself almost indistinguishable from the Egyptian goddess Isis.

Some time before this, our occult tradition, now well over 5,000 years old, had helped shape the Greek mysteries, though again we must take special care to distinguish between their exoteric form, the part known to classical scholarship, and their esoteric meaning. More form than meaning were some of the popular Dionysiac cults which, despite an interest in death and the after-life, seem often to have been an excuse for a communal booze-up in honour of the god of wine. Somewhat more dignified were the Eleusinian mysteries, their ceremonies based on the myth of how Demeter, the goddess of corn, searched for her daughter Persephone after Hades, King of the Underworld, had carried her off as his bride. Released only after her mother had threatened never to sanction another harvest, Persephone was found to have eaten a single pomegranate seed, symbol of death and rebirth, during the time she was held captive by Hades. As a result, she was condemned to spend a third of each year in her husband's underground kingdom before returning for the other eight months to her mother who, in return, permitted crops to flourish again. (Demeter's search for her missing daughter would later be used by Plato to illustrate the philosopher's quest for the truth, its goal being to reunite our spiritual nature with the real and eternal world of which the present one is but the insubstantial shadow.)

Of special interest is the esoteric content of the Orphic mysteries, their mythology linked once more with Dionysus, this time under the aspect of Dionysus Zagreus – whose mother, incidentally, was Demeter's daughter, the corn maiden Persephone. The teachings of Orphism were contained in a series of poems attributed to Musaeus, a pre-Homeric poet much admired by Plato and, according to legend, a pupil of Orpheus himself. Their chief concern was the moral responsibility of every individual and they recommend a pure and chaste life as the surest way to avoid repeated incarnations and so dwell in Elysium for ever. In the sixth century BC, these moral ideas and others connected with Delphi, were reintegrated into the mainstream of occult tradition by Pythagoras,[5] who had been introduced to its secrets, including, possibly, those dealing with the antediluvian worlds of Atlantis and Lemuria, while travelling in Egypt and India. For him and his followers, man was a spiritual being whose descent into a physical body was intended to give him the chance to earn by his own efforts the place reserved for him in the company of the gods. The aim of the mysteries was to help the initiate achieve this apotheosis all the sooner, by reproducing in his present life all the educative experiences that many earthly lives and many periods spent between death and rebirth would otherwise have to provide. Aware, too, of pre-earthly evolution, the Pythagoreans (like Rudolf Steiner after them) sought to describe in planetary terms the progression every human being had already undergone through different levels of being, what are called the archetypal, intellectual and formative conditions of proto-mundane existence. Ignorance of their real significance and a passing acquaintance with astrology prompted later commentators to interpret this as implying a literal descent from the stars, with the soul taking upon itself the characteristics of all the planets it passed on its way down to Earth. Likewise, on its journey back, the soul was thought to pass again through these same planets, surrendering in turn the characteristics it had previously borrowed from each.

Many of the same ideas, correctly understood but often expressed in a language that concealed this understanding from people not ready to share it, were taken over by Plato and his school. Among those who have since criticised Plato for his want of clarity is St Thomas Aquinas, who grumbled that 'he teaches all things figuratively and by symbols, meaning by the words something else than the words themselves mean, as when he said that the soul is a circle.' At that time the Church's 'Angelic Doctor' had not fully understood the difficulty Plato faced in trying to put into words truths he was intuitively aware of. When, in December 1273, he himself had a mystical experience, he stopped writing the third part of his *Summa theologica*, telling his secretary that 'all I have written is no more than straw compared with what I have seen and what has been revealed to me.' What Plato's language never conceals, however, is his total commitment to a spiritual reality behind the illusion of the universe, a reality whose particular manifestation in human beings constitutes the divine spark that makes each of us immortal. We have further to remember that because he preferred the spoken to the written word, Plato is certain to have disclosed the more esoteric of his teachings only to students attending the Academy in Athens. Acquaintance with these was a claim sometimes made (but never substantiated) by the neo-Platonists five hundred years later, though the existence of such teachings is at least partly confirmed by Aristotle who alludes to them on several occasions.

A contemporary of Plato who also drew on the theories of Pythagoras was the Greek thaumaturge Apollonius of Tyana who, like his master, is said to have journeyed to India in order to study the occult tradition brought there centuries earlier by Aryan migrants from the Tarim Basin. An account of his life, given by his pupil Demis and reproduced in AD 200 by Philostratus, records how Apollonius went about performing miracles – among them the raising of a young Roman girl from the dead – and preaching repentance, love and the forgiveness of one's enemies. (Some years later this account was to provoke a strident quarrel between pagans and Christians, the latter uneasy about the similarity it bore to the narrative contained in the Gospels.) A contemporary of Apollonius and a fellow Pythagorean was the Scythian philosopher Abaris whose long fasts and extraordinary feats of levitation are so like the exploits for which yogis and fakirs are famous that a connection with India seems once again likely.

The first major Roman author to deal with occult matters was the Pythagorean Nigidius Figulus (99–45 BC) who was a close friend and political ally of Cicero, despite the great orator's aversion to many occult practices, in particular astrology, which he condemned together with other forms of prophecy in his celebrated essay *De divinatione*. Apart from writing learned books on science and philosophy, Figulus earned notoriety as a magician and prophet, predicting among other things that the newly born son of a colleague in the Senate would grow up to be the emperor Augustus. By that time, a universal craving for the strange and exotic was already impelling Roman citizens, whatever their class, to seek admission to the mysteries which, like much else, they had taken over from the Greeks. Like much else, too, the mysteries were debased in the process, their individual characteristics – Dionysiac, Eleusinian and Orphic – slowly merging into a hotchpotch which, to lend it extra glamour, was placed under the exalted patronage of Isis. (So popular did Isis become in Rome, putting other oriental rivals like Attis, Cybele, Mithras and Baal in the shade, that her special protection was solicited by such diverse groups as cowherds, lovers, unmarried women and courtesans.) Many of the assemblies now professing to celebrate the ancient mysteries were in reality no more than secret societies dedicated to charity and good fellowship, their aims not altogether different from those of our own Freemasons, Elks and Buffaloes, though some – unlike these more recent counterparts – were not altogether averse to a bit of sexual slap and tickle on the side. Others, truer to Pythagorean ideals, had a more serious, esoteric character, with initiation ceremonies that required new recruits to confess their sins publicly before submitting to a ritual baptism that prepared them for a new and purer life.

Mention of practices which are so reminiscent of those later adopted by Christianity leads on to a curious distortion of occult tradition which that religion, itself an Eastern import, was to sponsor in Rome during the first century of its embattled existence. Known as Gnosticism, a name derived from the Greek word for 'knowledge', its main characteristic appears to have been a conviction that heavenly bliss is obtainable not by faith or good works but by knowledge alone. Starting from ideas already developed by Pythagoras, the Gnostics believed that inside each of us there burns a divine spark which, having 'fallen' from its true home with God, passed through the spheres of the planets until it reached Earth and there took up residence in the human soul. The only worthwhile ambition we human beings should cherish, therefore, is to take the same route and return whence we came. To do this, however, we have again to pass through the planetary spheres, each of them guarded by a spirit regent or Archon who – and here the distortion commences – is an implacable enemy of mankind and intent on barring our passage to the godhead.[6] Our only hope of overcoming this impediment is to obtain a knowledge of the pass-words, threats and blandishments that are needed if these angelic sentries are to be prevailed upon to let us through. Gnosticism furnishes precisely that knowledge. As for the unhelpful behaviour of the Archons, this is held as indicative of a wider conflict thought to prevail between all manifested existence (of which our soul and body are part) and the divine spark within us which alone belongs to the realm of unmanifested being. According to

Gnosticism, the creator of the universe was not the supreme and true god to whom we properly owe our allegiance, but an inferior deity, an impostor no less, whose authority we must at all costs strive to resist. To that end we have no choice but to scorn the world around us and, above all, to avoid bringing a new generation into it, for to do so would be to condemn others to an alien and comfortless exile on Earth.

These pessimistic themes are reproduced in a fifth-century Coptic text known as the *Pistis Sophia*. This records a conversation between the resur-rected Jesus and his disciples in which Jesus describes the ordeals he underwent when, after the Crucifixion, he had, like the rest of us, to ascend through the planetary spheres and was there confronted by their ill-disposed guardians. In the light of what healthy occult tradition has to tell us about the pre-earthly evolution of man, it is fascinating to observe how the Gnostics, ashamed of their natural attachment to worldly things and, possibly, to a cosmological theory more pagan than Christian, set about re-interpreting that tradition in their own sombre way. Their influence was to worry the Church until as late as the thirteenth century, when it gave rise to the Albigensian heresy whose adherents – the Cathars or 'Pure Ones' – were ruthlessly murdered, in the name of Christian orthodoxy, by order of Pope Innocent III.

More in keeping with traditional wisdom were the 'hermetic' speculations of the neo-Platonists who represented the last major school in the history of Greek philosophy. Particularly active in third-century Alexandria, the neo-Platonists endeavoured to arrange the esoteric knowledge at their disposal into a comprehensive and, above all, coherent system. Their pur-pose was to free initiates from the conceptual limitations in which their occupation of a physical body normally confined them. This encounter with Isis, as the subsequent expansion of consciousness was often described, then enabled them to behold a spiritual reality whose darkest corners out-shone all earthly brilliance or, as one of the texts puts it, to see the sun in the very depths of midnight. Only fragments of these hermetic texts sur-vive, many in translations whose lateness makes them suspect, but all contain doctrines that indubitably belong to the occult tradition. Most famous of them, perhaps, is the so-called Emerald Tablet or Tabula Smaragdina on which an essential tenet of hermeticism – the homogeneity of all levels of being – was supposedly engraved in Phoenician characters. One legend asserts that this precious tablet was discovered by Abraham's wife Sara, in a cave where the corpse of the pre-Adamic Hermes lay buried. Another names its discoverer as Alexander the Great, while yet a third maintains that Hermes presented the tablet to Maria Prophetissa, an alchemist living in Alexandria in the fourth century, who, reputedly the inventor of an improved type of spagyric furnace, has bequeathed her name to the bain-marie, still used in chemistry and cooking. Important to her, and to generations of alchemists afterwards, would have been the occult doctrine of reciprocity, summed up by the words 'as above, so below', which lies at the very centre of hermetic philosophy.

An early exponent of neo-Platonism was Plotinus, born at Lycopolis in Egypt, who, while travelling on a military expedition with the emperor Gordian III, spent some time studying among the Magi in Mesopotamia.[7] From AD 244 onwards he lived in Rome. Plotinus taught that there existed several layers or levels of reality, the lowest of them, matter, and above it three more: 'soul', then 'reason' (or spirit) and, finally, the realm of pure existence that is God alone (*τὸ ἕν*). Much of our knowledge of Plotinus we owe to his biographer Porphyry (AD 234–*c*. 305) who also edited his writings (the *Enneads*) and himself wrote a *History of Philosophy*, part of which – appropriately enough, a life of Pythagoras – still survives.

Other well-known neo-Platonists of that period were the astrologer Firminius Maternus and Simon Magus, the Samarian wonder-worker and, according to Iraenius, father of all heresies, whose story is recounted in the New Testament (Acts 8). Converted to Christianity on witnessing the superior skills of St Philip as he went about healing the sick, Simon is said to have hurled his occult textbooks into the sea, a foolhardy gesture for his conversion did not last long. As told by the Church Fathers (with every interest in discrediting the apostatic sorcerer) he met his end when St Peter's prayers brought him crashing down to earth after he had leapt from a high tower, intending to prove he could fly. Another version, given by Hippolytus in AD 230, has it that Simon, convinced that anything Christ could do, he could do better, instructed his followers to bury him alive. When, several days later, his planned resurrection had still not occurred he was dug up and found to be dead.

A more respectable end awaited another erstwhile neo-Platonist, Synesius the Cyrenian (AD 370–430), who ended his days as bishop of Ptolemais. Noteworthy, too, was the mystic Iamblichus (AD 230–325), founder of a Syrian branch of neo-Platonism but nowadays charged with complicating the system unduly by inserting intermediate categories between the different levels of reality its teachings already supposed. Author of a treatise entitled *On the Mysteries of the Egyptians, Chaldeans and Assyrians*, Iamblichus attempted in it to show how neo-Platonism was derived from a venerable tradition that was the source of all pagan religions. Later, in the fifth century, the zeal for systematisation which Iamblichus and other neo-Platonists seem to have shared was inherited by the Byzantine philosopher Proclus. His bold ambition, after throwing out much extraneous matter and tidying up the rest, was to offer occultism to the world as an alternative to Christianity. Disappointingly, there were very few takers.

Disappointing though this may have been, it was perfectly understandable, for true to its name, the esoteric tradition on which occultism depends had ever been the concern of a minority and, in any case, lacked the popular appeal of a religion like Christianity. It lacked, too, the powerful protection of the state which Christianity, despite occasional lapses, enjoyed after Constantine, having dreamt that his soldiers would be invincible provided their shields bore the Christian monogram Chi-Ro, decided that the Christian deity was a military ally worth having. (The superstitious Constantine, said also to have seen a cross superimposed on the midday sun, with the words 'By this Conqueror' emblazoned across it, had long hesitated whether to give his allegiance to Christ or to Sol, the Sun deity whom the emperor Aurelian had appointed to head the Roman pantheon, his festival following the winter solstice in December. Constantine chose Christ, thereby avoiding the need to elect a new date for Christmas.) In less than a hundred years, the emperor Theodosius would set about proscribing all non-Christian forms of religion, leaving the emperor Justinian to close the neo-Platonist school of Athens in AD 529 and so force its hapless members, led by the philosopher Damascius, to withdraw to the East, retreating from a new civilisation which in their eyes was 'a fabulous and formless darkness mastering the loveliness of the world'. Henceforth, but especially after the establishment of the Western empire under Charlemagne in AD 800, the Holy See of Rome would provide Europe with its only framework for faith and morals, as well as for knowledge and science, and be alert to all rival systems of belief, stamping these out whenever they dared to appear. Prudently, those in possession of arcane wisdom took care from then on to keep it to themselves: the slaughter of the Cathars, the Franciscan Fraticelli, the Stedingers and other heretics was reminder enough of what measures the Church would take to preserve the one true doctrine which, it claimed, it alone had been divinely authorised to teach. Even so, occult tradition – now more 'occult' than ever – did reveal itself from time to time, as in the mystical writings of Meister Eckhart (1260–1327) which contain so much lofty esoteric speculation that they earned him a wordy rebuke from the Pope. With the Inquisition formally established a few years previously, he was lucky to be let off so lightly!

It was the entry into twelfth-century Europe of Aristotle's work or, more precisely, of Arabic translations of it, accompanied by commentaries imbued with oriental and neo-Platonist thought, that was to re-introduce to Western scholars many of the theories that form part of esoteric teaching. Some historians express astonishment at this since to them the rational, scientific approach recommended by Aristotle cannot be other than completely incompatible with the feckless other-worldliness of which they judge Plato and his successors to be guilty.[8] Fortunately, the Islamic philosophers who had commented on Aristotle, among them Avicenna (980–1037) and Averroës (1126–98), did not share this modern prejudice and their open-mindedness did much to release the new spirit of inquiry that would succeed in permeating most of Europe by the time of the Renaissance. Also responsible for this renewed interest in neo-Platonism was a group of scholars attached to Chartres Cathedral, one of whom, Guillaume de Conches (1080–1154), wrote a celebrated essay, *De philosophia mundi*, in which he expertly summarised the views of Plotinus and Proclus. A similar task was undertaken by another member of the group, Bernard Sylvestris, whose special interest was the spiritual evolution of mankind which, like the Pythagoreans, he chose to describe in astrological terms. (These same terms would later reappear, applied to the nine spheres of Heaven, in Dante's *Paradiso*.)

By the middle of the fifteenth century, neo-Platonist ideas were to receive even more attention thanks to the enthusiasm of Cosimo de' Medici, whose reverence for Plato led him to set up an academy of his own in Florence. He, it was, who commissioned a young protégé, Marsilio Ficino (1433–99), to translate what had survived of the hermetic texts composed in Alexandria between AD 200 and 400.[9] Of these the most important was the so-called *Corpus Hermeticum*, consisting of thirty-seven fragments in which the triply wise Hermes expounded his teachings to his son Tat, to Asclepius, patron of healing, and to King Anmon. Many of them dealt with the relationship between ourselves and the macrocosm whose tiny replicas we seem to be, but one treatise, the *Pymander*, recalled in allegorical language how the spiritual monad inside us first descended into matter. From it we learn that one day primordial man chanced to lean out from Heaven and glimpse his own reflection in the waters of the Earth far below. So beautiful did it strike him that he edged farther out to get a closer look, only to end up falling down into the finite world of space and time. Here, Nature immediately fell in love with him and from their union humanity was born, first as a race of androgynous giants and then as men and women like ourselves, partly of this world and partly of a boundless one beyond it.

With the spread of hermetic philosophy, the notion soon became current in Europe that the physical world belongs to a much wider one which, though unseen, is every bit as real. As a result, many Renaissance scientists saw it as their proper task to investigate both worlds and, wherever possible, uncover the secret relationships between them. Soon, the more inventive among them had elaborated a series of analogies or correspondences by which denizens of the invisible world were supposedly linked to specific things in our own. In this way, the angels and demons (for there were good and bad among them) who inhabited either the unseen world or – the distinction is not always clear – our own world unseen, came to be grouped together according to an assumed planetary or spiritual rulership, one that they shared with particular metals, jewels, plants, colours, numbers, words and scents. Furthermore, because the universe, visible or not, was held to be the unity its name implied, with a law operational in one part (the physical world) equally operative elsewhere (the invisible world), it seemed to the hermetic scientist, mindful of the maxim 'as above, so below', that an action involving, say, the metals and plants assigned to any particular group automatically provoked a sympathetic reaction among the spiritual beings also grouped with them. From this was drawn the conclusion that by assembling the right objects and performing with them certain ritual actions, a dedicated experimenter might compel spirit forces to help him realise his wishes – the dedication a prerequisite if the ritual preliminaries, not to mention the rite itself, were to be performed as scrupulously as the grimoires or magical textbooks demanded. (The arduous preparation and tedious ceremonial, despite their occasional absurdities, have nevertheless the highly useful aim of concentrating the magician's will on the purpose of the experiment, thereby enhancing its chances of success.) Suddenly, magic – for it was nothing less than that – became intellectually respectable, and its validity, though challenged by people like Daniel Sennert and Johannes Kepler, remained a general presupposition of science and philosophy well into the second half of the seventeenth century.

Prominent among those to whom magic owed its new respectability was the Abbot of Sponheim, Johann Tritheim, better known as Trithemius (1462–1516), whose profound knowledge of hermetic science was to attract to him such celebrated pupils as Cornelius Agrippa (1486–1535) and Paracelsus (1493–1541). The former, born in Cologne and a student of theology, medicine and law, served briefly as a soldier before settling in Bonn where, after initial difficulties with the Inquisition, he published his three-volumed *De occulta philosophia* in 1533. In it Agrippa divided reality into three related kingdoms which he called elemental, intellectual and heavenly, these roughly corresponding to the formative, intellectual and archetypical states of existence long upheld by occult tradition. From here he proceeded to catalogue in immense detail the subtle correspondences between the visible and invisible worlds, as well as those obtaining between human beings and the cosmos, afterwards embarking on a discussion of ritual magic which contained enough practical advice to secure for the book a wide and avid readership.

Still more influential, though in the field of medicine rather than magic, was Paracelsus (Theophrastus Bombast von Hohenheim) whose adopted name served to proclaim his intention of carrying science beyond the stage at which Celsus had left it fifteen hundred years earlier and where it had lingered ever since. (From the patient's point of view, the 'hermetic' medicine taught by Paracelsus and others was certainly an improvement on the system then prevailing, much of it based on what Galen had taught at Pergamum around AD 150, and demanding total acceptance of the theories of Hippocrates and Aristotle, especially those dealing with the four humours alleged to rule the human constitution. Despite its own shortcomings, hermetic medicine did at least encourage an interest in curative plants – even if the choice of them was over-dependent on their appearance or astrological significance – and, because of its links with alchemy, in chemistry as well.) Central to the system taught by Paracelsus was again the view that human life is indissolubly linked (thanks to a mysterious substance, sometimes called 'mumia' but more often cryptically referred to as M) to the wider life of the universe, the latter understandable only through a patient study of the microcosm that is man. Paracelsus believed that the earthly clay from which human beings are made, the *limus terrae*, was a compound of all the chemicals in existence. Foremost among them were salt, sulphur and mercury, which in healthy people were harmoniously bound together by the Archaeus, a subtle life-force whose seat was in the stomach. Paracelsus often sought to heal his patients by immersing them in mineral baths so as to make good, presumably by a kind of osmosis, any deficiency in their chemical composition. He also believed that like cured like and that minute doses of medicine were often more effective than larger ones, beliefs which suggest that he practised homoeopathy centuries before the Viennese doctor Samuel Hahnemann perfected that system in the late 1790s.

Two other features were to characterise occultism – the public, but not necessarily true, face of esoteric tradition – in the period up to the seventeenth century. One was the practice of alchemy, the other a widespread curiosity in the kabbalah. Both are older than the fifteenth century, when interest in them was approaching its peak, but neither is as old as its supporters are sometimes fond of claiming. In the case of alchemy,[10] the earliest references to the manufacture of gold are found in China, notably in the *Shih-chi* (85 BC) and in ancient Greece, though it is not always clear whether they relate to transmutation or merely to a way of gilding metal in order to make it look like finest gold. We do know that in the third century a neo-Platonist called Zosimus (who claimed that the secrets of alchemy were revealed to Hermes Trismegistus by fallen angels and subsequently rediscovered, inscribed on stone tablets, by King Nechepso of Egypt) wrote twenty-eight books on the subject which, judging by those fragments still extant, appear to have offered practical advice on the techniques and equipment for the Great Work. Still earlier – possibly by as much as a century – are Chinese alchemical teachings, most of them concerned with personal immortality, attributed to the Huang-Lao masters, though it was not until AD 500–600 that alchemy, by then linked with Ko Hung and the *Tao Hung-Ching*, seems to have flourished in China. By that time, Western interest in alchemy had shifted to the Moslem world, where its most notable exponent was Djābir Ibn Hayyān, known to us more simply as Geber, who lived in the eighth century and wrote a famous book of instructions on how to produce the Philosopher's Stone, later translated into Latin as the *Summa perfectionis magisterii in sua natura.*

Three hundred years later members of the occult group at Chartres were themselves studying alchemy, while a century later, at Oxford, the Franciscan philosopher Roger Bacon (1214–92) produced his chief work, the *Speculum alchimae*, before being bundled into gaol on a trumped-up charge of trafficking with demons. So popular had alchemy become by the fifteenth century that the civil authorities, fearing that its results might upset the housekeeping of nations, banned it, first in France (1380) and later in England (1404) and Venice (1436), following an example already set in AD 209 by the Emperor Diocletian when he ordered the alchemical books of the Egyptians to be burned. (It did not take long, however, for spendthrift monarchs to realise that alchemy, the science of sciences, offered a convenient way of replenishing their coffers: Henry IV of England and, later, the Holy Roman emperors Rudolf II and Frederick III were among the rulers most eager to attract alchemists from all over Europe to their Courts.)

Among those tempted by the prospect of royal patronage was Edward Kelley (*c.* 1555–95), the friend and accomplice of Dr John Dee (1527–1607).[11] One account has it that when Kelley, then known as Talbot, was living in Wales, the landlord of an inn showed him an ancient manuscript recovered from the tomb of a Catholic bishop who was buried near by. The innkeeper had broken into the tomb in the hope of finding hidden treasure but instead discovered only the bones of its episcopal occupant, the manuscript just mentioned, and two balls made out of ivory. One of these the disappointed innkeeper had hurled against the church wall, causing the ball to break open and scatter a red powder concealed inside it. The other he gave to his small daughter to play with. A perusal of the manuscript was enough to show Kelley that it contained information on how to complete the Great Work and, further, that the red powder, of which a little had been preserved, must be the mysterious agent that converts base metal into gold. Within the hollowed-out interior of the remaining ball he found, too, a white powder, essential to the Opus Argenteum or Lesser Working, the middle stage in the alchemical process. For one guinea Kelley purchased the lot and some days later arrived with his prize in London where he got in touch with Dr Dee, thirty years his senior, a distinguished scholar, mathematician and favourite astrologer of Elizabeth I. Shortly afterwards the two of them, accompanied by their wives, quit England for the continent and, by 1585, had settled in Prague where, thanks to Kelley's manuscript and stock of coloured powders, they set about producing alchemical gold. Independent reports still exist of their experiments, in which – as in their reported commerce with heavenly spirits – Kelley played the leading role. Not that it did him much good: abandoned by Dr Dee in 1589, his gold-making failed to match the expectations of Rudolf II, who had him thrown into prison. Two years later while trying to escape, Kelley fell from a wall and was killed. Dr Dee fared scarcely any better, dying in poverty at his home in Mortlake.

Lest it be thought that all alchemists came to a miserable end, it is worth remembering the case of Nicholas Flamel, a long-lived Parisian alchemist who, in his book *Hieroglyphical Figures*, recounts how he purchased an old document called *The Book of Abraham, the Jew*, and twenty-one years later, while returning from a pilgrimage to Compostella, persuaded a learned doctor to decipher the alchemical instructions contained in it. As a result, Flamel succeeded in converting ½lb. of mercury into silver at noon on 17 January 1382, and mercury into gold a few months later. Helped by his wife Pernelle, he rapidly improved his technique and had soon amassed a considerable fortune, much of which he gave to charitable causes, endowing fourteen hospitals, seven churches and three chapels in Paris.

Strictly speaking, the purpose of alchemy was the manufacture not of gold but of the Philosopher's Stone or Scarlet Lion, the coveted powder that produced transmutation and, in certain circumstances, could be swallowed as an aid to health and longevity. One who is rumoured to have drunk the precious elixir was Nicholas Flamel, said to have been spotted at the Paris Opera on the eve of the French Revolution over three hundred years after his presumed death, at the age of eighty-seven, in 1417. Another was the Comte de Saint-Germain (*c.* 1710–80) who first appeared at the French Court in 1748 and thereafter retained the appearance of a perennial thirty-year-old, travelling to England in 1760 and, two years later, to Russia, where, like others before him, he captivated Catherine the Great. More travels were to follow before he settled in Schleswig-Holstein, teaching magic – he was the author of a treatise entitled *La très sainte Trinosophie*[12] – to a German nobleman, Landgraf Charles of Hesse-Cassel, until, some pretend, his death in 1780. Reports were to follow, however, that he was recognised in Paris in 1789 and, afterwards, elsewhere in Europe prior to his departure for India in 1822. He is even said to have turned up, still his elegant, fresh-faced self, at a diplomatic reception shortly before the last war.[13]

For the historian, alchemy sits none too comfortably on the border between science and magic. However 'magical' the literature on the subject may seem, it is abundantly clear that actual chemical processes are involved, even if from time to time these have been interpreted – as, for instance, by the Taoist writer Wei Po-yang and George Ripley, the fifteenth-century canon of Bridlington, in his *Liber duodecim portarum* – in terms of moral improvement. The first task facing the would-be alchemist, therefore, has always been to identify correctly the chemicals he was expected to procure, a task made more difficult by the fact that when alchemical authors spoke grandly of, let us say, Sulphur or Mercury (often referred to as Sol or Luna), they had in mind not ordinary sulphur (S) or mercury (Hg) but other substances in which, there is reason to suppose, unusually high concentrations of energy had been stored. The way in which this energy was employed may be easier to comprehend if we think of it as the chemical equivalent of what happens in modern physics when neutrons are used to activate an atomic nucleus and so change its constitution. The alchemical version of these neutrons would be Celestial Mercury – the Philosopher's Stone – which serves as the catalyst that induces transmutation without simultaneously disturbing the relative weight of the metals concerned.

Contrary to common belief, alchemy has not retired abashed before the supercilious advance of modern science. In 1896 a French chemist, François

Jollivet-Castelot, founded the Société Alchimique and, five years later, an alchemical journal called *l'Hyperchimie*. His book *Comment on devient alchimiste* (1897) together with its predecessor *l'Ame et la vie de la matière* had an enthusiastic reception. In them, the author (who counted the Swedish playwright August Strindberg among his admirers) emphasised the fundamental unity of matter and the vitality present throughout it, presenting the alchemist as someone who dared to imitate on a small scale the evolutionary and transformative processes God has sanctioned in the universe. Another alchemist, again a Frenchman, was Fulcanelli (Jean-Julien Champagne), who not only wrote several books but boasted of having perfected a method of making gold in less than six months. Sadly, Fulcanelli died a pauper in 1932, his literary magnum opus (*Finis gloriae mundi*) still unfinished. [14]

What alchemical textbooks reveal, as do surviving accounts of alchemists at work, is that the operation was more than just a chemical one. Significantly, the room in which the operation took place was described, not as a laboratory, but as an oratory, with the experimenter urged to keep on praying, as well as toiling, until his efforts were crowned with success. Esoteric tradition maintains that at a certain point in the exercise the substances trapped inside the Athanor or alchemical furnace were 'energised' by supra-sensible means. As a result, the Dragon asleep within the chemical ingredients – to copy the language of the art – was brought powerfully to life. Exactly how this was done, whether by chemistry or prayer, has always remained a secret, a requirement that accounts for the lack of clarity in most alchemical writings: from the allegorical nature of these and their infuriating tendency to give different names to the same thing or, worse, to present blatant contradictions within the same paragraph, it becomes clear that only to those entrusted with a key to their proper understanding could they ever have made any sense.

Typical of the more allegorical of such texts is a short novel, held by some to be satirical, entitled *The Chymical Marriage of Christian Rosenkreuz*. In explaining how its hero came upon the Philosopher's Stone, the author set out also to give his readers coded instructions on how they might do the same. The book appeared in 1616 but is thought to have been written several years earlier, by a Protestant clergyman named Valentin Andreae (1586–1654) who, after completing his studies at the University of Tübingen, wandered all over Europe and, so he was to claim, obtained admission to a secret society known as the Brotherhood of the Rosy Cross. Having married and settled down in Vaihingen, a small town in Württemberg, he lent his name to two pamphlets – expert opinion is that several friends helped him to write them – called the *Fama Fraternitatis* (1614) and, a year later, the *Confessio Fraternitatis*, the latter dealing with the social and political reforms the Brotherhood advocated and wished to see introduced into Europe. Similar concerns were present in the novel as well, but there, what was to impress its readers most of all was the story. This told how two hundred years earlier a certain C.R.C. (an abbreviation of Christianus Rosae Crucis), born in 1378, had travelled to Egypt and North Africa seeking occult knowledge from the many wise men he encountered on the way. Upon his return to Europe, where he tried unsuccessfully to interest academic circles in his new-found knowledge, he and three friends established the Brotherhood of the Rosy Cross whose members, sworn to secrecy, afterwards dispersed to heal the sick and do good works. A century later some of the brethren were busy repairing their headquarters, the House of the Holy Spirit, when they discovered a concealed and windowless chamber. Inside it, bathed in a mysterious light, stood an altar under which lay the entombed, yet perfectly preserved, body of their 'illustrious Father and Brother Christian Rosenkreuz' who had died at the age of a hundred and sixteen. With fresh heart the brethren then went back into the world, where their successors have continued ever since to be active in the service of mankind.

Nowadays, most historians regard this legend as no more than a symbolic account of man's perennial search for the Truth, though many concede that a secret society calling itself Rosicrucian existed in the seventeenth century. One of its most enthusiastic supporters was the English mystical philosopher Robert Fludd (1574–1637) who managed to write three books on the subject despite his commitment to weightier works like the formidably titled *Utriusque Cosmi, majoris scilicet et minoris, metaphysica, physica atque technica, historia* ('A history, metaphysical, physical and technical, of the one and other cosmos, namely, the larger and the smaller'). Fludd, who saw the universe as an immense chemical laboratory, was fond of arguing that Christ was the Philosopher's Stone inside each of us, enabling us to transform ourselves into worthy candidates for admission to the Rosicrucian brotherhood. (In his *Historico-Critical Inquiry into the Origin of the Rosicrucians and the Freemasons* (1886), Thomas de Quincey called Fludd the father of Freemasonry, where an order called the Rose-Croix still exists.)

What is clear is that from the point of view of that pristine occult tradition whose progress I have charted, Rosicrucianism is noteworthy because it shows how at times this tradition could be adapted to accommodate or conform with prevailing religious beliefs. In this case, under their emblem of the rose and the cross, Rosicrucians made of it a form of esoteric Christianity, one which they claimed was entirely consistent with the beliefs of the early Apostles.

Turning to the second important feature of Renaissance occultism, the kabbalah, we find ourselves restored to the mainstream of occult tradition. For the kabbalah – the word itself means tradition – endeavours to provide, in terms our intellect can grasp, a model of that ineffable reality which only spiritual vision, once the property of all, can ever perceive directly. To this end, the kabbalah offers us, as one writer put it, 'a philosophy as simple as the alphabet, profound and infinite as the Word; theorems more complete and luminous than those of Pythagoras; a theology which may be summed up on the fingers; an infinite which can be held in the hollow of an infant's hand'.[15]

Not surprisingly, a system as marvellous as this was given an origin worthy of its elevated aims. According to one version, God himself whispered its secrets to Moses on top of Mount Sinai, permitting him to impart these to seventy elders who in turn transmitted them by word of mouth to their successors, establishing a sequence that was to last until the sixth century when the earliest written texts started to appear. Of these the chief books of the kabbalists were the *Sefer Yetsirah* or 'Book of Formation' which is thought to date from the sixth century, and the *Sefer ha-zohar* (known as the *Zohar*) or 'Book of Splendour', which appeared in the thirteenth century and records conversations between a second-century mystic, Simeon ben Yochai (once believed to be the book's author) and his son, Rabbi Eleazar, though the true author of the book is now thought to be its 'discoverer', Moses ben Schemtob de Leon (1250–1305). Part of it, the *Sifra Di-Tzeniutha* or 'Book of Secrets', contains an allegorical account of the evolution of the cosmos, stressing the difference between the Absolute (*en sof*) and its manifestation (Shekinah) in the universe, teachings implicit in another important kabbalistic source book, the *Sefer ha-bahir*, which was probably written in the twelfth century by Isaac the Blind.

Most scholars now agree that in all likelihood the birth of the kabbalah coincided with the appearance of these first written texts, when certain Jewish initiates launched an attempt to restate the ancient teachings of occult tradition in the concepts and language of orthodox Judaism. By so doing, they hoped perhaps to make these teachings more acceptable to rabbinical authority. After a very short interval, however, devout Jews, many of them dissatisfied with the arid formalism of the Talmud, hastened to make the kabbalah their own and, by linking it to the Old Testament, place it firmly on the bedrock of divine revelation. In their eyes (often closed, it must be said, to the universal implications of the system with which they were dealing) the verses of the first four books of the Pentateuch offered a veiled account of the hidden processes of divine life. To the kabbalist, therefore, fell the sacred task of wresting from them their concealed meaning, largely by experimenting with the numerical value of particular words or of the letters that comprised them. Prominent among the cryptogrammatic methods employed for this purpose were a) *Gematria*: this involved converting the Hebrew letters into their numerical equivalents and substituting another word of the same arithmetical total. In this way the words 'and, lo, three men' (Gen. 18:2) could be reconstructed to become 'These were Michael, Gabriel and Raphael', an exercise greatly facilitated by the absence of vowels in the Hebrew alphabet; b) *Notarikon*: this required the kabbalist to form sentences by taking every letter of a given word as the initial letter of a series of words. Alternatively, the first or final letter of each word in a particular sentence could be used to form a new word: angelic names were usually discovered in this recondite manner; c) *Temura*: more complicated than the other two methods, this was a technique that enabled the kabbalist to decipher the many divine messages thought to be buried in the text and so discover a variety of hidden truths concerning God and his creation.

Understandably, Renaissance scholars who like Trithemius and Agrippa shared a passionate interest in magic, were not slow to press the kabbalah into their service. For in contrast to Christianity which, though admitting the existence of spirits, was reluctant to give details of their names and special powers, the kabbalah provided enough information on angels and demons to keep the most ambitious sorcerer happy. On this basis, one of Agrippa's disciples, Johannes Wierus (1516–88), was able, in his *Pseudomonarchia daemonium*, to list nearly seventy known demons, together with their respective offices and titles, while in a companion volume, *De praestigiis daemonium et incantationibus et veneficiis*, he gave detailed advice on their conjuration. Trithemius, too, had classified demons, in a book called the *Liber octo quaestionum*, and even put his knowledge to the test by undertaking to exorcise Mary of Burgundy, wife of the emperor Maximilian.

All this was part of the operative kabbalah (*kaballah ma'assite*) as opposed to the philosophical kind (*kabbalah iiounite*), though in fact the two were not irreconcilable, with several of the most well-known kabbalists combining both theory and practice in their work. Typical of them was Pico della Mirandola (1463–93) who asserted that the kabbalah led him not only to a deeper understanding of Plato, Aristotle and, if you please, the early Church Fathers, but also to a safer way of practising magic, one that enabled the wizard to retain full control of any fractious spirits he evoked. Under the influence of the works of magico-scientists such as della Mirandola, Trithemius, Agrippa and Wierus, kabbalistic terminology, together with its myriad signs, sigils and symbols, became an indispensable part of popular occultism, that uneasy contradiction whose connection with true occult doctrine is often of the flimsiest. As for the real meaning of the kabbalah, this was known only to a relatively small company of initiates, absent from which were many of the names most frequently mentioned in histories of magic.

Following its heyday in the Renaissance, occultism was never to recapture the widespread and gullible esteem it had briefly enjoyed among the savants and scientists of Europe. Already by the end of the seventeenth century, its fundamental notion, derived from hermeticism, of an animistic universe whose workings were governed by capricious spirit forces, had begun to sound rather silly. Meanwhile, waiting to take its place was the mechanistic world view that was to hold sway without challenge until recent times. Even so, there are signs that the change did not always occur without conflict, even in the case of so eminent a scientist as Sir Isaac Newton (1643–1727) who, while keen to depict the world as a great machine, nevertheless accepted that a spiritual reality, albeit one less obtrusive than that dear to the neo-Platonists, was the only true ground of creation. Indeed, in his later years Newton devoted much of his time to alchemical research and on several occasions referred nostalgically to the source of that occult tradition which is the subject of this chapter, regretting bitterly that the *prisca theologia*, the primitive wisdom of our ancestors, had been lost to mankind as a whole. [16]

Soon, however, a replacement for all this lost learning seemed at hand, as new discoveries, the result of direct experience and careful observation, began to transform the eighteenth century into the Age of Enlightenment. This was an age in which magic had no place, if only because people no longer felt the need for it, confident instead that life's remaining mysteries could be solved by the use of unaided reason. Nowhere is the decline of magic better shown, perhaps, than in England, where the Witchcraft Act of 1736 repealed penalties attached to the practice of the black arts (their effectiveness now officially refuted) and made it an offence only to *pretend* 'to exercise or use any Witchcraft, Sorcery, Enchantment or conjuration, or undertake to tell fortunes'. There is no cause to think that those genuinely acquainted with occult tradition did other than welcome many of these developments, for although their interest lay in a reality bigger than the clockwork universe disclosed to the senses, their investigation of it can only have gained from the rational, even sceptical, approach to knowledge fostered by the spirit of the age.

It says much for mankind's liking for the supernatural, however, that the old occultism, product of a more superstitious era, was not completely set aside. In France, for instance, the impact of Voltaire, Rousseau and Diderot was for a time matched by that of Cagliostro,[17] Casanova[18] and the Comte de Saint-Germain. There, too, while the greatest thinkers of the century offered subscribers to the *Encyclopédie* the most up-to-date information on science and the arts, seeking in the process to persuade them that empirical knowledge, derived from our senses, is the only worthwhile kind,[19] so other writers, none more so than Jean-François Alliette (1738–91), better known as Etteilla, were arguing just as persuasively that the Tarot cards (their true origin as recent as fourteenth-century Italy) were in fact the lost Book of Thot, an antique means of divining the future and, when linked to the kabbalah, of understanding how the universe functions. That same understanding was offered to his followers in Paris by Martines de Pasqually (1727–74), leader of a secret order known as the Elus Coëns (Elected Priests). Chief aim of this group, one known to the mystery cults of ancient Greece, was to restore man to that state of original grace in which his spiritual vision had still been unclouded, though when de Pasqually's secretary, Louis-Claude de Saint-Martin (1743–1803), succeeded him as head of the organisation, he adapted it to resemble orthodox Freemasonry, the latter by then popular all over Europe after the founding of the first Grand Lodge of England in 1717.[20] Elsewhere in Europe, other seers and visionaries were busy recording their experiences, among them Emanuel Swedenborg (1688–1712), William Blake (1757–1827) and Adam Weishaupt (1748–1830), founder of the Illuminati, while those of a more romantic than religious disposition were soon to indulge their imagination with a spate of Gothic novels, a craze for Ossianic verse and a Celtic, at times Druidic, revival.

A curious epitaph to this pursuit of the irrational, conducted in a century devoted to the service of Reason, appeared in 1801, when Francis Barret issued his *Magus or Celestial Intelligencer*, a ponderous compendium of demonic and magical lore, the inspirers of which are said to have been 'Zoroaster, Hermes, Apollonius, Simon of the Temple, Agrippa, Porta (the Neapolitan),[21] Dee, Paracelsus, Roger Bacon and a great many others'. Complete with portraits of thuggish-looking demons, possibly drawn or sculptured from the life, this lugubrious volume presented as a 'complete system of occult philosophy' contains a section in which the author offers his readers 'private instructions and lectures upon the Rites, Mysteries, Ceremonies and Principles of the ancient Philosophers, Magi, Cabalists, Adepts etc.' Those who would turn their mind to a contemplation of the 'ETERNAL WISDOM' were invited to present themselves at an address in Marylebone, London, between the hours of eleven and two. It is not known how many turned up. Certainly, the book itself is a poor tribute to the eminent authorities listed in it.

More instructive, if not always more readable, were the books written a few years later by a French occultist, Fabre d'Olivet (1768–1825) in an attempt to revive interest in esoteric tradition and, indirectly, the kabbalah.[22] Credit for that revival, however, belongs to another Frenchman, Alphonse-Louis Constant or Eliphas Lévi (1810–75), the latter a Judaicised version of his forenames which he adopted in 1845. Originally meant for the Church, Lévi quit his seminary in 1836 after falling in love with one of his young catechists (whom he subsequently married) and in 1841 was sentenced to eight months in prison for publishing a socialist tract, *La Bible de la Liberté*. In what many regard as his finest book, *Transcendental Magic* (1856),[23] Lévi set out to persuade his contemporaries that the sacred writings of ancient civilisations like those of India, Egypt, Assyria and Israel derive from a common tradition, thanks to which the esoteric meaning of the world's great religions has been the same at all times and in all places. Lévi's abiding interest, however, remained the kabbalah. Its methods, according to him, were as exact as mathematics and its speculation more profound than all other systems of philosophy put together, offering to the serious student not only insight into the cryptic teachings of Abraham, Enoch, Hermes and Solomon, but also power to control the unseen forces active all around us in the Astral Light. Although in his later books, written after an ambiguous reconciliation with the Church, Lévi was to warn readers against the practice of magic, he himself tried his hand at it in 1854 when, on a visit to London, he summoned up the shade of Apollonius of Tyana. Nevertheless, it was in gentler pastimes like reading Tarot cards that, in an appendix to one of his books, he offered instruction to those who cared to call on him. For this service he charged, of course, a modest fee:* even magicians must eat.

Notwithstanding the private tuition and occasional necromancy, it would appear that Eliphas Lévi put his occultism more into his books than

---

* Not so modest according to Mme Blavatsky, whose aunt once paid forty francs for one minute's explanation of the Tarot trumps. (See E. M. Butler, *Myth of the Magus*, Macmillan, London, 1948, p. 285.)

into his life, which may be why these are still enjoyable to read, the extravagance of their subject matter being well suited to the purple of their author's prose. Rather stricter and more scientific was the approach followed by one of Lévi's successors, Stanislas de Guaita, who tried in his book *Au seuil du mystère* (1886), as others before him had tried, to rid occultism of some of the spurious material it had accumulated over the past five hundred years. Associated with de Guaita were Joséphin Péladan who in 1890, with him, founded an 'Order of the Rose-Croix, the Temple and the Grail', and Gérard Encausse, who, under the pen-name of Papus, continued Lévi's attempts to reconcile the kabbalah with the arcana of the Tarot (which, in his book *Le Tarot des bohémiens*, Papus links to the gypsies). Something of an occult all-rounder, Papus became renowned for his skill in alchemy, healing, astrology and magic, earning new fame in the early years of the First World War (he died of tuberculosis in 1916) by predicting German strategy, often with remarkable accuracy. The members of his 'Ordre des inconnus silencieux' still meet in Paris and Lyons.

One of de Guaita's aims, more patriotic than occult, had been to make France the centre of esoteric activity in the Western hemisphere. To some extent, however, that honour had already passed to the United States where, on 31 March 1848, modern spiritualism came noisily into the world. Its exact birthplace was Hydesville, a village near Arcadia, a small town in Wayne County, New York, and home of John and Margaret Fox and their daughters Margaretta (Maggie), aged thirteen, and Katherine (Kate), two years her junior. That night the girls' parents heard knocks coming from the room in which the girls slept and, on going to investigate, found them sitting up in bed conversing with the invisible agency which, all were to assume, produced the phantom knocking.[24] Joined by curious neighbours, the grown-ups soon devised a simple code which enabled the spirit communicators to make themselves understood by responding with an appropriate number of knocks to any questions put to them. Within a couple of years the sisters were exhibiting their mediumistic talent in concert halls across the North-East, the entire country having been seized in the meantime by a veritable fever of knocking, rapping and table-turning. When this was at its peak, Maggie Fox, with her sister Kate's support, astonished the spiritualists by admitting that the whole affair had been nothing but a hoax. Obligingly, she now demonstrated in public — and the crowds were as great as those that ever flocked to hear the spirits — how she and her sisters (a third, Mrs Leah Fish, had been quick to join the team) produced the raps by cracking the joints of their fingers and toes. By then, however, the public, keener to be cheated than be cheated of its spirits, had turned its attention to other, more versatile mediums whose repertoire, soon to include such miracles as levitation, spirit photography and full form materialisations, far outclassed anything the toe-clicking Foxes had ever managed to achieve, though, to her credit, Kate Fox did briefly try her hand at materialising life-size spirit forms. Quietly, the three of them slipped off the spiritualistic bandwagon which they, more than anyone else, had helped set in motion. Maggie and Kate, having retracted their previous confessions, later found solace in drink. The bandwagon, as bandwagons do, rolled on without them.

Generally speaking, occultists were not among those who rushed to clamber on to it. Most of them questioned whether the phenomena reported were genuine and, even if they were, whether such indiscriminate confabulation with the dead was ever wholesome or worth while. This was certainly true among members of an English occult group known as the Hermetic Order of the Golden Dawn which in recent years has received considerable attention from historians of magic, though its membership, even at the height of its popularity in 1895, never exceeded a hundred. Its history goes back to the discovery by W. R. Woodward, leading light of a Rosicrucian group founded in 1868 and called the Societas Rosicruciana in Anglia, and a friend of his, W. Wynn Westcott, of old papers containing magical rites, the authenticity of which was subsequently confirmed by a mysterious German woman, Anna Sprengel, whose name and address appeared in the same papers and who, it turned out, was the Imperatrix of a Rosicrucian order in Nuremberg, known as the L ... L ... L ... (Licht, Liebe und Leben). Authorised to set up their own branch in London, Westcott and a third man, Samuel Liddell Mathers, established the Isis-Urania temple and supervised the initiation of, among others, the writers W. B. Yeats and Arthur Machen, the tea-heiress Annie Horniman and Shaw's sometime mistress Florence Farr. Mathers, something of a bully by all accounts, soon assumed control of the Order. Following his marriage to the sister of Henri Bergson, the French philosopher, he set up a temple – Ahathoor – in Paris as well. At one time there were also temples linked to the Order in Edinburgh (Amon-Ra), Bradford (Horus) and Weston-super-Mare.

Historians suspect that the story of old papers and a German Rosicrucian was never more than a fiction to provide some kind of pedigree to rituals which Mathers himself had manufactured, largely from material gathered from his researches in the British Museum. If so, then credit must be given to him for having put together a coherent 'magical' system, its parts drawn from neo-Platonism and the kabbalah, as well as from alchemy, astrology,

the Tarot, and classical mythology.[25] Especially notable about the procedures followed by the Golden Dawn was the emphasis they placed on the
psychological element in magical practice, their purpose being to awaken
the participant's mind to those levels of reality supposed by occult tradition. After Mathers' death in 1918, similar exercises in heightened awareness were conducted by his widow, Mina, who, to this end, founded a new
order of her own called the Alpha et Omega.

Of the Golden Dawn's members, the most notorious by far was Aleister
Crowley (1875–1947) or, as he liked to call himself, the Master Therion,
alias the Great Beast of Revelation, the number 666, or, less biblically, the
Wickedest Man Alive. Crowley's spiritual ancestry was only slightly less
impressive than his titles, for he claimed to be a reincarnation of the
priestly Ankh-f-n-Khonsu (26th Dynasty), Edward Kelley (Dr Dee's old
partner), Cagliostro and Eliphas Lévi, the last having died in the year
Crowley was born. His association with the Golden Dawn (which he joined
in 1898) had an abrupt and acrimonious end after more senior members
refused to allow him to climb the hierarchical ladder as speedily as he
demanded. Peeved, Crowley responded by founding an esoteric order of his
own, the Astrum Argenteum, in which his position was secure, if only
because it was second to none. Guided by astrology, the I Ching and, until
he deserted her, his wife's clairvoyance, Crowley travelled widely, visiting
America, Mexico, Egypt and the Far East, happily dabbling in magic
wherever he went. In 1920 he took a villa near Cefalù in Sicily and there
established his Abbey of Thelema, its motto, as in Rabelais's fictional
abbey of the same name, being 'Do As Thou Wilt'. (To be fair to Crowley,
these words were intended not as an endorsement of intemperance, but as
an acknowledgment of the power of the will.) Good intentions notwithstanding, rumours (certainly false) of human sacrifice were soon so current
in the region that Mussolini had Crowley expelled from Italy. From then
on, back in England, he did his best to maintain the reputation for beastli-
ness to which he attached such importance, though in reality he was all but
forgotten when he died at Hastings in 1947. Even allowing for the mis-
chievous way Crowley tried to shock his contemporaries by exaggerating
his own nastiness, much about this gifted man – he was no mean poet –
remained foolish, vain and downright unpleasant. Nevertheless a study of
his work, including his immensely readable *Confessions*,[26] shows him to
have possessed an enviable knowledge of occult tradition and, whatever
his faults, a sensitive awareness of its deepest meaning.

A more respectable graduate of the Golden Dawn school, though not of
the Order itself, was Violet Firth, better known as Dion Fortune, who was

attracted to magic when still a young woman. So swift was her progress in mastering the art that at some point or other she seems to have aroused the envy of the widowed Mina Mathers. The mutual ill-feeling these two ladies felt was to lead to something of an occult feud between them, their unseemly tussles on the astral plane solemnly chronicled in Dion Fortune's *Psychic Self-Defence*.[27] Here Mrs Mathers is accused of, among other things, conjuring up a plague of malodorous tom cats and, more seriously, of murdering one of her followers by psychic means. (This happened on Iona where a Miss Fornario was found one morning lying naked on a bleak hillside, the spot marked by a cross and circle carved in the turf. The only wounds on the victim's body — and here we return to the tom cats — were deep scratches all the way down her back.) When not fighting Mrs Mathers and her sharp-clawed familiars, Dion Fortune, who imagined herself to be the mouthpiece of Morgan Le Fey, wrote many books on occultism, some of them quite sensible, and a few novels which have an occult theme. She died in 1946, but the Society of the Inner Light founded by her continues discreetly to function.

By this point it will be clear, all too sadly so, that the stream of occult tradition with which this chapter started did not stay pure and crystalline for long as it ran its wayward course through the centuries leading up to our own. Still sadder is the fact that the closer we get to the present time, the muddier the stream appears to become. But just as the presence of mud cannot be blamed on the water it invades, so the shabbier aspects of occultism cannot be blamed on the occult tradition they presume to represent. Much of the fault lies with those human beings, as morally frail as the rest of us, whose task it has been to pass that tradition on: too often it has been judged in the light of their behaviour rather than on its own merit, something that should be particularly borne in mind in any examination of the case of Helena Petrovna Blavatsky. While her influence on contemporary occultism cannot be over-stated, Mme Blavatsky's life, far from blameless, is one which those hostile to esoteric matters always retell with great relish. Unfortunately, their hostility blinds them to the fact that what Mme Blavatsky had to *say* is a thousand times more valuable than anything this charming old fraud — if, indeed, such she was — ever *did*.

Helena Petrovna Blavatsky (née von Hahn) was born in the southern Russian city of Ekaterinoslav (now Dnepropetrovsk) on 31 July 1831. Her maternal grandmother, Princess Helena Petrovna Dolgorukova, was a noted botanist, her mother a writer of romantic novels containing mildly feminist ideas well in advance of their time. A boisterous, self-willed little girl, Helena exhibited psychic powers from an early age, often unnerving her playmates and the superstitious servants who took care of her. In 1849 she married Nikifor Blavatsky but left him a year later. She then made her way to Cairo, where she took lessons from a Coptic occultist called Paulos Mentamon. In 1851 she travelled to London, her twentieth birthday being spent in Ramsgate where, it seems, she met someone whom she later described in her sketch book as 'the Master of my dreams' and whom she would always claim was one of several Hindu sages committed to supervising her esoteric progress from their home inside Tibet.

By her own account Mme Blavatsky was to spend the next seven years travelling all over the world, returning to London in 1853 after trying unsuccessfully to enter Tibet from Nepal. Within a few months she was off on another grand tour, this time covering North America, Japan and India before managing, now with luck on her side, to penetrate a few miles inside Tibet. More sceptical biographers maintain, however, that the only touring Mme Blavatsky did in this period was around the minor opera houses of Europe, having by then become the mistress of an ageing bass named Agardi Metrovitch. (She is even said to have borne a child by him, a sadly deformed little boy who died in 1867.) Just as conflicting are the accounts that deal with the next few years of Mme Blavatsky's life. Some biographers, sympathetic to their subject, have accepted her claim that in 1867 she fought with Garibaldi at the battle of Mentana, and left again for the mysterious East a few months afterwards. On this occasion she is said to have finally obtained permission to enter Tibet, staying there for several months as the guest of Koot Hoomi, one of her Indian Mahatmas or Masters. (The Ramsgate Mahatma had been a senior colleague of Koot Hoomi's called Morya.) One biographer has described her stay there in the following marshmallow terms:

Helena lifted her eyes from the old manuscript of Senzar characters that she was struggling to translate into English, and looked through the window. She never failed to get a wonderful lifting of the heart from the mass of snowcapped mountains guarding the peaceful valley, from which no sound came save the occasional tingle of a distant cowbell or the warble of a bird in the trees near the house. This, she thought, must be *the* abode of perfect peace and happiness. Sometimes she had to pinch herself to prove that she was really there in the flesh, and not suffering another of those double personality experiences; that she was actually near Shigatze, Tibet, living in the house of the Kashmiri Adept, Kuthumi Lal Singh. His sister and sister's child were there too and, wonder of

wonders, most of the time under the same roof as herself was the great
Protector of her visions, the Master Morya![28]

The harsh reality – even biographers need to pinch themselves from time
to time – was that throughout the period in question, Mme Blavatsky was
loyally accompanying Metrovitch from one seedy hotel to the next, the
two of them ending up in Odessa where some of her noble relations were
living. (There she tried to make ends meet with a business manufacturing
and selling, first of all, cheap ink, and, then, artificial flowers.) By that
time, one witness has said, the couple presented a 'rather sorry sight, he a
toothless lion, perennially at the feet of his mistress, an aged lady, stout
and slovenly'.[29] Alas, it all must have seemed a long, long way from the
snow-capped Himalayas, and even if cowbells did sometimes tinkle in
Odessa, their sound can have brought only scant consolation.

Thereafter the contradictions are, if anything, multiplied in the story of
how Mme Blavatsky spent the remainder of her life. In 1871 she, but not
the unfortunate bass, was among seventeen passengers who survived the
sinking of a ship carrying the pair of them to Cairo, though she would
always insist that Metrovitch had been poisoned in Egypt by Jesuits. What
seems certain is that in 1873 she set sail from Le Havre to New York and,
having found her feet there, renewed an involvement with spiritualism she
had earlier begun in Cairo. Though fully accepting the genuineness of the
raps and knocks that were then resounding in seance rooms up and down
the East Coast, she would later pour scorn on their 'spooky' origin, and
demonstrate how she could obtain the same, if not better, results without
ghostly assistance. By 1873 she had already attracted some devoted
admirers, none more so than Colonel H. S. Olcott (1830–1907) who, through
all the vicissitudes to follow, would be her lifelong partner and, until their
estrangement some ten years later, her dearest 'chum'.

The Theosophical Society she and others established in November 1875
aroused little interest at first. This changed in 1877 when Mme Blavatsky
produced her first book, *Isis Unveiled*, purportedly an esoteric history of
mankind and religion. The real turning point in the Society's fortunes,
however, came in 1879 after she and Colonel Olcott had settled in Madras.
There, within a short space of time, the Society gained a large membership
in which all the racial and religious divisions of the sub-continent were
represented – a rare event in colonial India. Part of the Society's success
was due to Olcott's missionary zeal but most was due to Mme Blavatsky
herself, since, to the envy of the Christians and the embarrassment of pious
Hindus, her psychic gifts enabled her to produce signs and wonders in

considerable profusion. Most commonplace among these were the so-called Mahatma letters, missives written and dispatched by the Masters in Tibet either as a result of a request telepathically conveyed to them by Mme Blavatsky or on their own enlightened initiative. Sometimes these letters arrived through the post, at others they simply dropped from the ceiling or materialised in all sorts of unexpected places. Controversy has raged over their true authorship, as well as their unconventional means of delivery, ever since the first of them arrived postmarked Philadelphia and addressed to Colonel Olcott in New York. This epistle was penned in gold ink on dark green paper by a certain Tuitit Bey, scribe of Section V of something called the Brotherhood of Luxor. Little more was heard from the Brotherhood once Koot Hoomi and his Himalayan colleagues began their own prolific correspondence from Tibet. Tuitit Bey's letter, like several written by the Masters, was an attempt to revive Olcott's flagging spirits: life with Madame, one feels, would have tried the patience of the saintliest Mahatma. It need hardly be said that most Theosophists stoutly defend the Mahatmic origin of all these letters while others, more circumspect, point to the lapses of grammar and spelling they often contain, all of them identical to errors Mme Blavatsky was herself accustomed to make. Even handwriting experts could not – and still cannot – agree on whose writing the letters contain, whether Madame's own or that of somebody else.

In 1874 and already suffering from Bright's disease, Mme Blavatsky returned to Europe. Among those charged to take care of the Society's headquarters in the Madras suburb of Adyar was a Levantine woman, married to a Frenchman, called Emma Coulomb. This faithless person – Mme Blavatsky had befriended her in Cairo – presented herself one day at the home of the Reverend George Patterson, a local Presbyterian minister and, more to the point, editor of a journal called the *Madras Christian College Magazine*. To him the fickle Emma handed letters in which Mme Blavatsky seemed to be requesting that Emma and her carpenter husband help fake the psychic phenomena that had made the Society famous. This help had included impersonating Koot Hoomi and fixing sliding panels at the back of a 'shrine' or wooden cabinet suspended against a wall separating the so-called Occult Room from Mme Blavatsky's bedroom. (An aperture in the bedroom wall then made it easy for anyone to deposit inside the locked cabinet the Mahatmic letters or small objects that kept miraculously appearing there over the years.) As if this scandal were not enough, the newly-formed Society for Psychical Research, after questioning Mme Blavatsky and Colonel Olcott in London, dispatched a young investigator, Richard Hodgson,[30] to Adyar, and in the light of his sceptical report, passed the following judgment on our heroine: 'For our own part, we regard her neither as the mouthpiece of hidden seers, nor as a mere vulgar adventuress; we think that she has achieved a title to permanent remembrance as one of the most accomplished, ingenious and interesting impostors in history.'[31]

Impostor or not, Mme Blavatsky was still to produce her crowning achievement, *The Secret Doctrine*, subtitled 'The Synthesis of Science, Religion and Philosophy', which appeared in 1888. And it is for this and her other writings (including, arguably, the disputed Mahatmic letters) that Mme Blavatsky deserves our gratitude and our respect. Possibly she deemed it necessary, early in her career, to invent her Himalayan Masters, though this is unlikely, and then fake the epistles attributed to them, inventing, too, the ancient texts in long-dead languages which she pretended the Masters had shown her, a deception that was meant to lend more weight to the message she wanted to give to the world: without these, she may have feared, nobody would bother to listen to the teachings of a 'stout and slovenly' émigrée Russian. 'What is one to do', she is said to have asked her compatriot Solovyoff, though we have only his word for it, 'when in order to rule men, you must deceive them, when in order to catch them and make them pursue whatever it may be, it is necessary to promise and show them playthings? Why, suppose my books and *The Theosophist* [the Society's magazine] had been a thousand times more interesting and serious, do you imagine I should have anywhere to live and any degree of success unless behind all this there stood "phenomena"?'[32] On the other hand, it is possible that a conclusion of this sort misjudges Mme Blavatsky completely, that the Masters and the miracles were genuine after all. Were that so, I for one would be delighted to let her have the last laugh.

At the time of Mme Blavatsky's death in 1891, the Theosophical Society had as many as 100,000 members scattered all over the world. The following years were turbulent ones, with schisms[33] and numerous defections from its ranks. As a movement, however, Theosophy has managed to survive these difficulties just as its Adyar branch was to survive the 'Christianisation' inflicted on it by Annie Besant (1847–1939), a member since 1889, and 'Bishop' Leadbeater (1847–1934), not to mention the desertion of Jiddu Krishnamurti (b. 1895) who as a young boy had been hand-picked by Mrs Besant and Leadbeater to be the new Messiah.[34] These reversals were for many years to leave Theosophists somewhat over-sensitive to criticism but by now there are welcome signs that they are discovering the robustness and good humour which Mme Blavatsky, above all, would surely have wanted them to have.

One of the most important defectors from the ranks of the Theosophists was the Austrian Rudolf Steiner. [35] Born in 1861, Steiner studied in Vienna and received a doctorate from the University of Rostock for a thesis on the theory of knowledge. Afterwards he moved to Weimar where, at the age of thirty-three, he became responsible for editing the first complete edition of Goethe's scientific works. Ten years later he was in Berlin, editing a literary review and giving lectures at a working men's institute. Like Mme Blavatsky, Steiner had always enjoyed a private awareness of what he called the spiritual world and his sympathy for Theosophy, though never complete, was such that he eventually became leader of its German section. In 1913, however, Mrs Besant expelled him from the Society, aggrieved by his persistent and, worse, public refusal to endorse her infatuated sponsorship of Krishnamurti, her action provoking Steiner's followers to establish their own society, dedicated to Anthroposophy or spiritual science. Anthroposophy has been defined by Steiner as 'a path of knowledge, to guide the Spiritual in the human being to the Spiritual in the universe. It arises in man as a need of the heart, of the life of feeling and it can be justified only in as much as it can satisfy this inner need. He alone can understand Anthroposophy, who finds in it what he himself in his own inner life feels impelled to seek. Hence only they can be anthroposophists who feel certain questions on the nature of man and the universe as an elemental need of life, just as one feels hunger and thirst.' [36]

From then on Steiner threw himself into the task of spreading his teachings, writing and, above all, lecturing all over Europe, while the Society's membership grew rapidly, principally in German-speaking countries, in England and in The Netherlands. After the First World War, the Society erected its headquarters at Dornach in Switzerland, though the building, known as the Goetheanum and constructed entirely of wood, was mysteriously burned down in 1922. A new building, this time of concrete, took its place but had not been completed when Steiner died, largely through overwork, in 1925. By that time, his talks to teachers, farmers, doctors and artists had prepared the way for the important contributions Anthroposophy, unique among modern occult groups, has since made to medicine, nursing, education, agriculture, painting and drama. Steiner's talks to Protestant clergy even produced a religious branch of the movement known as the Christian Community, a development not altogether surprising, given the emphasis Steiner, unlike Mme Blavatsky with her oriental preferences, put on the central role Christ's incarnation had played in the history of the human race and of our planet. Without what Steiner terms the Mystery of Golgotha, the spiritual impulse that descended into the physical world when it first came into being would by now have become so enmeshed in matter that its ascent back to its source would no longer be possible. From these considerations it at once becomes evident that Anthroposophy belongs to the 'Western' form of occult tradition which, as we saw earlier, had already given rise in the seventeenth century, if not earlier, to Rosicrucianism and the mysteries it taught.[37] For these mysteries Rudolf Steiner, not unexpectedly, always had a special regard.

Over the intervening years, esoteric tradition has lacked a defender from its own ranks (as opposed to sympathetic outsiders) with sufficient energy and talent to do it proper justice, though there has been no shortage of occultism about, with astrologers, tarot card readers, and assorted mystery-mongers plying their trade more busily than ever. In the 1950s there was even a revival of witchcraft, its supporters claiming that theirs was the ancient pagan religion of Europe. In reality, however, its beliefs and ceremonies were a curious pasticcio of hermeticism, popular folk lore[38] and dubious anthropology, with just enough sexual innuendo (nudity was *de rigueur* among worshippers) to attract a host of converts. Possibly, some of those participating in these hybrid rituals genuinely believed in their antiquity, and if, thanks to them, they came into contact with realities beyond the sense world, then so much the better for them. By now, the 'old' religion seems to have all but disappeared, a victim perhaps of the sexual revolution of the last fifteen years: with topless bathing on our beaches, the sight of a bare-bosomed priestess is presumably less of a thrill than it was. Meanwhile, more modestly covered, as well as high-minded, the Spiritualists, Theosophists, Anthroposophists and assorted Rosicrucians still manage, if not to flourish, then at least to stay in business, while the odd black mass still turns up from time to time to titillate the readers of certain Sunday papers.

It was in the 1960s, amidst the flower power, macrobiotic food, Zen Buddhism and endless talk of peace and love, that there appeared to be signs of an occult renaissance, with young people determined to make the transcendental a part of their everyday lives. There was, of course, nothing new in this; the novelty was only that with the widespread decline of religious belief this perennial yearning for the numinous could no longer be satisfied, as it had been in the past, by organised religion. As a result, large numbers turned to occultism in the hope of encountering the supernatural without any of the theological preconditions their intellect was not prepared to accept. In doing so, however, the majority soon left their intellect behind, blithely forgetting that all experience, be it of this world or, more importantly, of other worlds, has always to be subject to critical appraisal. Instead these starry-eyed converts to occultism went their own happy, hippy way, accepting all they came across at its face value: flying saucers, horoscopes, ghosts, ghouls, Atlantis — all had their unthinking supporters, people who needed to believe in them as much as others needed subconsciously to believe in the fairy-tale sagas of Professor Tolkien. A few even sought help from drugs and mistook the hallucinations offered to their distorted awareness for a veridical revelation of some transcendental reality. Far from being the promised 'dawning of the Age of Aquarius', what had flared up was an aurora borealis which, like all false dawns, quickly fizzled out. The only consolation, perhaps, is that no false dawn is possible without a real one with which to compare it.

When that real dawn finally comes, the source of its light will be the esoteric tradition talked about in this chapter. It is a light that has been burning darkly inside us ever since the human race began, though few of us turn our gaze inwards to behold it. Occultism, drawing on knowledge that is older and more admirable by far than those who proclaim it, shows us how to rediscover this inner light, knowing that in it we shall see revealed our true, eternal selves. 'Open your eyes', says a Graeco-Egyptian papyrus containing the teachings of the triply-great Hermes,

and you will see that the door is unclosed and the world of the gods lies within; and your spirit rejoicing in this vision, will find itself drawn onwards and upwards. Now pause awhile and draw the divine essence into yourself, your eyes fixed upon the light. And when you are ready, say 'Approach Lord'. With these words, the light will shine on you and as you gaze into its centre, you will behold a god, very young and exquisitely formed. His hair will be like the sun and his tunic as white as snow.[39]

That god is yourself. It is time now to see how we can find him.

V

The Attainment
of
Occult Knowledge

As I was going up the stair
I met a man who wasn't there.
He wasn't there again today.
I wish, I wish he'd stay away.

HUGUES MEARNS, *The Psychoed* (*Antigonish*)

Having glanced — from the outside, as it were, and then only briefly — at the history of the world and of humanity, as well as at the occult tradition that purports to supplement the evidence available to us from more conventional sources, we have now to delve more deeply into this tradition to see if it really does offer us a better understanding of the how, whence and whither of our existence. Before doing so, we ought perhaps to ask ourselves if occultism, involving, as it does, a search for information concealed from our senses, merits the effort required. We should, in other words, try to satisfy ourselves that the likelihood of there being any such information to hand and, if there is, of our being able to obtain it, is strong enough to make the search for it worth while: an occult wild-goose chase is doubtless just as futile as any other sort.

One of the claims made by occultism is that it does not demand that we take its teachings on trust. Instead, it boldly declares that the veracity of its tenets can be confirmed in the light of our private experience, and has not to be accepted simply because, for instance, Mme Blavatsky (or, for that matter, Koot Hoomi), Rudolf Steiner *et al.* have at some time or other announced that it is so. Fundamental to this claim is the assumption that the heightened awareness which enables certain individuals to perceive levels of reality beyond the physical world is something all of us can cultivate if only we take the trouble to do so. It is an assumption that may at first appear questionable, given our tendency to equate reality with sense experience and nothing else. This tendency, however, is itself open to question.

Our awareness of the world about us, as any physiologist will confidently explain, is a product of the action wrought by energy or matter on our sensory nervous sytem. If, therefore, I were at this moment to say that I 'see' the desk in front of me, what I mean is that my eye or, rather, its retina has registered the impact of the electro-magnetic energy reflected to it by a certain object, enabling my optic nerve to carry the resulting impulses to my brain. That organ starts at once to analyse these and, having done so, informs my consciousness that the object responsible for them is what experience has taught me to identify as a desk. So far, so good. At this point, the confidence of our physiologist will start to waver slightly, if we go on to press for details of the analytical process conducted by the brain, asking, for example, whether it is a knack we acquire in infancy or one with which we are born. Confidence will soon yield to impatience if, after listening, we then inquire about the precise relationship between the desk and the image of it – the percept – which our conscious mind retains. That kind of speculation, the physiologist will tell us crossly, is for philosophers to deal with.

Such impatience would be understandable. After all, speculation of this nature must sound like a fuss about nothing, for we are accustomed, without ill effect, to treat what we 'see' – in this case the desk – as an accurate mental 'photograph' of the object standing before us. Those physiologists and philosophers who care about their sanity happily go through life accepting, like the rest of us, the brain as a kind of camera which, aided by the sensory system, registers the things we encounter in a trustworthy way. Mistakes admittedly occur from time to time, as happens with any camera not always properly focused, but in general we have learned to rely on the apparatus put at our disposal.

Only when we pause, as we seldom do, to consider how much the image finally presented to our consciousness depends on the structure of our brain and sense organs, do we begin to realise how personal and subjective it is. Far from being the mirror-image of reality we fondly supposed it to be, it is in fact a mere simulacrum, the extent of its resemblance to the thing itself (what Kant called *das Ding an sich*) determined by the processes responsible for its construction. Had my eyes been equipped with a different set of lenses – perhaps those given to a house fly – then the smooth brown surface of my desk would be a ridged and rugged landscape made up of dense wood fibres, with colours like red, green, black and yellow competing with a dozen shades of brown. And had those lenses been sufficiently microscopic, then the entity I know to be my desk would dissolve into a swarm of unstable molecular components. The choice we have to make, therefore, in deciding which of these constitutes the 'real' desk serves only to indicate how naïve it is to believe that our percept of an object reflects that object's natural — and thus veridical — appearance. Moreover, because we are all made differently, the result may be that each of us, looking at things in a unique way, spends his or her conscious life in an idiosyncratic world which can be shared with others only because a common vocabulary artificially endows it with universal meaning.

That some sort of world, however much we misrepresent it, does exist outside us is, fortunately, something few people are disposed seriously to challenge, though among those who do, even if their challenge is more academic than real, are idealistic philosophers who would, for instance, argue that the desk in front of me is no more than an idea — a hallucination, if you like — I have created in response to a spontaneous and private experience going on inside my brain. The outside world is thus an illusion. But, I may then ask in reply, if the world outside myself has no real existence, how can I be sure that I and my brain have one? It is, to say the least, presumptuous to make my own existence the sole exception in a world that does not exist! Some philosophers have tried to settle the issue with a compromise that concedes some validity to the world we are aware of. For them, our personal experience of an object is the product of sensations which *represent* rather than reproduce its nature. These sensations derive not from the object but from sense data relevant to qualities such as its texture, colour, sound, taste, smell, etc. It is they that then stimulate our sensory nervous system to convey to the brain the information it needs to prepare a composite picture of the related object. The trouble with this explanation is that the existence of sense data is not sufficient reason to suppose the existence of a physical object behind them. Indeed, we can dispense with it altogether. Neither does this 'representational' theory explain how hallucinations, based on no sense data whatever, are able to occur. Small wonder, therefore, that most of us are only too content to accept that our brain, in collaboration with our senses, registers the outward presence of some kind of reality, the true nature of which may correspond but little to whatever appearance we give it.

To discover what its true nature is, we have again to enter the *Alice in Wonderland* world of micro-physics. (Readers reluctant to venture down the rabbit hole or who have no conceptual difficulty with occultism's idea of paraphysical levels of reality may prefer to skip the sixth-form science of the next few paragraphs.) It was inside this queer, microscopic world, you will recall, that the compact and stable entity I naïvely took to be my desk disclosed itself to be a loose conglomeration of elementary particles, with all the delinquent behaviour characteristic of them. Investigation of this sub-atomic world shows that only when we start observing the position and velocity of an elementary particle does it assume a definite existence within space and time: before then, like the wave it sometimes is, it fluctuates at random along a curve of indefinite possibilities. This means that by our observation, we may be said to have conferred on it, as particle, a discrete existence, in place of the irresolute and indeterminate one which, as wave, it enjoyed up to then. We have, as scientists would put it, caused its wave function to collapse.

This process is comparable with what happened on a far larger scale when my eyes, faced with a swarm of particles in front of them, informed my brain that what they could see was a desk. To some extent, therefore, it is correct to say that our observation of what lies outside us brings relative fixity to the universe we live in — relative because that fixity declines the closer our observation gets to the sub-atomic level and meets there the true physical nature of what is being observed. Relative, also, because each observer, whether ourselves or the instruments we use, is likewise composed of elementary particles, each of them subject to the same existential ambiguity as the elusive particles that are under observation.

This all-embracing ambiguity forces us to ask, among other questions, whether the measurements on which scientists base their observations can ever be trusted when even the needle that records them has a molecular constitution as indeterminate and changeable as whatever is being measured. Some physicists, among them Niels Bohr, the Danish Nobel Prize-winner, have answered the question by saying that reliable measurements are in practice possible because the uncertainty prevailing on the sub-atomic level is virtually eliminated on the macro-physical level, thanks to the confluence of statistical probabilities represented on it. A more alarming argument used to defend the validity of any measurement recorded would have us believe that the collapse of wave function which follows once the velocity of an elementary particle is observed does not in fact happen, since *all* possible measurements are coincidentally observed — somewhere! In the universe occupied by our present consciousness only a single one of these possible measurements, the one we have succeeded in noting, has, of course, taken place, but, in an infinite series of 'alternative' universes, formed by the Law of Realised Potential, other measurements are being simultaneously observed by an infinite, carbon-copy series of ourselves, each little self oblivious of the rest. Here, too, in what we might term Superspace, Napoleon may have emerged victorious from Waterloo, the *Titanic* never sunk, and Adolf Hitler spent a happy retirement scoffing cream cakes and listening to Wagner records at his home south of Munich.

Before we get lost, as Alice did in a landscape scarcely curiouser than this, let me conclude by saying that what our senses imperfectly perceive is the 'particle' side of reality, one that is consubstantial with our sense organs as they engage in the act of observation. Putting it in simplistic terms, it could be said that in sense-awareness matter is responding to matter. What must not be overlooked, however, is that outside the specific event which makes up this response, there persists the 'wave-aspect' shared by the observer and what he or she observes. It persists because the wave, no less than the particle, is an integral constituent of each elementary particle and, as such, cannot do other than pursue *concurrently* its own erratic career, despite the discrete and fixed existence which our observation has imposed on its complementary 'particle'. Here, at these multiple levels of existence, there is ample room to accommodate all the alternative universes that physics presumes to suggest, as well perhaps as the paraphysical realities, tame in comparison, which occultism has never ceased to proclaim!

That these paraphysical realities make no impact on our senses should by now tempt no one to disbelieve that they exist: we have seen that the limits of perception to which our sense organs are subject are matched by the limited reality available to them. We have seen, too, that in quantum physics even material objects have something equivocal about them; like a man with one foot inside the house and one still on the pavement, elementary particles straddle a threshold between our familiar three-dimensional world and another where different conditions are bound to prevail. For centuries occultism has pioneered the study of these conditions, though it must be admitted that science is rapidly catching it up, discovering, as Aleister Crowley once put it, 'odd scraps of magical information and making a fuss about its own cleverness'.

While most of our knowledge is assembled from what our senses have told us, as far as they can, about the physical world, it is of course our brain that does the really hard work of sorting, sifting and correlating the jumble of information delivered to it. To identify the process with the passage of RNA from one grey cell to the next or to compare it with what happens inside a computer, is to deal with only part of the story. Admittedly, as far as concerns much of our behaviour, this part will suffice: information is received by the senses and swiftly conveyed to the brain, which in turn decodes it and, if appropriate, relays a signal to that part of the body required to take action. Our instinctive, unreflective behaviour – what psychologists call 'motivation' and, for convenience, locate in our basal brain – is probably explainable in this mechanistic way. The same is not true of what, by analogy, may be said to go on in the brain's cortical region, its development, with all its myriad convolutions, far more complex in the human race than in any other species. There, the biochemical or other processes that accompany thought are susceptible to the conscious direction of what for the moment we can best call mind, meaning by this, something that is greater than the sum of the properties owned by the brain. Even materialists have had to recognise the mind's important role in our thinking, though they then go on to tie themselves in knots trying to explain it away. Their most popular explanation is that the complex structure of the brain is itself sufficient to generate new properties which far exceed those attributable to the neurons that comprise it. Here, once again, we meet the old holistic argument which, if carried this far, would mean that a large enough group of novice musicians could finish up sounding better than the Berlin Philharmonic.

One of the most valuable achievements of psychical research has indeed been to rehabilitate the mind, a result anticipated in 1888 by Professor Henry Sidgwick, first President of the Society for Psychical Research (founded in 1882), when, referring to 'the preponderant tendency of modern psychology . . . to treat the life and processes of any individual mind as inseparably connected with the life and processes of the short-lived body that it animates', he went on to declare his belief in 'an important body of evidence – tending *prima facie* to establish the independence of soul or spirit – which modern science has simply left on one side with ignorant contempt; and . . . in so leaving it she has been untrue to her professed method and . . . arrived prematurely at her negative conclusions'.[1] Since Sidgwick's day, further research has succeeded in demonstrating that the mind is not uniquely dependent on information picked up by the senses and passed on to the brain by our nervous system. This, as far back as the 1920s, led Dr J. B. Rhine, founder of the Parapsychology Laboratory at Duke University in North Carolina, to conclude that the mind might also receive information by non-physical means and he coined for this purpose the term 'extrasensory perception' (i.e. perception *outside* the sense system). Few of his fellow researchers, for whom mind was simply the product of cerebral activity, were prepared to accept Rhine's conclusion, and, accordingly, busied themselves looking for some physical medium to explain how mind-related phenomena such as telepathy, precognition and telekinesis were possible. For a time, they suspected that electro-magnetism might provide the materialistic explanation they were seeking, but in the event were unable to turn up any evidence to prove it, though Soviet parapsychologists, perhaps for ideological reasons, reportedly still hope to find it. Indeed, what evidence there is, showing for example that telepathy is unaffected by distance, tends only to confirm that *psi* activity, as scientists like to call such things, is not physiological by nature. Or, as occultists have always maintained, that our mind is equipped to discover more than what our senses and the physical world have between them to offer.[2]

Having said all this, it is perhaps useful to add by way of postscript that occultism would never deny that a physical process – chemical, electromagnetic or whatever – normally accompanies our thinking. It is realistic to suppose that any other kind of process would not only be inappropriate but ineffective as well, if only because we currently occupy physical bodies and inhabit a physical world. It came as no surprise to occultists, therefore, when recent research showed our brain to be divisible into two segments, the one so different from the other that the term hemisphere, now used to describe each side, seems entirely appropriate. The right side of the brain is the poet and mystic within us, the left the schoolmaster and scientist. It would seem that several thousand years ago the left side managed to gain the upper hand and has since then kept its gentler neighbour firmly in check. Before then, the two had lived in harmony together, while earlier still the visionary right-hand side may even have held sway, enabling our remotest ancestors to communicate with realities whose existence the logician on the left would never suspect, still less acknowledge.

Legacies of that past are the myths and sagas surviving from these very early times. By now it will, of course, be clear that this novel theory is no more than a restatement of how humankind came to lose the natural clairvoyance – the *psi* faculty, as science squeamishly calls it – which occultism sets out to help us recover. Its job, alas, is not an easy one, for no amount of pleading will at this late stage reawaken the clairvoyant faculty dormant in the right half of our brain: merely to reach it, we are obliged to channel our entreaties through the left, which in its own selfish interest makes sure that its neighbour never receives them or else withholds from us whatever response we are offered. Neither will persuasion serve us any better, not least because the intellectual quality of our arguments will be lost on the more dreamy right side of the brain, even if it has the chance to hear them. Other, less conventional, ways have therefore to be sought.

To discover what these ways might be, we have first to consider what occult doctrine teaches about the way our mind works. Not unexpectedly, it says nothing, at least not to my knowledge, about the left and right sides of the brain or the RNA that seeps mysteriously through them: its terminology is far older than discoveries like these. What it does insist upon is the contribution made to our thinking by the astral body and the ego, two of the elements which, together with our physical and etheric bodies, combine to make up every human being.

The astral body has neither bodily nor starry characteristics. Its true nature, as far as language can ever describe it, is expressible only in psychological terms, none of which, I fear, is likely to advance our understanding very far. However, as it seems possible to manage satisfactorily in the physical world without ever observing, let alone describing, the true nature of what it contains, we shall hardly fare worse if, in order to understand the astral body better, we treat it as if it were a quasi-physical part of us. As for the ego, it is to this that we owe our individual selfhood, the categorical 'I' that each of us *is* uniquely to oneself. By its action on the astral body and, in a different way, on the etheric and physical bodies as well, the ego gives rise to the lively self-consciousness that distinguishes human beings from the rest of material creation. Animals, deprived of an active ego, have no self-conscious life, though their possession of an astral body does assure them of consciousness as such, unlike the plant kingdom whose inhabitants, occupying etheric and physical bodies only, exist in a sleeplike or, truly, vegetative state. Turning finally to the mineral world, we find there a physical body and no indications of anything else. It should, however, be noted that plants and minerals do possess what might be called an *indirect* consciousness, located on the mental or 'devachanic' plane of being. Indeed, plants and minerals (and even, to some extent, invertebrate animals) may be thought of as the sense organs through which a collective or archetypical consciousness becomes aware of the physical world.

An important function of the astral body, though not its only one, is to act as an intermediary between our inner life and all that is external to it. By so doing, it makes us aware of things happening outside us, a process observable in the physiological impulses – engaging our senses, nerves and brain cells – by which we and animals obtain knowledge of our environment. It might even be correct to state that the real home of our senses is the astral body, since from there we transfer to our etheric and physical bodies those feelings of pleasure, pain, desire, repulsion, etc., which the astral fabric experiences as a result of its contact with the waves and particles that combine to form matter. The plant, of course, knows little or nothing of such feelings, as its lack of an astral body means that its etheric and physical bodies are in turn deprived of the consciousness needed to induce them.

As far as animals are concerned, the feelings which their experience of the outer world stirs in them, though plentiful, are forgotten as soon as the particular event that produced them has passed, though some pet lovers may be shocked by the suggestion that animals have a different kind of 'memory' from ours. What, many will ask, of the dog that rejoices every time it is reunited with its owner? The answer is that the dog then renews an experience that also brought it pleasure in the past. Between experiences, however, it does not relive these pleasurable feelings – any more than Pavlov's dogs salivated between experiments. The same is true of the dog that grieves for its absent owner. It is reacting not to the conscious memory of its owner, but to a need – its owner's company – which, with time, has become as important to it as hunger and thirst. In human beings, on the other hand, the gift of self-consciousness ensures that our feelings are remembered and, moreover, that new feelings may be born inside the mind *without* the necessity for any external stimulus. For this, again, our ego must be thanked since having assured us of our individual selfhood, it now provides us with an inner life which memory invests with sturdy, though subjective, permanence. It goes further even than that, for having given us this inner life it permits our consciousness to work freely on the material our memory has stored in it. In short, it emancipates us from the sense world and makes each one of us the regent of our own soul.

If 'soul' is a word fit to describe the activity of our astral body, then 'spirit' may be applied to that of our ego. Together, both represent what Indian philosophy calls manas, especially when our self-illuminated consciousness (vijnana) reflects on the content of sense-derived information.[3] At such a time it is mainly 'soul' activity the astral body is engaged in, whereas once our attention turns to concepts not directly related to sense experience, it is spirit that begins to dominate our thinking. From here it is but a short step to a still higher form of consciousness when, to revert to Indian terms, bodhi or enlightenment permeates the manas and makes our mind more receptive to realities outside the realm of sense experience. Recovery of this intuitive faculty – that supersensible awareness our race was born with millions of years ago – is the first aim of esoteric training.

Training of any kind requires self-discipline and effort, none more so perhaps than esoteric training whose task is all the more difficult because it sets out to awaken in us, and that in relatively no time at all, a spiritual capacity that fell into desuetude countless generations ago. And its task does not end there, for it has also to persuade our intellect, whose stewards on the left side of our brain,

> . . . too fond to rule alone,
> Bear, like the Turk, no brother near the throne,*

to accept an outlandish newcomer in their prim and proper midst. Small wonder, then, that it expects us to give it all the will-power we possess.

While methods of esoteric training may vary, in almost all of them apprentice occultists have to start by improving their powers of concentration, aided by exercises that teach them to direct their undivided attention on an object or specific event, either actual or remembered. Before this, however, they will probably have learned how to relax their body so that no messages come from it to harass and distract them. They will also have been taught how to set aside (which is not the same thing as to repress) unwanted thoughts which, if unchecked, would invade their conscious mind and likewise attempt to distract them. At the same time, they will certainly have received advice on ways of controlling their breathing, including techniques that help to clear the mind and later monitor their thinking, though at this point no major change in breathing habits will be condoned lest the altered oxygenisation of the blood – the vehicle of our incarnated ego – result in physical or psychic discomfort. Only when these preliminaries are over will students get down to concentration proper.

Throughout this initial period, their instructions will be to concentrate *impartially* on the object of their choice, keeping their feelings about it as neutral as possible. This will also happen when students graduate to visualisation, a type of concentration which, with its emphasis on image building, will develop in them a more pictorial, less verbal, manner of thinking, one which psychologists, adopting a term first used by Erich Jaensch, now call eidetic and compare with the way we all used to think as small children. In esoteric training its special importance stems from its usefulness as a means of translating impressions received intuitively into concepts our conscious mind, reared on sense experience, will be capable of grasping. The paradox is that, while supersensible forms of reality differ from anything found in the physical world, we have nevertheless to convert

* Pope, *Epistle to Dr Arbuthnot*. Prologue to the Satires, lines 180–1.

them into pictorial concepts relevant to that world if we want our consciousness to acknowledge their existence.

Students begin their visualisation by concentrating on a simple object, perhaps nothing more than a pattern drawn on a sheet of paper, and then, with eyes shut, re-creating the image of it inside their head, with all its details true to the original. Once expert at this, they will again be asked to re-create an object mentally but this time as if viewed from an angle other than one from which they had earlier observed it physically. They might, for instance, look at an ordinary matchbox for a few minutes, close their eyes, and then visualise it first from one angle, then from another, sometimes from above and sometimes from below, but always in complete and colourful detail. From here they may be invited to try such refinements as mentally installing themselves *inside* the matchbox or, more challenging still, viewing it from all sides at the same time. They may even be persuaded to exteriorise the image by opening their eyes and projecting it on to the scene in front of them, its appearance so life-like that they can, should they so wish, inspect the visualised matchbox from any angle they care to choose. Soon the moment will have come to involve the other senses just as much, learning first of all to 'feel' visualised objects by touching the real thing and afterwards reliving in their mind the original tactile impression. Similarly, they must learn to 'smell' visualised flowers, 'taste' visualised food and 'hear' sounds like the ticking of a visualised clock. Once able to perform such feats with ease, they will at last be allowed to advance from single objects to groups and from groups to entire scenes, visualising, for example, a walk along a windswept seashore, where they can both hear and see imaginary breakers crashing on the beach, taste and feel the salt spray on their lips and smell the briny air blowing off the waves.

The aim of all this is to make the students' mind or, in this case, their imagination – meaning the faculty for image-building, not fantasy – as supple as the body of a well-trained gymnast. Moreover, just as a gymnast learns not only to develop his or her muscles but to make them, singly or together, responsive to every wish, so has the occultist's mind to be no less obedient. Through their skill at concentration, therefore, esoteric students, while enhancing their powers of imagination, are at the same time bringing their mental processes under the dominion of the will, focusing their dispassionate attention with growing precision (and consequently force) on things external to themselves. Only in the next stage of their training, as they learn the art of meditation, will they allow their thoughts for the first time to encompass themselves, and that will be only the beginning, for the ultimate goal of meditation is nothing less than the complete fusion of observer and observed, a state of liberation which the *Upanishads* call the turiya-avastha or fourth state of the soul. This lies within our reach because the ego that constitutes our essential selfhood is identical to the spiritual reality underlying all manifested existence, a relationship that permits us to 'become', as it were, the object of our meditation: 'Thou canst not travel on the Path', Mme Blavatsky once wrote, 'before thou hast become the Path itself.' At the end of this path, though most students will stop far short of it, there awaits the extinction of all feelings of separateness between ourselves and the universe, feelings which Buddhists call the heresy of sakkayaditthi, one of the ten fetters that bind us to existence. When that goal is reached, our becoming will be transformed, in full consciousness, into the blissful nothingness of absolute being.[4] We shall, in short, have found our way back home.

The reconciliation of each individual spirit with its universal complement is also the goal that yoga — the word itself means union — sets out to reach, its similarity to methods followed in the West easily understandable now that we know a little about the central Asian origins of occult tradition. The fact that yoga was already ancient in the second century BC when, as most scholars believe, the *Sutras* of Patanjali were first written down makes it reasonable to suppose that it sprang from knowledge carried into India in pre-Vedic times by invaders from the North, possibly by early post-Atlantean immigrants from Takla Makan or their Aryan descendants, by then spread over the plains of the Caucasus. Since that time different approaches to yogic fulfilment have emerged, the best-known paths or margas being karma-yoga (the yoga of good works), hatha-yoga (the yoga of effort or discipline), bhakti-yoga (the yoga of devotion) and mantra- or yantra-yoga, based respectively on the meditative use of words and symbols. Noteworthy, too, are laya-yoga and its close relation, kundalini-yoga, the first useful for mystical, the second for psychical, development, and the philosophical system called sankya-yoga (sanky = reflection or discernment) which has a cosmology closely related to that of occult tradition, envisaging manifold reality as having evolved (parinama-vada) from a single undifferentiated substance (prakriti). These different approaches have developed largely in response to the preferences and aptitudes of those aspiring to attain fulfilment, so that candidates whose temperament is, for example, loving and compassionate may opt for bhakti-yoga, the way of devotion, while others, more intellectual, will favour jnana-yoga where it is wisdom, above all, that unites the adept with the timeless being of Brahman.

The steps along the way towards this mystical union or samadhi are

eight in number – the astangas or 'eight limbs' of true yoga, set down in
the *Yogatattva Upanishad* – and commence with the ethical teachings of
yama ('self-discipline'). Here, students (sadhakas) are taught to abhor the
five negative principles of violence, dishonesty, theft, intemperance and
greed, while the second step, niyama ('observance') applies these lessons
to their own moral life and urges purity, continence, spiritual ardour,
contemplation and devotion to God. The third step, asana, last of those
in the outer court, deals with posture and strives not only to make the
physical body healthy and supple but to put its owner in control of its
behaviour, just as the two previous steps were intended to subdue its
natural weaknesses and passions. By then students are qualified to embark
on the two inner quests (antaranga sadhana) beginning with pranayama
and pratyahara. The first, concerned with breath control, introduces them
to the rhythms of inhaling (puraka), exhaling (rechaka) and retention
(kumbhaka), all invaluable aids for the exercises in contemplation which
the second quest, pratyahara, requires them to perform. In combination,
these two steps should enable them to subdue the clamour of their senses
and listen to the 'voice of the silence' by which their supersensible facilities
will make themselves heard. Deaf to all else, their entire being at ease with
itself, they are now ready for the next step, dharana, where their powers
of concentration will receive further training. After it, they will be ready
to peer deep into their innermost self and merge their wakeful consciousness
with the ego (atman) that resides there, surrendering to it the unique selfhood it alone gave them in the first place. This step, the seventh of the
series, is known as dhyana. From it there flows an awareness of the fundamental unity between the yogi's own spirit and that of everything there
is, an awareness which, in samadhi, the eighth and final step, unites them
consciously with that total reality from which, in fact, their true being has
never been sundered. On entering the absolute Independence (kaivalya)
to which the highest form (asamprajnata) of samadhi finally brings them,
each one will at last have come home.

Most esoteric students, we have already said, stop short of these mystical
heights, their training at this stage intended only to show how supersensible knowledge may be obtained. Referring to yoga – and the reference does not mean that yoga, a discipline proper to India, is the only path
or even the most desirable for Western feet to tread – we might say that
students have arrived at dhyana, the step of meditation. There, thanks to
the mental training they have undergone, they can already contemplate
their own inner being and examine the spiritual faculties that lie dormant
inside them. In so doing they retain that impartial detachment which the

practice of concentration is designed to encourage. This will in due course permit them to analyse their discoveries with philosophical scepticism, something occult tradition in both West and East (notably in the Buddhist system of meditation known as Satipathana)⁵ has always insisted upon, eager at all times to guard them against self-delusion or vain ideas of their own importance.

Nowhere is this detachment more necessary than in the period following meditation, particularly because of the fusion of perception and perceived that meditation normally entails. Beginners will also need all their detach-ment — and their sang-froid! — for that moment in their progress when they have for the first time to confront their inner self, the sum total of their past, an event occultism describes as a meeting, sometimes the lesser meeting, with the Guardian of the Threshold, meaning by this term a personified amalgam (the 'Shadow' of Jungian psychology) of all those ingredients, conscious or not, that make up the personality we currently own. (The Higher Guardian is the same in relation to our total past, being the aggregate karmic debt acquired over *all* our previous incarnations, a subject that will be considered later in more detail.) Meanwhile, never will aspiring occultists lose sight of the practical aim of their training which is to 'energise' their astral body by transfusing it with the new ego-consciousness that is theirs, now that they have introspectively 'become' their true self. The word 'individuation' was used by Jung to describe, in terms of psychology, a state of mind closely akin to this, its realisation comparable to the transmutation that occurs when base metal turns into gold. A similar alchemy of the soul occurs inside every student who successfully completes a course of esoteric training, the reunion of the inner sun and moon re-opening his or her mind to the myriad wonders that time has made it forget. Indeed, the term hatha, as in hatha-yoga (self-realisation through self-discipline), means exactly this, its combina-tion of ha (the Sun) and tha (the Moon), implying that solar and lunar energies — again perhaps, the left and right sides of our brain — need to be brought into balance. (In esoteric biology, solar energy is said to travel along a hidden channel called pingala which passes through the right nostril and thereafter down the right side of the spine, while a parallel channel on the left, known as ida, acts as a conduit for lunar forces.)

Happily, the actual techniques used by esoteric training to revive this primitive clairvoyance are sufficiently interesting to make the entire business less arduous than the description just given may possibly suggest. The supersensible organs of the astral body, for instance, are often identified with the chakras or psychic centres which hatha-yoga relates to various parts of our physical body, though in reality they interpenetrate the etheric and astral bodies as well; six in all, according to Swatmarama, author of the *Hatha-Yoga-Pradipika*. A seventh has been added to these by other experts, among them certain occultists whose obsessive attachment to that magic number has already been remarked upon. Starting with the sacral region, we find there two chakras specifically linked with our physical body, one (muladhara) at the base of the spine, the other (svadhisthana) in the region of the pancreas where prana, here meaning soul, rather than breath, has its ethero-physical abode. Next come three chakras with links to our more subtle bodies: to the etheric and, as far as concerns its lower or 'soul' activity, to the astral body also, belongs mani-puraka, its physical home in the solar plexus, while to the astral body's higher or 'spirit' activity belong, first, a chakra named anahata, located at the heart and, secondly, vishuddha at the front of the throat. The two remaining chakras, ajna and sahasrara, situated respectively between the eyebrows and on top of the head (but both in reality deep inside the skull), are closely linked with our spiritual life.

Although some of these chakras are alleged to govern various bodily functions, often those attributed to our endocrine glands, or particular nerve centres, their precise psychosomatic effect has yet to be established. For the purpose of meditation, they are traditionally depicted as lotus blossoms, flowers sacred throughout Asia and, as the secret dwelling place of Ra, especially important in Egyptian magic, where they (𓇳) represent the manifested universe (𓏺𓋹). The various colours of the chakric lotuses, clairvoyantly observed, do not always correspond to what has been recorded (shown in brackets below) in such Indian classics as the *Satchakra Nirupana*, where each flower has two colours, that of its petals and that of certain symbols and Sanskrit letters written on them, but this difference need not worry anyone unduly. The first lotus, corresponding to muladhara, lowest of the chakras, has four copper-coloured (crimson) petals, and the second, at the pelvic chakra, six vermilion petals, while the next two, manipuraka and anahata, have in turn ten light, greenish-blue petals and twelve of palest lilac (orange-red). The sixteen petals of the fifth chakra, vishuddha, are a rich crimson (purple) while between the eyebrows grows the white two-petalled lotus of ajna, part of whose activity is to foster psychic awareness. The seventh and noblest of the chakras, the pylon gateway to mystical life, is sahasrara which, at our approach, changes, white and shining, into a glorious, thousand-petalled flower. In their meditation on this and on the others, students will be invited to open the petals tenderly and look for the jewel that lies buried in each flower's heart: Om mani padme hum.

For those less florally-minded, the chakras may also be thought of as wheels, each having the same number of spokes as the petals (except ajna with ninety-six and sahasrara with ten times as many). Esoteric students have then to meditate on these wheels and imagine them spinning so fast that sparks fly off and light up the darkness inside them. Another way of activating the chakras is to evoke the vital force known as kundalini, often related to the virgin force of Shakti, female aspect of the divinity and described here as the 'Princess who sleeps at Brahman's gate'.[6] Kundalini, better known as the Serpent Power, coiled three and a half times at muladhara, the chakra at the root of our backbone, will, when roused from its slumber, streak up the subtle equivalent of our spinal column (sushumna), following the citrini nadi, one of 72,000 nadis or occult channels connecting our physical, etheric and astral bodies. Viewed clair-voyantly, kundalini, once awake, resembles a vertical blue jet, emitting red flames from one side and yellow from the other, though the two are often intermingled. (The red flames are usually to the left side in men, on the right in women.) This high current of cosmic energy ascends in a spiral through each of the chakras and brings them into harmonious and tuneful life (the first syllable of kundalini – the word itself denotes a coil of rope – is one of the Sanskrit words for 'sound').[7] After traversing all the other chakras, the kundalini fire at last ignites sahasrara and, to adopt the imagery of Hinduism, transforms that final chakra into the marriage bed of Shiva and Shakti, their divine ecstasy symbolic of our blissful release (moksha) into absolute being.

As for the working of kundalini on those chakras sympathetic to psychic development, notably anahata and ajna, this is what is customarily de-scribed as the opening of our third eye. Many occult writers, none more emphatically than Mme Blavatsky,[8] have associated this organ with the pineal gland, its location inside our skull (more precisely, behind the right ventricle of the brain) corresponding to that of the chakra sahasrara. To anatomists the exact function of this humble gland still remains a puzzle, though recently some interesting theories have emerged about its hor-monal action on a substance called serotonin, an inhibitor of certain brain activities and, as such, perhaps the chemical agent that keeps our third eye dark. As long ago as 1650, Descartes was proposing that the pineal gland might be the junction between mind and body, while for occultists it has long been the cerebral centre (one of seven, each connected with a specific chakra) where akasha or, in this context, space as undifferentiated substance – what Eliphas Lévi, copying Paracelsus, called the Astral Light, and his nineteenth-century successors ether – is individualised within every human being. Among the meditation techniques recommended by some esoteric schools is one designed to activate the pineal gland or, at least, its ethero-astral counterpart. In this technique the gland is visualised as a brilliant emerald glowing with akashic fire, while a reciprocal luminescence radiates from the pituitary gland at the base of our brain (seat of the ajna chakra), its own function, according to occult anatomy, to help us translate supersensible impressions into the pictorial form our conscious mind needs – at least to begin with – in order to apprehend them.

While it is true that the techniques favoured by occult schools to stimulate our faculty for supersensible awareness are much the same everywhere, the imagery and terminology they employ may differ from system to system. This is just as well, for it entitles students to choose the system most congenial to them. Hence those who feel ill at ease with oriental symbolism can turn their back on lotus blooms and chakras, and meditate instead on, say, the Goleuad, an old Celtic system based on legends nowadays associated with the Holy Grail, though these did not acquire their present Christian gloss until the late Middle Ages, largely under the influence of French courtly romances such as *Perceval or Conte du Graal* by Chrétien de Troyes. In its more primitive, Celtic, form, the sacred vessel depicted in them is still the miraculous cauldron of Ceridwen which turns old into new and dross into purest gold. Within it, the seeker after knowledge undergoes a ritual death – his encounter with his 'I' – which is symbolically linked to the death of Mabon Yr Ail, Prince of Gwynedd, who after falling into a lake called Llyn Cerrig Bach on the island of Anglesey, emerged from its waters refreshed and, above all, renewed, having become an adopted son of the fairy goddess Danu.

A more popular system, this time kabbalistic, is one that requires the student to meditate on a diagram known as the Tree of Life (Etz-hayim) said to depict at one and the same time the microcosm that is the human being and the macrocosm that is All. Inherent in this system is the doctrine that the universe grew from God's awareness of himself, a cosmogenic event portrayed as a sequence of ten divine thoughts, expressible in terms of light, and representing the various cosmic forces active in and around us. The last of these thoughts or creative emanations resulted in the world of dense matter (Asiah) shown in the diagram as a circle or sefira (pl. sefiroth) to which the name Malkuth is given. (The other 'worlds' that make up the realm of manifestation are known as Atziluth, Beriah and

Yetzirah, representing in turn the archetypical, creative or intellectual, and formative planes of existence that we came across earlier.) Because the diagram represents an inverted tree, its base, Malkuth, is in fact at the tree's crown, while its roots lie in the uppermost sphere, labelled Kether, which is said to reflect the primary manifestation of God's creative impulse. Between these two extremes the diagram contains a further eight spheres, the three that form a column on the right (the Black Pillar or Pillar of Mercy) being positive and initiatory, the three on the left (the Silver Pillar or Pillar of Severity) negative and passive. Central to both are two remaining spheres which, appropriately enough, mediate between their neighbours on either side.

In their quest for supersensible awareness, students of the kabbalah will learn to meditate on a human figure, the Adam Kadmon or Primordial Man, which is superimposed on the Tree of Life.[9] This serves to remind them that the forces present in the universe are present also in them so that by exploring their inner world, using the sefiroth as their guide, they will become aware of the spiritual ferment in the wider world outside. By reflecting in turn on all thirty-two paths that link the sefiroth (the equivalent of charting kundalini's progress through the chakras) they are able to advance from Malkuth, the sphere of Earth, to the starlit sphere of Yesod, and thence through the seven remaining spheres to the throne-room of Kether where, symbolically, the One that *is*, the formless 'en sof', first found dynamic self-expression. Like the eight limbs of yoga, therefore, the branches of the Tree can serve as a ladder not only to higher knowledge but to a higher state of individuated being, at once the origin and the consummation of our everlasting selfhood.

So much for the mechanics involved in developing supersensible awareness – and very pretty they all seem – but they do leave two important questions unanswered. How, we might ask, does all this marvellous knowledge make itself known? And, secondly, where precisely does it come from? The first question, simple though it is, permits of no simple answer. Just as one student of music may choose to play the piano while others find their talent better suited to the trombone, harp or cello, so do we find that in occultism, knowledge, like music, adapts itself to the special abilities of the individual. For some, the first signs of progress are an increase in spontaneous experiences of ESP or extrasensory perception. These may even be accompanied by physical phenomena usually of a mildly poltergeist nature, though if anything of the kind happens, natural causes should always be sought before supernatural ones are assumed – the sisters Fox and their percussive toe joints should never be forgotten! In any case, however weird and wonderful such experiences may seem, it is important not to take them too seriously for they are usually devoid of real meaning *in themselves*. This is true also of any day-dreams or visions that may invade our conscious mind at this stage in its development: involuntary hallucinations, most of them at least, belong to mental illness, not to serious esoteric training.

Strangely enough, it is in our nightly dream-life that the first intimations of occult knowledge often come. Strange, because in general our dreams make very little sense, and, in any case, are purely subjective, even though some of their commonest causes – such as too much supper or too many blankets on the bed – are physical in origin. These, however, are only the dreams we remember, whereas occultism is concerned mainly with those we forget. According to occult teaching, the onset of sleep permits our astral body and ego to abandon the ethero-physical organism, its daytime companion, and proceed every night into the supersensible regions to which they belong. The trouble is that our memory of these nocturnal excursions rarely survives once our two higher elements are reunited with their denser partners and, as a result, we wake up. No sooner does this happen than our conscious mind, impatient of all it judges irrelevant to the sense world it has to deal with by day, rejects any recollections we may have brought back with us from a sleep world where, according to esoteric teaching, there occurs a complete reversal of what we are accustomed to. Whereas, when awake, we react to the world outside us, the distinction between that world and us no longer persists once we enter the sleep state, and, instead, become one with our surroundings, with all the mutual inter-play of cognisance and feeling to which this homogeneity gives rise. Even this, however, does not provide a complete picture of our sleep experience, for by night we also resolve into ourselves all that exists outside us by day – as if our sleeping self were to expand to include the macrocosm whose miniature each one of us in a special sense is. In other words, the relation-ship between us and the world is turned inside out, even to the extent that it is we who impress ourselves on our surroundings and not they on us, as happens in our ordinary, everyday sense experience.

In contrast, however, to those dreams, often imperfectly recollected, which preserve the memory of our sleep experience, our other dreams, the totally subjective sort, are not so quickly forgotten because they arise only when the detachment of our astral consciousness from our etheric and physical bodies is less than complete, allowing our mind, still partly 'awake', to pursue its whimsical way and, later, remember the fanciful adventures it has had. This ambiguous situation is most likely to occur when a physical cause – be it indigestion or heavy bedclothes – competes for our attention or when we find ourselves returning to the physical body, neither fully in nor fully out, immediately prior to waking, a time, incidentally, when most of our dreaming is done. By making our conscious mind – the left side of our brain – more tolerant of supersensible knowledge, esoteric training allows us to recollect the objective experiences of our sleeping life as vividly as we do the flotsam and jetsam of these subjective, more commonplace dreams. Better than that, it enables us to distinguish easily between the two.

The separation of our higher and lower selves which, for instance, accompanies sleep, does not necessarily mean that we are transported to other realms of existence. Sometimes we remain in the physical world, though freed of its natural constraints. Such an occurrence is known in parapsychology as an out-of-the-body experience and, when self-induced, involves a technique many students are taught as part of their occult education. That it can also happen spontaneously is attested by frequent reports of hospital patients who claim to have left their bodies and then been able to observe these lying in bed or being tended by doctors and nurses. Similar examples crop up all the time in the annals of psychical research, often involving the apparition of someone at the precise moment he or she met with an accident or even sudden death. An example I can cite concerns an acquaintance of mine who had been involved in a motorway accident and described to me how he had detachedly watched himself sitting dazed at the side of the road while an ambulance man bandaged his head. It is, of course, arguable that experiences like this are no more than unusual states caused by stress or serious illness, but my friend told me that while out of his body he had suddenly thought of his wife. At once he had found himself watching her making pastry at home, the whole picture so clear that he had even noted a clock on the wall showing the time to be twenty-past four. Later when he returned home he found that his wife had been frantically telephoning local hospitals and the police, having glimpsed him in the kitchen, shaken and bandaged, just as she got the weekend baking ready for the oven. The time had been twenty-past four.

From accounts of this kind, it would seem that when our physical resources are seriously depleted, for example by injury or fatigue, the consciously motivated astral body may become detached and, once freed from the limits of time and space, manifest itself in a spot other than that currently occupied by the physical body. Exactly the same dislocation occurs during sleep, though our spirit-mind then shuns the world of matter and ascends to another world whose incorporeal nature is identical to its own. It is the task of esoteric students to recollect the experiences they meet in that world every night and, at a later stage, to live such experiences while still wide awake.

The spatial terms which, in default of anything better, I have used up to now to describe how supersensible knowledge is gained, are implicit in the second of the two questions put earlier: where does this knowledge come from? The question assumes a special urgency once we begin to have direct acquaintance with the paraphysical realities this knowledge embraces. Understandably, our sense-educated mind expects these to be 'located' somewhere, the more so in view of the solidly 'physical' appearance they they take on whenever we perceive them. It was to satisfy this expectation that many occultists spoke in the past of multi-dimensional reality, inviting their listeners to visualise hypothetical objects like the 'tetteract', an imaginary solid formed by mentally moving an existing object at right angles to each of its three dimensions of length, breadth and depth. The result, it was then alleged, typified conditions in the 'astral' world, the supersensible plane closest to ours − closest, that is, because it had only one extra dimension, unlike its neighbour, the 'mental' plane which had two, and, next to that, the 'spiritual' plane which had three.

It used also to be said that by experimenting with a non-Euclidean form of geometry like that developed by Georg Riemann in the nineteenth century, it was possible to render such notions more conceivable than could ever be managed by words alone. [10] Meanwhile, those whose geometry, whether Euclidean or not, had fled with the passing of their school days, were able to savour the impact of a new dimension by imagining how the third of our three spatial dimensions might affect a creature condemned to know only two. To appreciate this, we might for instance imagine that this page has a conscious life and that somehow or other we were able to pass through it a cone-shaped object. While the page, aware only of length and breadth, would then experience no more than a series of expanding (or retracting) circles, our awareness of an extra dimension, in this case depth, would enable us to observe both the cone and its gradual passage through the paper. Fortified by examples of this sort, generations of students have been encouraged to think that the aim of esoteric training is to expand their consciousness until it admits realities composed of more than three spatial dimensions − first the four proper to the astral world, followed later by the five and six that characterise respectively the mental and spiritual levels of being. Even scientists, following the discovery of two sub-atomic particles called the W and the Z by researchers at CERN

(Centre Européen de Recherche Nucléaire) are speculating that space, though dominated by the three dimensions familiar to us, may in fact consist of as many as ten dimensions, their properties, unrecognised by us, comprehensible only in mathematical terms.[11] Still more ambitious is Stephen Hawking, Lucasian Professor of mathematics at Cambridge, whose research team is reported to be striving to perfect the ultimate theory of everything, known as $N = 8$ Supergravity, and likely to involve no less than thirty-six dimensions!

The occultist who thinks in this way, however, falls into the error of transporting paraphysical realities to the physical world, since even if it were possible to multiply the dimensions that are natural to space, these would, presumably, be all of the same space-related kind — with not a single astral body anywhere in sight! In other words, we would find ourselves forever adding to our three-dimensional world something more, even something new, but never, never something *different*. Or, to put it more accurately, we would spend our time adding something extra to our own perception of that world since, as our example of the cone has shown, a supernumerary dimension adds nothing to the world as such but only to the observer's awareness of what it contains. While it may to some extent be true that esoteric training attempts to alter the novice occultist's awareness by adding to it a new dimension, this new dimension, possibly one of several, relates to a supersensible reality which does not share the spatio-temporal dimensions peculiar both to the student and to the physical world he or she lives in. On the whole it is better not to speak of dimensions at all.

Before we follow this advice, it is worth noting that the one extra dimension — that of time — which quantum physics has donated to science does much to help us rid ourselves of these misconceptions. From its earliest beginnings, esoteric tradition has always maintained that space and time, united in akasha, are one and the same, a view not shared by Newtonian physics which, until well into the present century, attributed a separate and absolute value to each. Not surprisingly, therefore, the two — space and time — are shown to be inseparable in the many ancient systems which occult tradition has inspired all over the world, among them that taught by Aghamarsana, a Rishi of the Vedic age, for whom time was the source and sustainer, *sine qua non*, of three-dimensional space. Other typical examples include the Aztec legend of how the god Omotéotl dispatched subordinate deities, the Tetzcatilipos, to four cardinal points so that behind them would be formed space and time, while far away in China the interdependence of both, implicit in the *Treatises of Seng Chao*, is beautifully

symbolised by the conditional existence which the masculine Yang ($\equiv$),
meaning time, in contrast to the absolute presence of Ch'ien ($\equiv$),
voluntarily leads as the loyal consort of Yin ($\equiv\equiv\equiv$), or created space.

The intimacy between time and space, represented in India by the sacred
syllable *Om*, was scientifically proven when quantum physics established
that time has no absolute meaning (something poets and lovers have long
suspected) but is conditioned by the situation of whoever lives through it.
This proof, based on the interaction observed among nuclear particles
moving at velocities close to the speed of light (186,000 miles per second),
allows us to suppose that if two clocks were perfectly synchronised and
one left standing while the other moved away at extremely high speed, the
time shown on each would be different when the second clock returned to
its stationary partner, even though both had been – and still were –
ticking along at exactly the same rate. Thankfully, none of us is aware of
the relativity implicit in the passage of time for we all move at speeds far
slower than light, but it has by now become accepted as an integral part
of our universe, and is known to science as the Einstein-Minkowski block,
a quaternity composed of the three dimensions of space plus the extra
dimension of time.

What scientists have been able to prove by observing the behaviour of
sub-atomic matter does no more than confirm what psychologists, following the lead of Jung, have also concluded, namely that the deeper we
recede into ourselves – where space has no more relevance – the less does
time retain any meaning, our sense of past and future finally dissolving
in an actual, all-inclusive now. This subjective timelessness is what esoteric
training sets out to achieve when, in the oriental terminology beloved of
certain occultists, it replaces the space-related awareness of kama-manas
with the more spiritual buddhi-manas that serves our atman or higher
self.[12] For the ancients its achievement produced that sublime moment
(*illud tempus*) in the Orphic mysteries when the candidate for initiation,
about to be reborn as the Lord of Time, could echo the resurrected Osiris
who was heard exultantly to shout, 'I am yesterday, today and tomorrow'.
For such a man, as the *Chandogya Upanishad* succinctly put it, '... the
sun never sets. For him it is daytime for ever.'

If the individuated consciousness that occult training brings is able to
transcend time, then it follows, given their interdependence, that the three
concomitant dimensions known to govern space are likewise left behind.
Yet instead of vanishing with them, our consciousness continues not only
to function but, as those with experience of it unanimously agree, to
function with new-found clarity and vigour. And it is when this comes

about that esoteric students will be encouraged to direct their attention from their own inner self to those extra-dimensional realities that share its qualities and, like it, lie beyond space and time. To inquire about their location, therefore, is to ask an improper question, for by their nature they have none. It is only because we ourselves *do*, that, in talking about them, we pretend that they exist 'somewhere' as well. For the same reason we have likewise to pretend that the beings that populate these insubstantial landscapes are no different, when our mind's eye sees them, from those of our own four-dimensional world. This, however, need give us no cause for concern. We have seen, after all, that the objects revealed to us via our senses bear little resemblance to their true natures, yet we still feel at home in the world as we find it. Thanks to occultism, the same is true of worlds which our senses know nothing about.

VI

A Many-sided
Nature

In the ancient world candidates for initiation were required to undergo a ritual death which imitated the death and resurrection of some heroic or semi-divine figure. An early example, central to the Egyptian mysteries, was the legend which described how Osiris was murdered and later dismembered by his brother Set. From Egypt this legend travelled to Greece where its hero, changed into Dionysus, was said to have been torn to pieces and eaten by the Titans — an event that formed the basis of the Orphic mysteries, just as the similar death suffered by Orpheus himself at the hands of the Maenads became part of the cult named after him, while the mutilation and murder of Cashmala by his three brothers were commemorated in the Cabirian mysteries of Samothrace. By his ritual death and rebirth, therefore, each neophyte was expected to bid farewell to his former, sense-orientated existence and, thanks to his new-found ego-consciousness, acknowledge both his higher self and the higher realities to which his mind would henceforth be receptive. His 'death', in short, was the lych-gate to a fuller life.

Nowhere was this made plainer than in the Eleusinian mysteries, which told how Persephone, daughter of the goddess Demeter, was held captive by Hades in his subterranean kingdom until her mother was able to secure her release for part of the year. Here, Persephone stood for the spiritual element within each human being, its true home outside the 'underworld' in which our flesh-and-blood self is currently exiled. The mysteries were divided into the lesser and the greater, the nine days needed to celebrate the former corresponding to the nine months that pass between conception and birth. Throughout these nine days attention was paid above all to Persephone's abduction and imprisonment, indicative both of our descent into matter and of the earth-bound life our day-time self is now forced to lead. In the greater mysteries more importance was attached to Demeter's search for her missing daughter, with the goddess shown carrying two torches, one a symbol of reason, the other of intuition, both of them faculties we ourselves must deploy if we are to attain the enlightenment promised us by occult tradition. Interestingly enough, the link between this tradition and the mysteries is corroborated by the valediction *Konx Ompax*, which, according to some authorities, derives from Sanskrit and which brought the biannual celebrations at Eleusis to a jubilant close.

To summarise the esoteric content of the mysteries, we might say that they strove to teach initiates how to recover in full consciousness the un-remembered awareness they enjoyed during sleep and – hence the persist-ent references to death – would continue to enjoy more lastingly after the physical body had ceased to function altogether. In other words, the blessing bestowed was access *while still alive* to the kind of supersensible knowledge which, in our present stage of evolution, only our post-mortem self normally acquires, a privilege that earned for the initiate the title 'epoptes' (ἐπόπτης) or 'one who has seen what is hidden'. For this reason a convenient way of introducing the paraphysical realities I mentioned earlier, but have been somewhat loath to describe, is to examine what happens to us after we die. That something does indeed happen, meaning that our mind can survive the decomposition of the flesh, should by now astonish no one, for it is implicit in all I have said so far about the human constitution.

That we die at all is due to the fact that during our earthly existence certain natural forces are bent on attacking the elements that combine to form our physical body. Evidence of Nature's destructive power (the god Shiva, as destroyer of the world, in Hinduism, and the sphere of Geburah on the kabbalistic Tree of Life), these hostile forces are in perpetual, yet fruitful, conflict with others whose aim is constructive and, from our point of view, more benign. In the wear and tear of living, we constantly expose ourselves to their baleful influence, escaping it only by night when our astral body and ego are able to withdraw to a more congenial – and salubrious – environment. Thanks to the brief convalescence they have there, both come back refreshed every morning to revitalise the ethero-physical organism with which they are then reunited. Nevertheless, like old car batteries which grow progressively weaker, no matter how often we charge them, our depleted resources can never be topped up to the level of the day before, with the result that at some point all of us, without exception, succumb to old age or to an illness we no longer have strength enough to resist.

To put it more accurately, our *physical* body succumbs to one or other of these. Our mind, in contrast, being able to function independently of the brain, remains alive and well inside the two invisible bodies which, together with our ego, comprise what is left of each human being. Occult tradition maintains that with the advent of death our etheric body, doing for the first time what our astral body and ego have done every night, withdraws from its physical partner which, deprived of its support, starts there and then to decompose. (The etheric body, you will recall, is the individual force-field that co-ordinates our molecular structure and thus preserves our physical identity – doing so, it might be noted, even though our cellular brickwork changes completely every seven years.) People who have been close to death, among them those resuscitated after being pro-nounced clinically dead, provide us with a valuable account of what this transition involves, though all protest that human language is inadequate to describe the experience.[1] It is nevertheless reassuring to find that most of them claim to have enjoyed an overwhelming sense of peace and happi-ness, even if some do admit to being startled on discovering that they are still able to think, though no longer occupying their physical body. Many of them go on to speak of having travelled through a dark tunnel at the end of which shone a brilliant white light, the source of such powerful feel-ings of warmth and love that some took it to be a spiritual being and others a glimpse of the world such exalted beings might inhabit.

Also common to a majority of these accounts is an experience in which the individual's life appears before him or her in vivid pictorial detail, much as a drowning man is reported to see his entire past in a single instan-taneous flashback. Long before interest was shown in accounts of this kind, occultists had consistently taught that a biographical retrospect always follows death and lasts for anything between a few hours and two or three days. In this period (measurable only from our position in the here-and-now but in itself timeless) the etheric body surrenders to the mind all the con-scious and unconscious memories which, in conjunction with the physical body, it accumulated during the latter's lifetime. By doing this, it surrenders also its own individuality and so becomes free to dissolve again into the amorphous 'ether' from which it first drew tenuous substance.

The panoramic vision of the past that precedes the loss of our etheric body is important because the memory of it imprints itself on our astral consciousness, enabling us to enter the next world with a clear recollection of who we were and what life was like in this world. Because of that and, especially, because our personality has to such a large extent been conditioned by our senses and what we learn from them, our new surroundings seem at first hardly to differ from those we left behind, which is one reason why Sufism calls them 'the world of similarities'. (In reality, of course, there is no such *place* as a 'next' world, still less one with characteristics similar to those of our Earth!) As a result, newcomers find themselves in an environment which, though they may not realise it, is but the thought-product of those who pass through it, one whose fabric they, too, will soon learn to shape according to their preferences. Not surprisingly, a lifetime spent on Earth means that settlers in this corner of what occultism calls the astral world quickly turn it into an idealised version of the world they remember, which is why so much of Spiritualist literature consists of rose-tinted descriptions of a 'Summerland' on the other side of death, the beauty of its lakes, forests and mountains surpassing anything found in travel agents' brochures. These are places where 'musically minded people gather in vast halls to listen to spirit orchestras, doctors pursue their researches in well-equipped spirit laboratories (without recourse to vivisection), great writers write and where, since someone must keep the lawns trim, spirit gardeners garden away contentedly. We even have reports of animal-lovers running rehabilitation centres for cattle slaughtered in the Chicago stockyards and suddenly transported, much to their bewilderment, to lush spirit meadows!'[2] In much the same way – though without the lawns and string quartets – the borderland (Yuh-Kai) of Bardo, the other world of the Tibetans, was also said to resemble the physical world, much to the confusion of those newly arrived in it, while the lower regions of the Egyptian Amenti, like the Moslem paradise, promised a store of earthly delights to everyone who reached them – all, did they but know it, of their own wishful thinking. The unspiritual character of these descriptions – a spirit purporting to be Sir Oliver Lodge's dead son even commented on the availability of astral Havanas[3] – is bound to arouse our scepticism, even derision, unless we bear constantly in mind the subjective, psychogenic nature of the region and the many pleasures it offers.

Appropriately enough, this thought-created province is known in occultism by its Indian name of Kamaloka or 'place of desire'. Paradoxically, however, it is a place in which our desires, at least those relating to the physical world, are slowly abandoned since we come at last to realise that the lovely things around us do not impinge on us at all: it is we who create them and create also the feelings of pleasure they bring, relying for this on the memory of pleasures we once knew in life. By degrees, therefore, every deceased person learns that without the use of a physical body, wants and emotions are doomed to stay unfulfilled. From then on, over a period said to equal, in earthly terms, a third of the life gone by, our astral body becomes purged of the sympathies and desires which, as the seat of our feeling and willing, it up till then harboured. A faint recollection of this experience is discernible in the Roman Catholic doctrine of Purgatory where the soul is purified before it makes its entry into Heaven.

Another adventure awaiting our astral consciousness during its stay in Kamaloka involves a second recapitulation, in this case regressively from death to birth, of the life just completed, though now we experience the *effects* of our previous actions, just as others, not only human beings but the rest of nature as well, experienced those effects when we were alive. No punishment is meted out to us beyond the grave but, on reflection, none seems necessary, for it is not difficult to agree with occultists that a biographical review of this inverted kind never leaves us unmoved or unready to compensate for what, knowingly or unknowingly, we may have done to harm others and, by so doing, impede the spiritual progress of the universe. Interestingly enough, this is the conclusion reached by Dr Raymond Moody, whose pioneering studies of near-death experiences have done much to corroborate the occult account. Speaking of the effect such an occurrence would have on people involved in atrocities of the sort that result 'in awful degradation, in years of hunger, wars and torments for their victims', Dr Moody adds, 'If what happened to my subjects happened to these men, they would see all these things and many others come alive, vividly portrayed before them. In my wildest fantasies I am totally unable to image a hell more horrible, more ultimately unbearable than this.'[4] Small wonder, then, that the outcome is always repentance, mixed with an urgent wish to make amends.

Esoteric tradition goes on to tell us that no sooner have we made this moral commitment than our astral body, purified of its earthly attachments, brings its work to an end. All that remains for it to do is transmit to our ego or higher self (Atma-Buddhi-Manas) the refined essence of the personality we bore in our previous life, after which it is free to follow the example of our etheric body and leave us, eventually dissolving in the astral fluidum around it. This separation of our astral body and 'I' is known to occultism as the second death, since once it is past, our ego, rid of its 'kamic' or Earth-related ballast (itself a death of sorts), can ascend unburdened into the spiritual world, something the Egyptian mysteries described as the entry of Osiris-Ani, his lower self devoured by the serpent Urhekh, into the cloudless kingdom of Sekten.

The disintegration of what, heedful of its tenantless state, we might call the astral shell may, in cases where the desire element was particularly strong, take time, since its substance, though no longer vivified by an ego, still contains a residual memory of the personality it served. Obedient to this, it may well resume in the astral world some of its former habits and, being denied there all prospect of satisfying its wishes, loiter in the borderland between that world and the physical one it previously knew. Such is its nostalgia for its old haunts that it may even return to these – many ghosts and apparitions are caused in this way – or else frequent Spiritualistic gatherings where it often passes itself off as the person whose memory it keeps and whose mode of behaviour still comes naturally to it. (Alternatively, it may lay claim to be the spook of someone famous: Shakespeare, Chopin, Pasteur and Marilyn Monroe are among the diverse and garrulous revenants reported by Spiritualist journals to have turned up at recent sittings.) Only with time does it become clear that the 'messages' an astral shell gives, however lofty their language, possess nothing that is new, still less of value, to those who receive them, their very banality one of the reasons why Spiritualism, despite its prodigious claim to reunite the living and the dead, has become the vast irrelevance it is.

In addition to the recently deceased in Kamaloka and the empty shells of those who have moved on, the astral world is home to other beings, for whom life there is part of their evolutionary cycle in the way our human existence on Earth is part of our own. Among these are the devas or angels whose mixed company includes entities who have completed their human evolution on Earth, as well as others, mostly out of reach, whose descent into matter and subsequent development occurred on planets outside the solar system. Also to be found are other devic beings – Hindu tradition puts their number at 330 million – some of whom, the kamadevas, are true natives of the astral world, while others, the rupadevas and, higher still, the arupadevas, are mere visitors from the spirit plane or Devachan. It is the kamadevas, formidable but harmless, whom the practising occultist is likely to come across when making an astral journey, though more likely still is the chance of encountering the lower devic orders which, as nature spirits, have a subsistent relationship with natural phenomena in our own familiar world. Tradition divides them into four groups and, more for the sake of .convenience than scientific exactness, associates them with the four simple elements proposed by Empedocles, introducing us to salamanders (fire), sylphs (air), undines (water) and gnomes (earth) – medieval-sounding names which become less off-putting once we regard them as a means of classification and nothing more. In any case, this fourfold division bears no relation to the gross constitution of the 'elements' just mentioned in brackets, but refers instead to the noumenal reality behind them. This was understood in the fifth century BC by Empedocles, who saw the elements as stages in the sequence through which manifested existence must pass on its journey into dense matter. 'From them', he wrote, 'flow all things that are or have been or shall be; from them sprang trees, men and women, wild beasts and birds, and water-nourished fishes, and the gods themselves, long-lived and most worthy of honour.' It is hardly surprising, then, that Mme Blavatsky, speaking of the same four elements, would tartly observe: 'It required long millenniums before they found themselves finally, in our cultured age, degraded into simple chemical elements.' [5]

As soon as one attempts to discuss elemental forces present in the astral world, it has to be admitted that their intrinsic qualities are inconceivable. So too, of course, are the qualities of any forces present in the universe, even those that manifest themselves on the physical plane, since though real enough in themselves, it is only their activity, notably their effects upon matter, that can be observed. It used, for instance, to be said that Newton discovered the law of gravity because an over-ripe apple chanced to drop on his head, while a non-scientist like myself knows that there exists a force called electricity only because, thanks to it, the living-room light comes on when I flick the appropriate switch. Nevertheless, it is undeniable that gravity and electricity exist as entities separate from their occasional manifestation. While, therefore, all of us can affirm that forces like these are at work round about us, this brings us no closer at all to envisaging what they are like.

Clearly, the same has to be true – even more so – of the forces that operate in the paraphysical conditions of the astral world and, in most cases, never deign to work upon matter. As a result, it is impossible to recognise them by the sort of events – be they falling Granny Smiths or incandescent lightbulbs – that physical forces from time to time produce or even by the reaction of scientific instruments, however sensitively tuned. Due to their constitutional aloofness, such forces are bound to remain inconceivable – as well as unkown – to all except those occultists whose esoteric training allows them to study their behaviour in the astral world. Even occultists, however, have no choice but to use words borrowed from the sense world, though totally inapt, if they wish later to describe what they have seen, hence the need for forbearance on the part of those they talk to: few modern occultists, when referring to gnomes, seriously believe that rosy-cheeked dwarves in green tunics are toiling deep inside the Earth – not even under Zürich!

Yet gnomes, if we are to accept the name given to them by Paracelsus, are among the elementals most active in the physical world. More often than not, however, these forces are not truly astral in origin but synthetic thought forms generated by the natural processes which take place here on Earth. While the initial impetus responsible for them, such as the one that turned the first acorn into a sapling, may well have involved a devic force indigenous to the astral world, this smartly heads for home as soon as its task is done, leaving the process it has begun to produce its own elemental consciousness, one that frequently combines with others to form the oversoul of a specific locality such as a valley, wood or mountain top. Sensitive persons can often 'feel' this elemental presence, sometimes hostile, sometimes friendly, though the beings responsible for it, formerly visible to our ancestors, nowadays survive only as the fairies, elves and goblins of popular folk lore, having earlier been, for the ancient Egyptians, the semi-divine Khnumu who assisted Ptah in his work of creation, and, for the Greeks, the nymphs of mountain (Oreads), wood (Dryads) and stream (Naiads) whose commerce with mortals recurs so often in classical mythology.

Tradition has it that nature elementals of this kind, being no more than creations of the created, eventually cease to exist and, sooner or later, begin to sense that they are doomed. From this has grown the rather touching belief that elementals, in particular those of earth and water, look to us for help, and hope that by noticing them and caring for their plight we shall teach them how to gain the individuality they need to make themselves immortal. Through the sympathy we show them, they find a way to think for themselves and so establish an identity distinct from the relentless activity in which they are engaged. For our part, we may feel nothing more than a vague attachment to a certain object or place – a stream, a single flower or even our own back garden – but our feelings are said to break the spell that binds the elemental concealed there and so make it the arbiter of its fate.[6]

Other elemental forces, this time proper to the astral world, have always been used in alchemy, where their transfer on to the ethero-physical plane provided much of the energy the Great Work demanded, just as, more

mundanely, electricity is used in the twentieth century to bring heat and
light into our homes. Magicians, too, were said to tap the same elemental
source and draw from it the power their rituals could not be without, if
success was to attend their performance. To this end, they would sometimes create their own artificial elemental and make it do their bidding, a
practice which gave rise to the notion of witches' 'familiars'. Tibetan sor-
cerers or ngagspas were reputed to be especially adept at fabricating
thought-creations of this kind, all endowed with varying degrees of permanence and often called tulpas, a word related to tulku (avesha in
Sanskrit) and expressive of the psychic faculty involved in their creation.
Generally speaking, however, experiments in this field, all of them requiring a form of mental activity known in the East as kriyashakti, are
extremely ill-advised: too often the resulting thought-forms have con-
trived to get the better of their maker and, after being good servants, have
soon become bad masters. This was the lesson learned by the French
explorer Mme Alexandra David-Neel, who on one of her visits to Tibet
managed after several months of effort to create a tulku of her own, a fat
and jolly monk.[7] After some time, however, he became self-willed and
menacing, and could only be got rid of with considerable effort. 'My mind-
creature', its chastened begetter has noted, 'was tenacious of life'.[8]

The plain fact is that elemental forces do not belong to the same order
as ourselves, even if many of them do assume human shape when perceived clairvoyantly, and, because of this difference, they are best left to
their own innocent devices. Neither do they possess an intelligence that is
comparable with ours, their consciousness, such as it is, being dedicated
totally to the execution of whatever task their angelic betters have set
them. Unable by their nature to question what they do, they consequently
lack the moral sense that only free will can bring, though some have been
known to affect an impish, but nonetheless charming, independence when
met for the first time. To be sure, therefore, of treating them correctly,
avoiding undue deference on the one hand and disrespect on the other, the
apprentice occultist is encouraged to think of them in impersonal terms
and then only in relationship to the particular stream of cosmic life to
which they properly belong.

If the majority of elementals found in nature can be described as artificial creations, then so can many other entities dwelling in the astral
world. Shaped from the residual energy of our thinking processes, these
survive there as thought-forms and, by feeding on the elemental forces
most compatible with them, may feign for a time a quasi-independent life
of their own. Not that every one of our thoughts can lay claim to an astral

form: most of them are so weak and fleeting – though none, as we shall see later, gets lost for ever! – that they quickly lose their plastic force or else join up with others of their kind to produce a composite astral shape. Many of these shapes, expressible as symbols, have remained in existence for centuries and make up the powerful archetypes that Jung identified in the collective unconscious of the racial and cultural groups whose forebears once fashioned them.

A similar impermanence awaits the astral bodies of dead animals which, deprived in their lifetime of any self-consciousness, shed without delay what individual characteristics they ever possessed. Slightly more durable are the astral bodies of family pets and even some domestic livestock which, like the nature elementals, have become more individualised as a result of prolonged contact with human beings. It should always be remembered that because the monadic ground of all existence is in the course of evolution, members of the mineral, plant and animal kingdoms will transcend their present states just as we shall transcend ours in some future manvantara. There is a rather charming story of how an elderly priest, a member of the Tendai Buddhist sect of Japan, was seen watering a clump of irises with such tender care and devotion that those observing him felt constrained to ask why. 'One day,' the old man replied, 'these flowers will also be Buddhas.'[9] We would do well to remember this truth in all our dealings with nature.

From what we have so far learned about the bizarre world of astral shells, thought-forms, elemental spirits and devic beings, it might seem that intruders risk getting lost or even hurt there, since not all the flora and fauna they meet will be well disposed towards them, any more than are those found in Africa or places still closer to home. Yet passage through the astral planes is part of every occultist's education. For many occultists, the path they follow into the spiritual world, the goal of their mystical endeavour, is one that takes them through this intermediate realm and, though unlikely to linger there, they cannot avoid some acquaintanace with its strange topography. For those of a more inquiring mind, in particular students of magic, the characteristics of the astral world are of interest in their own right, if only because they reveal so much about the hidden workings of our own. Accordingly, before entrusting the tyro occultist with the key to this strange kingdom, his teacher (or her, as the case may be) will have made sure that his daytime consciousness is able to cope with its inhabitants just as expertly as his nocturnal self has learned to cope with life in Devachan. He will, for instance, have studied the symbols that serve as his guide, their purpose to ensure that everything he

'sees', presents itself to him in shapes and colours whose significance he
can understand, enabling him at all times to know where he is and what
kind of company he keeps. The increased awareness of his inner self – his
ego-consciousness – that esoteric training brings will likewise come in useful now that the moment has come for him to cross that nebulous area
where his individual mentation not so much ceases, as edges gently into
the collective mind all about him.

Even if astral travel were no more than an exploration of our own inner
psyche, as some psychologists contend, it would still not be without risk,
for its route would again lead us to that same fortified place where by day
our consciousness bars access to the cloacal thoughts that incessantly
plead for admittance. Every journey into the astral world demands that
the portcullis of our mind be raised and the moat around it cleared, if we
are to venture out into the countryside beyond. Even there, with sirenic
influences waiting to greet it, there remains a danger that unless well prepared, our consciousness will rapidly succumb to their blandishments and
allow them to destroy its cohesion, something the mysteries symbolised in
the dismemberment of heroes like Osiris, Orpheus and Dionysus. It is
these same forces which in other circumstances, the result perhaps of drugs
or faulty brain chemistry, can induce mental illness. For the trained occultist, let it be stressed, the danger just described is a slight one, but for others
the gate that holds out the astral world is the gate that holds out madness,
whence comes the need to keep its key in safe hands.

Despite all precautions, that key can sometimes fall into the possession
of someone who is neither looking for it nor has any knowledge of the
reality to which it offers surreptitious entrance. This, I remember my
father telling me, once happened during his boyhood in Wales to a party
of women who had set off to gather bilberries on the bleak and lonely slopes
of Plynlimon. Throughout that afternoon, warm but unsunny, the air had
been remarkably still and it was through this opaque, oppressive stillness,
at around five o'clock, that there travelled odd, yet pleasing, cadences
which, though not musical – on this all were later to concur – nevertheless
left the listeners with the memory of a tune none could ever forget or,
stranger still, bring herself to sing aloud.

At first the women listened to these curious harmonies without any
sense of alarm until one of their number, taking fright, implored her companions to leave, saying that the spot must be haunted by tylwyth têg or
fairies. Within no time her fear had spread to the rest, quickened no doubt
by the arrival of twilight, at which all gathered up their baskets and hastened to make tracks for home; all, that is, except a teenage girl named

Wenna whose ears, by then enchanted, were deaf to the nervous chatter going on around her. Her only thought was to discover the source of the sound, and with this in mind, she abandoned her friends and set off in the direction it came from. 'Of course, she really heard nothing,' my father would say, 'at least not like the way you hear me when I'm talking.' He was right. What had happened was that on that peaceful afternoon something had intruded on Wenna's adolescent world which in normal circumstances would have stayed well outside it. Unknown to her and the others, their search for berries had led them to one of those places — I know of several — where the everyday world and the wider one beyond it are drawn so close together that they briefly overlap, bringing the supersensible so near to us that we imagine we can see it or, as in Wenna's case, hear it. Our ancestors knew better than we do where such places exist, building monuments on them, and later, the first Christian churches. It is even suggested that if lines linking these ancient sites were plotted on a map, a distinctive pattern would emerge, its paths representing secret channels of tellural power identical to those already mentioned in connection with Atlantis. Be that as it may, Wenna and her friends had inadvertently found such a place and all, except her, obeyed their best instincts and fled.[10]

Four days were to pass before Wenna reappeared, seemingly none the worse for her experience. Only later was it plain that she had left her mind on the mountain, though even then her madness was not all that obvious, being more in the nature of a quiet withdrawal to some secret, day-dream world of her own, one she found more agreeable to live in than the familiar world she had known up till then. Within six months she was dead — 'Debility' was officially, if imprecisely, blamed for it — and her last words to her mother were ones she had repeated often since her return from Plynlimon, the only words in fact that came from her mouth. Even they appeared to make little sense: 'I want to go back there,' she had whispered, 'I want to go back.' It is perhaps understandable that those who mourned her chose to think that in the end her wish had been granted.[11]

Unlike the demented Wenna, experienced occultists do not stumble into the astral world by accident. Neither do they seek admission to it simply for the pleasure or excitement that travel there affords them: they know that its scenery, though spectacular, is only thought-created, mirroring in its peculiar way the physical world behind them. (Also mirrored in it, we have noted, is Time, since it is here that the akashic chronicle stands open to disclose our cosmic past to the few entitled to peruse it.) No, the primary aim of occultists as they venture on their expeditions is to draw closer to the higher intelligences that overshadow the regions they hope to traverse;

though 'overshadow' is not quite the right word, given that light, not shade, is what their proximity brings. From our present standpoint, the astral plane is essentially a causative one, an intermediate region where purely spiritual influences can be adapted to physical conditions (much as an adapter modifies electrical currents to suit the equipment to hand), thereby enabling these to be conducted on to the plane of dense matter. Because our universe is itself the conglomerate effect of these influences we can, by going behind the scenes, as it were, see in the astral world the cause that determines each effect, the potential behind the real, and, most edifying of all, the intention behind the causes. Here, in short, is a window into that spiritual world to which, when we left it, our posthumous self was about to ascend from the moonlit world of Kamaloka, the realm of extinct desire.

In contrast to Kamaloka which, for descriptive purposes at least, could be compared with conditions found on Earth, the spiritual world or Devachan is *utterly* different from anything our mind can at present conceive. (The word, a mixture of Sanskrit and Tibetan, means 'realm of light', being a combination of Deva, 'light', and Chan, 'abode'.) In reality a self-contained state of contemplation on – to revert to oriental parlance – the Atma-Buddhic plane, a state in which the self is united without loss of its integrity with the All, it is tempting to describe Devachan as a condition in which our emancipated self will find unalloyed bliss and, having said this much, leave it at that. Once we go on to add something, for instance that our bliss will include (since we are not alone there) the good companionship of others, we begin to suggest things – in this case a Saturday night knees-up at the local – which detract from the understanding we were trying so hard to promote. Rudolf Steiner could not escape this danger in the many lectures he delivered on the subject, describing in them how the ego, having entered Devachan, journeyed from the lunar precincts of the soul world (Kamaloka), first to Mercury (by which, to increase the confusion, he meant what you and I call Venus), then to Venus (i.e. Mercury) and from there to the Sun. After disporting briefly with the solar beings that live there, the ego proceeded to Mars and, lulled by the Music of the Spheres, moved on past Jupiter and Saturn towards the fixed stars, having by then – understandably – dropped off to sleep.[12] All of which may be to describe, as competently and clearly as anyone can, the sort of experiences the ego lives through in the spirit world: the imagery of the planets is, after all, common among the neo-Platonists and Gnostics who used it to indicate the reconciliation of microcosm and macrocosm brought on by the all-embracing self-awareness we enjoy after death. But, alas, it must be admitted that to a generation brought up on *Star Wars* and Challenger spacecraft, the imagery of interstellar travel does not appear at first sight to be helpful in increasing our comprehension.

Yet we cannot for long avoid objective, even spatial, terms if we are to convey any clear idea of the Devachanic experiences that follow our so-called second death. Speaking earlier of Kamaloka, I explained that our discarnate self sheds there the grosser elements of its previous personality before assimilating what is left into its 'I'. Had I wished to describe the process differently, and, it might be argued, more helpfully, I might have said that it begins in Kamaloka to distance itself from the sphere of Earth, meaning by this not that our ego plunges suddenly into space but that it starts to withdraw (again a spatial term) from its former, Earth-related attachments. It is by no means odd, therefore, that Rudolf Steiner, echoing the neo-Platonists, found himself saying that in Devachan our 'I' or atman (with a small 'a') is now reunited with a spiritual part of itself that never incarnates and, as Atman, journeys through the solar system — whose miniature, if we accept the hermetic maxim of 'as above, so below', each one of us essentially is. To talk, therefore, of the Sun and the planets, not to mention the stars and the Music of the Spheres, is to describe in objective terms of time and space a series of inner experiences which has nothing directly in common with either. Much the same thing happens when an encephalograph records, as lines on a sheet of paper, the dream life of the person hooked up to it, its waves and squiggles conveying nothing of the actual experiences being lived through.

The reference to the planets has another esoteric significance also. Whereas in Kamaloka we were said to watch a re-run of the incarnation just completed, being ourselves affected by all it contains, in Devachan we rediscover the *totality* of our past and become conscious once again of our enduring selfhood: that trans-personal 'I' which experience, distilled over many incarnations, has made of the monadic essence we first brought into matter. Indeed, our past stretches back even farther, as was evident from the earlier account of the prehistory of the universe, each of whose previous manifestations coincided with a particular stage in our collective pre-human development. Though not themselves directly involved in all this — it happened before they were formed — the visible planets of our solar system, so occultists claim, are the materialised (one might say 'mineralised') detritus of this cosmic operation. Each is a memorial to the activity of certain forces, all of them intelligently directed by higher beings, and to the contribution these beings have made to our evolution. Nothing is more appropriate, therefore, than to describe the reabsorption of our total past which the 'I' progressively achieves in Devachan as a voyage among the planets that are closest to our Earth.

If Kamaloka could be described as part of the wider astral world, so may our individual experience of Devachan be depicted as a province of that spiritual world which many occultists prefer to call the mental plane. The name is appropriate since in it there flourish all the archetypal ideas which in due course find their concrete expression in the physical world, working towards this end through the multitude of evolutionary processes forever taking place there. The blue-print for these – the universal intention they combine to realise – already exists in its entirety on the upper Devachanic levels, but its translation into material form by angelic, devic and elemental agencies is a gradual process occurring only in time. For the spiritual beings responsible for the execution of it, this task represents a special kind of challenge, one whose successful accomplishment will help them in turn to advance their own evolution. Even so, because they are neither omniscient nor omnipotent, they do sometimes make mistakes and, interestingly enough, it is these that produce the false starts and failures which have led many scientists to view evolution as a haphazard affair, subject only to the accidents and contingent necessities that chance imposes on it.

Pressed for details of this archetypal world, called by Plato the realm of ideas, the occultist will declare that it is filled with the ceaseless activity of spiritual beings, their collaboration so harmonious that it can best be thought of in terms of sound, be it as choirs of angels or, indeed, the Music of the Spheres. Some, however, go on to warn that we ought not to confuse these celestial harmonies with the sounds we know on Earth. To add to our conceptual difficulty, we further learn that on the seven levels of the mental plane there exist not only archetypes of form but also those of life and feeling, not to mention archetypes of archetypes as well. It is fortunate, therefore, that the hierarchies appointed to supervise this cosmic ideation are much cleverer than we are! In modern occult literature the name commonly given to them is Dhyan-Choans or divine intelligences, a generic term (meaning 'Contemplative Lord') which is attributed to beings who have completed the human stage of evolution and whose present status has to be deduced from the context in which the term is used. (The early Vedic hymns use the word deva in the same all-embracing way.) Other writers, just as often, lapse into what seems like polytheism and refer to them simply as 'gods', including in this august category all spiritual beings whose job, higher than that of the angels, is to be the architect and chief designer of manifested being.

The experience our posthumous 'I' enjoys in Devachan, identical to the experience each initiate hopes to capture in his or her lifetime, entails a reconciliation of the self with the overall oneness of the manifold universe. This notion of unity, let it be said, does not mean that from our vantage point in Devachan the diversity of creation suddenly ceases, to be replaced by an all-encompassing uniformity. On the contrary, the unity we perceive on the mental plane or, better still, *live* there (since we ourselves are part of it) is, to paraphrase Descartes, 'not the one in many but the oneness of the many'. We obtain, as it were, a snapshot of the evolutionary goal towards which everything, according to its nature in the current manvantara, is sedulously working, though once again it must be stressed that the Absolute we 'photograph' is not a *single* perfection but the sum-total of the perfections appropriate to the parts. To this differentiation we owe the fact that our visiting ego, anticipating its own perfection and that of the whole human race, is still able to remain itself and is not, as followers of the Mahayana school of Buddhism declare, extinguished 'like a candle in the wind'. (To be fair to the Buddhists, the annihilation thus implied may not mean total extinction since it probably describes a situation we cannot yet begin to conceive, a situation attainable only when the entire universe reaches its own end or 'moksha', its final deliverance from the successive 'incarnations' it lives through in the rhythm of its existence. There will then prevail a unity beyond unity and plurality, as we now understand them, one in which we and all else will be assumed into the non-dualistic being of the Absolute. This will be the true apotheosis of the All.)

To sum up, then, the mystical fusion of our essence with that of all else which life on the mental plane brings about does not compromise either the individual self or the oneness of which it is part. In the spiritual world, therefore, we might be said to follow the injunction of Jan van Ruysbroek, the fourteenth-century mystic, who recommended that 'we should feel ourselves living wholly in God *and* wholly in ourselves', something that is less a matter of becoming one with the Absolute than of discovering the Absolute present inside us. To say more on the subject would require us to tread warily along the *via negativa*, to say what our Devachanic experience is *not*, rather than what it actually is. Even that road would not take us very far since no matter what is said on the topic, whether negative or affirmative, we have to make do with remote analogies harvested from the narrow fields of time and space. In retrospect, therefore, it might still have been sensible, when treating Devachan, to have mentioned its existence and added nothing else. Those who earnestly wish to know more, need only take up occultism; those who do not, have only to wait ...

I cannot leave the subject, however, without returning to the disembodied ego whose voyage into space will by now have carried it to what, in astronomical terms, is the outer edge of the solar system, where in its enlightened state it is said to illumine the midnight darkness all around it. Here, too, at this farthermost point from the Earth, there is suddenly born in it a wish to return to our planet, an experience Hinduism calls trishna (Pali: tanha) or the thirst for personality. From then on it begins slowly to retrace its journey through the planetary spheres and, on the way, loses the recollection earlier given to it of its all-embracing past. Henceforth, its attention will be directed only to the future, as it assents to the plan being made for its impending return to the physical world. What it makes of its life there will be its own business – our mistakes and successes are of our own doing – but at least the time and place of its next incarnation will have been planned by higher beings so as to offer it ample opportunity for progress.

Part of the same plan is the irrevocable commitment each of us will have made before our second death in Kamaloka, to compensate for past deeds that were detrimental to the harmony our universe is always striving to attain. By this commitment we voluntarily submit to the law known as karma, a Sanskrit word meaning, suitably enough, 'action', since karma is the moral force responsible for the changes through which all manifested being has to pass, some so vast and others so minute as to escape our perception completely. In the *Brihadaranyaka Upanishad* which dates from 500 BC, the secrets of karma or the law of life (as the Pali Canon calls it) were stated to be known only to the highest-ranking initiates, though apparently even they were more familiar with its workings than with its true nature. Occultists believe that one of the noblest achievements of Gautama the Buddha was to reveal to humanity the universal scope of karmic law and, more particularly, its relevance to the spiritual progress of every human being. So rigorous and comprehensive is its application, ensuring that all events in life are more or less determined by antecedent causes, that karma ends the need for a god who passes judgment on our behaviour. Indeed, to many of those who hold karma accountable for the vicissitudes of our human condition, it removes the need for God altogether.[13]

It has long been an error in the West to confuse karma with necessity or fate, and so treat it as a mechanical law which we poor mortals are powerless to change. Those who defend this view often point disapprovingly to the resignation with which the masses in India have for centuries endured the hardships of their life – though it is hard to see how resentment and despair would make them any happier. The truth is that the absence of bitterness discernible in societies that believe in karma is due not to passive indifference but to the lively certainty people have in their ability to control its operation. To grasp this, we need first of all to remember the voluntary assent our post-mortem self gives to the karmic obligation to make good its past mistakes in some future life. Secondly, we need to bear in mind that the misfortunes, like the blessings, we encounter in our present incarnation are the result of actions freely taken in a previous one: our past deeds, the *Mahabharata* declares firmly, will seek us out as surely as a young calf seeks out its mother in a herd of cows. Also to be borne in mind is the freedom we enjoy in each life to direct our thoughts and actions so that our behaviour creates for us the effects we shall meet up with in lives yet to come. In every incarnation, therefore, the chance is ours not only to redeem karmic debts already incurred but, at the same time, to choose what the future balance sheet will look like. Oriental teaching accordingly recommends that a judicious mixture of renunciation (nivritti) and activity (pravritti) should govern our conduct, with the *Bhagavad-Gita* exhorting us to perform conscientiously our social and other duties, albeit with a certain detachment, while dedicating our every effort to the service of God (Ishvarartha).

Although karma, unseen and unknowable, dispenses its rewards and punishments impersonally, it does so with absolute equity, its constant aim being to redress an imbalance which we ourselves have brought about. It is not a blind force or even a ruthless one since, as we have observed, it supposes that the human race is capable of self-improvement and, given this, it co-operates with us in the pursuit of moral perfection. Neither does its prearrangement of so much we encounter in life mean that karma inhibits our subjective freedom: if, for example, we meet again in this life – as we regularly do – the people we knew in a previous one, both sides now bring to the relationship a different personality, with all the new insights and responses this will foster. Far from prejudicing the independence we cherish so dearly, karma allows us to be *self-determining* and, since it applies to our spiritual evolution as a whole, to be angels and gods in the making. Initially set in motion by the descent of our spiritual element into the conditional world of time and space (samsara), karmic law sees to it that we reincarnate again and again (samtana) until our spiritual progress is such that we merit liberation (moksha) from the wheel of rebirth. When that day comes, we shall be entitled to dwell in Nirvanic bliss until the last of our fellow human beings have finally caught up with us,[14] an event which can only mean that the next stage of our evolution, this time post-human, is about to begin – 'And Earth is but a star, that once had shone.'* For the moment, however, our many failings and those of most other human beings mean that our resplendent Earth will keep on shining for a long, long time to come.

Belief in reincarnation is by now fairly common in Europe and America, though what has been taught for nearly 2,000 years by orthodox Christianity about 'the resurrection of the dead, and the life of the world to come', in particular St Paul's statement that 'it is appointed unto men once to die, but after this the judgment',[15] conceals the fact that before then, belief in reincarnation was widespread in the West, as well as in the East. A heritage of that distant age when humankind still had supersensible knowledge of such matters, it was taught in the mystery schools of Greece and Rome, and, so Julius Caesar tells us in his *De bello Gallico*, was also professed by the Druids. Later it was revived by the Manicheans and the kabbalists, though by then it had passed from popular favour. Nevertheless individual thinkers, among them Hume and Kant, continued to proclaim their acceptance of it and when, in 1780, G. E. Lessing defended reincarnation in his *Education of the Human Race*, he found many supporters, among them Goethe, Fichte, Benjamin Franklin and, later, Schopenhauer. Since then, interest in the subject has grown, especially as a result of our wider acquaintance with oriental thought and its traditional attachment to punarjanma or rebirth, though for every serious student, there are a dozen enthusiasts claiming to have been Egyptian princesses, Chinese courtiers and Roman centurions in lives gone by. Among erstwhile princesses, the most voluble has been Joan M. Grant whose book *The Winged Pharaoh*[16] caused a small stir when it was first published just before the Second World War. It was followed by other books, all of them based, their author claimed, on her recollections of past incarnations and all reminiscent of the kind of historical extravaganzas Hollywood once was famous for. (The same failing was known also in earlier times and satirised by Lucian (AD 115–200), notably in the story of Micyllos the tanner who was preached at by a talking cockerel that claimed to be a reincarnation of Pythagoras.)

Somewhat less exotic have been the past lives remembered by individuals who, under hypnosis, have apparently regressed to a time preceding their birth. This technique was pioneered by a French hypnotist, de Rochas, several of whose hypnotised subjects gave plausible accounts of their previous incarnations, often with circumstantial details, the accuracy of which could later be confirmed.[17] Such experiments, assuming the absence of

---

* James Elroy Flecker, *The Golden Journey to Samarkand*, Prologue.

fraud by those taking part in them, often reveal an element of the paranormal but rarely, it must be said, provide irrefutable evidence of reincarnation, if only because we now know so much about the multiple personalities that may be locked up inside a single mind.[18] Given our fondness for self-dramatisation, it is not surprising if under hypnosis these personalities take immense delight in presenting themselves as characters from times long past, their modern knowledge of the chosen period, in part unconsciously acquired, lending a degree of verisimilitude to the tales they tell. Their case is comparable with that of an amateur medium, known by the pseudonym Hélène Smith, who was investigated at the turn of the century by the Swiss psychologist Théodore Flournoy. This young lady purported to give messages from the deceased son of one of the sitters, who had been reincarnated on Mars, the medium supplementing the routine tittle-tattle with lengthy examples of the language spoken on that planet. At first this language, as consistent and complex as any earthly one, seemed entirely new, but careful analysis was to show that its structure and syntax were unmistakably those of Mlle Smith's native French, and its provenance like that of the Martian who spoke it, her own inventive subconscious. More close to home were the previous incarnations the medium commandeered for herself: the first was Marie-Antoinette, ever a favourite in reincarnationist circles, and the second, a sixteenth-century Indian princess called Simondini who, for good measure, delivered whole sentences in Arabic and Sanskrit, all of them traceable, alas, to books found in the library of Mlle Smith's father and unconsciously memorised by her.[19]

It is alleged by those who have made a study of reincarnation that the behaviour and special interests of young children will often yield clues to their previous lives, though Western parents might be expected to overlook these, being unaccustomed to the idea that their mewling and puking offspring may have several grown-up lives behind them. In the East, possibly because of its matter-of-fact acceptance of reincarnation – Gandhi is reported to have said casually that he could remember up to a hundred former lives – many strange cases involving small children occur, though a single well-authenticated case will suffice by way of illustration. It concerns a small girl named Shanti Devi who at the age of four announced to her parents in New Delhi that she had once lived in the town of Muttra, at that time unknown to her, and had died there twelve years previously, on the birth of her second child. The name of her former husband she gave as Kedar Nath, her own as Lugdi, and subsequent inquiries by her teacher and others were to lead them to a widower of that name in the town mentioned. Tested further, the child described her previous home and offered many details of her private life. Taken for the first time to Muttra she dug up a box buried under some floorboards and expressed disappointment on finding it empty. The box, the bemused Kedar Nath informed his visitors from New Delhi, had once contained money but he had removed this following the death of his wife.[20]

In matters of this sort, the testimony of small children is considered by psychic researchers to be more reliable than that of adults, since their limited experience does not contain the mass of information which the rest of us assimilate, consciously or not, with the passage of the years. Interesting research in this field has been conducted by Dr Ian Stevenson of the University of Virginia, who has investigated cases all over the world, often with startling results.[21] Nevertheless, occultists,while not discounting the possibility of recalling past lives, know too much about the akashic record and the mimicry in which astral shells indulge to accept as proof of reincarnation the small balance of recorded cases not attributable to suppressed emotion, self-deception and, to be frank, downright fraud. In the end, it is doubtful whether reincarnation can ever be 'proved' by the kind of evidence parapsychologists are presented with from time to time.

Quite another question, however, is whether previous lives, though the related personalities have long ago been shed, can sometimes be remembered at will. According to occultists they can, though the methods to be followed, many involving access to the akashic record, are divulged only to initiates whose curiosity is justified and possibly has a worthy purpose such as trying to overcome difficulties – their own or someone else's – which relate, for example, to one's private life or one's health, and whose karmic cause needs to be established. These methods range from straightforward meditation, often centred on the sefira of Hesed on the Tree of Life, to more elaborate procedures like the old Egyptian rite known as A Khonsu, heq t'etta, said to date from the 4th Dynasty, that of the royal pyramid builders Snefru, Cheops and Chephren, and performed either on the first day of the Sothic year (the first new moon in our present July) or on the fifteenth day of any lunar month, preferably the ninth, that day having been held sacred in the ancient world. Even certain herbs are rumoured to help jog one's memory as well![22]

Whatever the chances of success, it is certain that no conscious memory of our past lives remains with most of us when we start a new life here on Earth. The longing for this, you will remember, is what drives our ego down through the spheres and back to the threshold of Devachan. By the time it reaches there, the circumstances surrounding its re-entry into the physical world – family, hereditary disposition, social background and even looks –

will have been determined, providing the soil, as it were, in which the incipient personality will take root. In occult terminology the seeds of that personality are often called skandhas, a Sanskrit word which refers, strictly speaking, to the five attributes of phenomenal existence, but here, micro-cosmically, relates to the karmic predisposition through which our emergent consciousness will function after birth. Looked upon as the moral residue of the thoughts and actions of our previous incarnation, skandhas may be pictured as a kind of micro-chip that has been programmed according to our individual karma. As we cross from Devachan into the astral world, we find the skandhas waiting patiently for us, ensuring that our past always catches up with us at last. This, then, is the karmic burden we bring with us, though oblivious of what it contains, when on the seventeenth day of pregnancy or, since opinion is divided, at the instant we draw our first breath, our 'I' unites itself with the physical body and the ethero-astral vehicles of the baby in whom we are due to born.[23]

To some initiates that birth, like Persephone's descent into the Underworld, represented a kind of death, since it exiled us from the spiritual realm in which our true self comes fully and gloriously to life. Others, not so pessimistic, welcomed this re-entry into matter as a chance to start a new incarnation, trying this time to do better and so win eventual liberation from the cycle of death and rebirth. Modern occultists tend on the whole to share this positive approach, comforted by their knowledge that the objects around them contain, as they themselves do, a spiritual essence that is on its way back to its source. Curiously, even as it opens our eyes to realities beyond the physical world, occultism serves also to bring that same world closer to us, coupling our destiny with its own and making us love it, cherish it and care for it more devotedly than ever before.

VII

First Steps
Along
the Path

...the end of all exploring
Will be to arrive where we started
And know the place for the first time

T. S. ELIOT, *Four Quartets*

Never has it been the intention of occultism to distract us from the physical world. Rather, it has sought to rekindle in us a feeling for the sacramental nature of that world, as an outward and visible sign of God's self-awareness, similar to the feelings many of us had towards it in our childhood. I consider it to have been a fortunate coincidence, therefore, that my first introduction to esoteric tradition took place when I was still a young boy, my mind free of those shades of the prison house which adulthood is said to bring.

In describing this tradition and what it consists of, I have taken care up till now to exclude my own experiences. The moment may have come, however, to say a little about them, if only because occultism, whatever serious claims are made on its behalf, risks being treated as moonshine unless its teachings are matched by personal experience. Wisely, the custodians of the ancient mysteries were never content merely to preach at those who came in search of enlightenment but led them, in the course of their initiation, to a direct awareness of the luminous truths that lay unremarked inside them. Nowadays, with the mystery centres long since closed and fallen into ruin, the modern inquirer has little choice but to seek out these truths without priestly guidance, assisted only by the kind of mental training occultism offers to those determined enough to find it and pursue it to the end. In this way alone can esoteric doctrine, its subject matter beyond our senses and reason, be put to the test: without that possibility, a description of our post-mortem life would be just about as credible, perhaps not as much, as claims for the imminence of Armageddon or the historicity of Noah's Ark.

By experience, I mean, of course, the first-hand kind, but as no book can ever hope to offer that, a few references to my own experience, admittedly a poor substitute, will have to suffice. The scene of it was the Welsh country-side and not some remote and colourful corner of the world where occult adventures, though not necessarily believable, are nevertheless so much a part of the exotica one half-expects to find there, that they cease to be shocking. Sadly, one has to admit that weird, inexplicable events, like home-grown prophets, tend to be without honour when they turn up close at hand: what goes down well in Kathmandu is just plain daft a few miles north of Cardiff. Understandably, then, it is with some diffidence that I now invite you to relive with me my first encounter with occultism. In previous dealings with the topic I have taken care to keep it at arm's length, favouring, wherever possible, a detached and lofty view of things and even having the odd snicker at those individuals like Simon Magus, John Dee, Mme Blavatsky and Dion Fortune (she of the ubiquitous tom cats) who actually dabbled in signs and wonders instead of merely talking learnedly about them. Now the time has come for me to join their ranks and, by so doing, risk appearing every bit as dotty as they do.

With that unwelcome prospect and all these excuses in mind, let us proceed at once to a farm called Tanrallt (the name means 'under the hill') that nestles in a desolate valley not far from the Welsh market town of Aberystwyth and close to the summit of Plynlimon, its rolling hills by then fully stretched to a modest 1,300 feet above sea-level. For centuries this has been wild, sheep-farming country since neither the soil nor the harsh climate is conducive to anything else, though some years ago the Forestry Commission did begin to clothe a few bare slopes with experimental fir trees, bred from a race inured to the rigours of Scandinavian winters, but even these sturdy plants found it hard to survive. It is as if the area, jealous of a primitive independence, resents all human interference with its bleak dignity; as if, too, it fears that any compromise with humanity will force it to give up a secret of which it has for centuries been the guardian. Often, as a boy, I paused on my way down from the summit, with not a cottage or farmhouse in sight, watching the grass around me welcome the darkness like a long-lost friend, listening to the sympathetic murmur of the wind and the mournful cry of curlews, and I ached to know the secret of those ancient, sullen hills.

Only John Isaac James who lived in Tanrallt Farm, as his parents and grandparents had done before him, felt completely at home among them. He respected them, loved them and they in return conceded him the right to be there and to graze his sheep along their slopes. If, when I think of Mr James today, 'supernatural' is the word that promptly springs to mind, it is not because of the paranormal gifts he was reputed to possess, but because of his physical appearance, a generous nature having endowed him with a frame whose dimensions exceeded what is natural to the common run of men. Over six foot in height, with shoulders like a stocky Welsh black bull, his presence invariably dominated, at times blotted out, any company in which he found himself. About him, everything was larger than life: his hands, roughened and reddened by outdoor work, were too big, as were his feet, while his head rested massively, if a trifle unsteadily, on a neck the size of another man's thigh. And yet there was nothing grotesque about Mr James for, despite his build, he did not move in an awkward, clumsy manner. On the contrary, his movements were characterised by a delicacy that left the spectator with an impression of gentleness, an impression which his bulk seemed in a curious way to reinforce and not to contradict, just as a circus elephant performing feats of balance suggests a lightness its appearance belies. By this I do not mean that there was something graceful about Mr James: anything elephantine about him belonged to the jungle, not the tinsel of the circus ring. His manners, too, were as rough as his hands, and the voice that boomed out from his huge barrel chest used a language far beyond the limits of what was deemed respectable in Aberystwyth and its staunchly Methodist environs. [1]

I was thirteen when I began spending my Saturdays with Mr James at Tanrallt. A faithful customer at the grocer's shop my father kept – the two of them often went out shooting rabbits together – he had by then become a friend of the family. Already in his seventies and alone in the world, he welcomed my help around the farm and, still more perhaps, the company it brought him. My parents welcomed the arrangement as well, believing it did me good to get away from my school books, especially in summer, and spend as much time as I could out of doors. Admittedly, my mother had a few reservations to start with, all due to Mr James's notorious use of bad language, but after warning me not to listen whenever he swore (which would have meant missing every other word he said), she quickly overcame them. 'The fresh air', Mr James promised her, 'will bring some colour to his cheeks, and he'll get a chance to earn a bit of pocket money' – promises only half kept, for while a healthy glow came to my face, the pocket money was somehow forgotten.

To reach Tanrallt I had to cycle from Aberystwyth, past the town cemetery and the eleventh-century church of Llanbadarn, and follow the road that led through Lovesrove Woods to the hamlet of Capel Bangor. There, the road began a slow, but not over-arduous, ascent to Goginan, its row of terraced cottages staring blankly down at a valley scarred by disused lead mines. From then on the scenery grew rapidly wilder, with exposed moorland spreading out in all directions, and far fewer trees to be seen, most of them sparse hawthorns bent low by the wind, and sometimes an alder or dwarf mountain ash. On either side of the unfenced road, reeds and rushes flourished in the wet, marshy ground, their monotonous green intermittently enlivened by clumps of purple loosestrife or vivid yellow toadflax. Downhill, the air cool against my face, I would freewheel at last into the village of Ponterwyd, only to proceed uphill again, past more abandoned lead mines until suddenly, to the right, like a gash in the landscape, a deep narrow valley opened up between two sharp bends in the road. Driving by car one might easily miss it. Certainly one would miss the way that led down to it, marked by an old wooden gate, with 'Tanrallt' painted in uneven white letters on the topmost bar.

The asphalt surface beyond the gate soon yielded to rough gravel and that, too, was replaced before long by a twin-furrowed track, the width of a tractor's wheel span, with reeds and coarse grasses growing in between the ruts. Provided I steered carefully, I could ride along one of these furrows and, apart from a bump or two, this final leg of the journey was perhaps the pleasantest of all, bringing me after ten minutes to the slate-slabbed yard in front of Tanrallt. There, a Rhode Island cockerel lived with a harem of twelve assorted hens and, though I never knew if the polygamy extended to them, a trio of bad-tempered Old English bantams. If I heard the dogs barking as I approached, the odds were that Mr James was at home, since they and he were normally inseparable. Uncounted cats, two ponies, half a dozen small beef cattle and a few hundred sheep made up the rest of the livestock.

In a setting like this, occultism, whenever Mr James talked about it, could not help but assume a naturalness that made its subject matter as real and immediate as the grass that grew underfoot. For him, the super-sensible world was not 'occult' in the sense of being far removed from this one, to be looked for down dark alleys like hooch in the days of Prohibition, but was an integral part of life, 'occult' only to the extent of its being concealed from our senses. Thanks to this approach, Mr James saw the phenomenal world imbued with the presence of what neo-Platonists like to call the 'intelligible world', that archetypal realm of ideas which, according to

Plato's *Republic*, education should teach us how to rediscover. Required of us for this purpose is a shift of consciousness identical to that achieved in meditation so that our perception of objects and events becomes infused with a kind of empathy, a new awareness of our involvement in whatever we happen to be looking at. Far from being just a spectator, therefore, Mr James felt himself to be a participant in the natural processes going on around him, compassionately aware of the 'becoming' he and they shared in Time, and the 'being' awaiting both of them beyond it.

To him it was a matter of profound regret that contemporary science preferred the opposite view, its beginnings traceable to the fifteenth century when, so he told me, the post-Atlantean history of humanity entered a new psychological phase or, as other occultists have put it, a new period of soul development. Around that time, marked in Europe by the Renaissance, the human ego finally came of age, its new-found maturity enabling human beings to view the world for the first time with dispassionate curiosity as something totally distinct from themselves. Indulgence in this novel ability by subsequent generations has resulted today in most scientists finding it natural to withhold their feelings from the things they observe, believing that only complete detachment will permit them to draw from the object of study the conclusions it warrants: the less they involve themselves in the exercise, the better will be the result.

So successful has this approach been (and no occultist would deny it the credit it deserves) that most people, ignorant of its limitations, believe it to be the only one possible. Not so the minority to which Mr James belonged and whose conviction it is that our understanding of reality cannot be made to depend on whatever pieces of it scientists put beneath their microscopes or scalpels, any more than the effulgence of light in Turner's paintings can be appreciated by a chemical analysis of the pigments used in their composition. What is not realised by most scientists, especially those currently engaged in the search for the secret of life, is that by the time they have succeeded in reducing matter to its smallest components, their quarry has long since absconded, leaving only the basic mechanics behind. The fact is that the wonder we call life resides not in the behaviour of individual cells but in their common activity and the vitality thus imparted to the organism they collectively serve. And even that is only half the story.

Our intellect alone fails to recognise this. In a sense it is as dead as the laboratory specimens researchers dissect in order to extract the kind of data it feeds on. Only if we bring to living things a way of thinking that is correspondingly alive, can we ever hope to penetrate the mystery of their true nature. Goethe, who was both an artist and a scientist,[2] is among the few thinkers – his contemporary Kant was another – who realised this and called the required faculty 'intuitive discernment' (*anschauende Urteilskraft*), with the result that Goethean is the term applied by some occultists (none of whom was keener on it than Rudolf Steiner) to the 'vital' thinking needed for the proper study of nature.

Whether Mr James, Tanrallt, was familiar with Goethe I cannot say but the German writer's 'wide and luminous view', as Matthew Arnold once called it, matched his own. He refused to accept that experiment and minute analysis were in themselves sufficient to give us a full understanding of the organic world and, since life may be latent there also, much of the inorganic world as well: far from lifting the veil of Isis, such methods merely concentrate on the texture of the cloth. Moreover, it was his firm belief that in studying nature, be it alive or apparently dead, we have to take account of the formative forces directing the changes through which living things pass in the course of their evolution. Never did Mr James forget that these changes are indications of the Earth's progress within the mode of time towards the realisation of an idea pre-existing in the archetypal world, making of our planet an objective spiritual reality on its way to perfection. 'Mighty, manifold and magnificent', enthused Rudolf Steiner on the same theme, 'are indeed the spiritual effects that continually approach man out of the things of nature when he walks in it . . . it is something that constantly streams towards him as a supersensible spirituality poured out over nature, which is a mirror of the divine-spiritual.'[3]

In this same mirror each of us beholds our own reflection. It is there because of the mysterious analogy, a favourite topic in occult literature, that subsists between us and the universe we live in, between the microcosm and the macrocosm stretching beyond it. At once it should be emphasised that this analogy does not mean, and never has meant in esoteric circles, that each of us is a miniature copy, *mutatis mutandis*, of the physical world or the solar system, though it has often been interpreted in this simplistic fashion. There are, it is true, many interesting and, from the hermetic point of view, highly significant correspondences between us and the phenomenal world, so many in fact that the temptation is strong to regard every human being as a concise epitome of the All.[4] Our physical constitution did, after all, evolve through the mineral and plant kingdoms before entering that of the animal, and we still carry traces of these inside our bodies. (Some occultists even allege that the special relationship between the universe and us has been corroborated by the discovery, part of the Uncertainty Principle proposed by Werner Heisenberg in 1927, that the mere act of observation induces micro-physical changes in whatever is observed. These subtle changes, together with the fact that elementary particles appear to enjoy a discrete existence only when we apprehend them, may well mean that on the sub-atomic level it is we ourselves who determine, albeit involuntarily, much of what goes on.)

Nevertheless, when occultism speaks of the human being as a microcosm, what it sees in it is an image of that supersensible reality which is the ground of all things, itself and the macrocosm included. The coincidence between the two is thus an intrinsic one, our awareness of it due to the consciousness we have, as human beings, of our individual selfhood, the spiritual centre that reveals to us not only our essential nature but that of all else as well. Because of this relationship between the part and the whole, those initiated into the mysteries were always taught that in endeavouring to realise their individual destiny, they were at the same time helping the universe to realise its own.

Let me repeat that not for one moment did Mr James, though mindful of supersensible realities, ever disregard, still less disrespect, the objective world his senses showed him daily: as a farmer and shepherd he could hardly afford to do so.[5] Yet at the same time his spiritual awareness was such that he always saw behind it the etheric forces (or 'formative powers', as he preferred to call them, using the Welsh expression *nerthoedd lluniol*) by which an immanent spirituality strives untiringly to transform matter in accordance with specific evolutionary impulses. In the plant and animal kingdoms these impulses, known in the East as dharmas, flow from the archetypal world where the 'oversoul' or collective identity of a particular genus or species struggles to attain perfection on the physical plane. In human beings, on the other hand, an *individual* identity, the product of our ego, means that the urge towards, in our case, spiritual perfection flows from within, its eventual realisation due to our own efforts and, as we saw earlier, to the harmonious operation of karmic law. In the East, it is called our Devayana, our inner pathway to the gods.

From this it cannot but follow that the entire world, no less than its parts, as supporters of holism would have to concede, is subject to the same evolutionary direction. Taking this in a literal sense Mr James told me on several occasions that the planet we walk on is itself an organic, will-impelled entity and not a lump of dead rock on whose surface living forms happen to thrive. (On the mental plane, you will recall, its consciousness is nourished by the collective experience of plants, minerals and invertebrate animals which act together as its sense organs on the physical plane.) 'Listen,' I have heard him whisper at midday, 'the Earth's breathing in again.' When I used to admit to having heard nothing, he would try to explain to me that evidence of this respiration (involving one complete breath every twenty-four hours and covering in turn all parts of the world) could be found in the movement of mercury inside a barometer, its rise and fall, like those of sap inside trees, due to changes in the etheric body that our Earth, in common with other living things, was equipped with. That body, he further assured me, possessed four complementary, but separate, qualities and, though the image was certainly inapt (since 'ether', in so far as it had substance, was composed of 'non-matter'), [6] this quaternity could be thought of as successive layers or skins, each associated with one of the four basic elements and each responsible for four basic shapes (circular, semi-crescent, square, triangular) that combined to form the rudiments of matter. Inside its shell (and enclosing a central core of 'fire' ether), our planet was permeated by 'earth' ether with, around it, a mantle of 'water' ether and, on top of this, the remaining zones of 'air' and 'fire' ether, the last two pervading the atmosphere – though not in the quasi-physical way once attributed to the 'ether' of old-fashioned physics. In the course of the Earth's respiration, 'water' ether rose from its surface in the morning, as if exhaled, and invaded the home of its neighbour, 'air' ether. This went on until midday when, because of it, barometric pressure fell to its lowest level, at which point the 'water' ether started descending to its own habitat, drawn back, as it were, by the inhalation that locally took place.

The atmospheric changes produced by this breathing are said to be responsible for the maximum levels registered on barometers at sunrise and sunset and for a variety of meteorological phenomena. Even the Earth's rotation, Mr James affirmed, is attributable to rhythms connected with quasi-organic processes going on inside it. On a microcosmic scale, the same etheric forces also impose their rhythm on us, for instance on our breathing and on the circulation of our blood. Here, it should be noted that because ether moulds for its purposes the matter it works through, such bodily organs as our lungs and heart originated as a functional response to rhythms transposed on to the physical plane. Our blood, in other words, does not travel through our veins and arteries because our heart has always acted on it like a pump but because its own molecules move to a rhythm inherent in their etheric constitution. Meanwhile, on a macrocosmic scale, there exists – and this was my starting point several chapters back – a cycle, too great for human conception, through which the entire universe passes, its current expansion but a phase in a centripetal and centrifugal sequence which occult tradition long ago likened to the way we – and our planet – breathe in and out.

So it was that during the Saturdays I spent in Tanrallt, Mr James taught me how to recognise the wheels within wheels by which nature, 'but art unknown',[7] moves slowly towards self-fulfilment. By observing and sharing in the changes wrought by the seasons or even the growth and decay of a single small flower, I learned to discern how etheric forces active in matter sustain a plan, said by the late Christmas Humphreys, Q.C. and former Vice-President of the World Fellowship of Buddhists, to be 'too wide for the intellect to grasp . . . an equally vast machinery of involution and evolution . . . cycles too large to follow and, within them, others too small to see, and somewhere within them all . . . the complex entity, at once supremely real and utterly unreal which we, with a blend of deep humility and arrogant pride, call Man.'[8]

In spite of these elevated, all but mystical insights, I have to confess that part of my reason for going to Tanrallt every week arose from Mr James's reputation of being a witch or dewin, it being well known in the district that he could lift the evil eye from ailing cattle (and, rumour said, put it back again, if his services were insufficiently rewarded), as well as help people cursed with bad luck or crossed in love. His power to foresee the future by peering into a crystal ball was also well-attested, as was his knack of finding water and missing objects with the aid of a forked hazel twig. It was, however, as a herbalist that my parents solicited his help from time to time: he had rid me, as a small boy, of worms caught, it was suspected, from the family cat, and had cured my father of a nasty bout of shingles. Even the local doctor, far from resenting this challenge to his own, more orthodox, skills, had been known to swear that Mr James's herbal tonic, made from balm, marjoram, rosemary and marigolds, was the finest spring-time pick-me-up anyone could wish for.

Sad to report, not once in all the time I spent at Tanrallt did I witness any of the magical skills Mr James was popularly thought to possess. Whatever may have happened the rest of the week, on Saturdays, at least, no anxious cattle breeders or star-crossed lovers ever turned up in search of assistance, and, with water plentiful everywhere on Plynlimon, the need to divine its whereabouts never arose. Even the mysterious crystal ball stayed frustratingly hidden from sight. To my disappointment, the only visitors to the farm were people wanting a cure for their illnesses or chronic aches and pains, but it was by listening as Mr James talked to them that I began to learn how, for him, each individual patient, with his physical, etheric and astral bodies, not to mention his karmic inheritance, was every bit as important as the malady complained of. I learned, too, how the formative forces responsible for movement, growth and life in the physical world could in many cases, none more so than in cancer,[9] be responsible also for the outbreak of disease.

To describe Mr James's therapeutic methods, at least in the kind of detail they deserve, would take too much time, but two characteristics of them should perhaps be mentioned since they directly relate to the etheric forces I have been discussing. The first concerns his method for recognising which plant was best suited to help cure a particular disease. In many cases, of course, these plants are already well known and are listed in every herbal pharmacopoeia, but thanks to his 'living' approach to the natural world, Mr James was able to confirm the medicinal value of each plant by identifying what sort of etheric force was predominant in it and relating this to a corresponding function in human beings. Occultists have been doing this for years, though some have proceeded to link the practice with the now discredited Doctrine of Signatures, by which a plant's external appearance is held to reveal its therapeutic use.[10]

Though he spoke of such signatures, the great Paracelsus (whose intuition led him to describe the medicinal uses of foxglove) was careful to stress the subjective nature of the process: 'The mind', he wrote in his *De natura rerum*, 'need not concern itself with the physical constitution of plants and roots. It recognises their powers and virtues intuitively thanks to the signatures they carry inside them.' We hear the same from George Fox (1624–90), founder of Quakerism, who narrates how, at the age of twenty-four, 'the creation was opened up to me; and it was showed me how all things had their names given to them according to their nature and virtue. And I was at a stand in my mind whether I should practise physic for the good of mankind, seeing the nature and virtue of all creatures were so opened to me by the Lord.'[11] Even today, as I learnt in Tanrallt, there are still people in country areas so in love with nature that she, responding, unveils her secrets to them.

Because of the influence etheric impulses have on many diseases, Mr James often administered his herbal remedies homoeopathically and in minute doses, progressively diluting each substance until its presence in a neutral solvent such as water became too weak ever to be detected by chemical analysis. While the medicinal value of such a solution swiftly declined, given the decreasing amount of active ingredient still in it, this trend was reversed when, at a certain point, the corresponding etheric forces ('negative matter') began to replace the departed physical ones. With their arrival, a remedy is said, in the language of homoeopathy, to be 'potentised', and the more the subsequent dilution, the greater its potentisation. (Not that the process can go on for ever: eventually the potenisation comes to a halt.) Instructing me in the preparation of such remedies, Mr James explained how they acted primarily on the patient's etheric body and, through it, on the physical body where they could achieve a cure without inhibiting that body's own ability to heal itself or co-operate in the remedial process taking place. Effective though modern drugs are, it cannot be denied that many of them (ironically, on account of their very effectiveness) act against the sufferer's long-term interest by eliminating physical symptoms, sometimes at one fell swoop, without requiring more from the patient than the appropriate physiological responses. Asked to do no more than passively react, the organism ends up having no role to play in overcoming the sickness that afflicts it, thereby losing in time its ability to cure itself, even when required to do so. Here again, Mr James would have argued, we have yet another instance of that 'dead' science which, among other things, leads researchers to view disease as a kind of mechanical breakdown and doctors to see in their patients machines in need of repair.

In need of some repair, it is true, but with nothing machine-like about her, was Mrs Sophie Price, the Paragon — the appendage referring not to that lady's qualities but to the name of the shop she kept a few miles out of Aberystwyth — who on a Saturday in early July descended on Tanrallt in her nephew's Austin Seven, scattering the poultry, just after Mr James and I had returned from treating a pair of ewes badly crippled by foot-rot, a condition the wet, marshy ground on Plynlimon is notorious for causing. The day was memorable because I was due to stay overnight at the farm, something I had never been allowed to do before because of my mother's anxiety that the beds there might be damp. (I might not end up with foot-rot but, loath to take risks, she had insisted I bring with me a pair of well-aired sheets from home.) At seven o'clock Mr James had lit the fire, explaining how even in summer it still got chilly at nightfall in a stone-built cottage like Tanrallt, and going on to add that in any case an empty grate was a cheerless sight, whatever the season. That job done, the two of us were just finishing a late tea of cheese and pickles when Mrs Price arrived at the door in search of something for her dropsy.

Cumbersomely overweight, Mrs Price seldom budged in those days from a chair behind the counter of her shop, expecting callers to help themselves to whatever they wanted and deposit their money on the till as they left. (This was long before self-service stores had brought the practice into fashion.) In between, customers were welcome to stay as long as they liked, to gossip with the proprietress who sat in her chair, serenely munching liquorice allsorts all day long. 'I'm eating up my profits,' she often used to laugh, baring several liquorice-yellowed teeth, 'but we all need one little weakness, God knows!'

Mr James disagreed. In the sternest of terms he condemned her over-indulgence in food, particularly her avid consumption of sweets: liquorice was not bad in itself, he explained, being especially good for lazy bowels (though he did not put it quite as delicately as that) but in the quantities consumed by Mrs Price, it could not fail to add more pounds to her already excessive weight. This, combined with her aversion to exercise, imposed an intolerable strain on her heart and provoked the dropsy of which she complained. He agreed, however, to give her some herbs to relieve the swollen ankles, giddiness and puffiness under the eyes that were its main symptoms, but warned her that only a change in her eating habits would effect a radical cure. Ten minutes later off went his patient with a diuretic mixture of larkspur, nettle and tansy, to which Mr James had thoughtfully added some hawthorn to strengthen her over-burdened heart. Profuse in her thanks, Mrs Price slipped a ten-shilling note into a box labelled 'Missionary Work' that stood on a small table by the front door. All callers were expected to do the same, though none really believed that the indigent heathen ever caught a glimpse of the money thus collected.

'I'll do as you say, Mr James,' panted his grateful patient as we helped to reinstall her in the car. Mr James grunted. He knew that before the Austin came within sight of the gate, she would be deep inside her bag of liquorice allsorts looking for the black ones to which her addiction was greatest.

'A foolish woman,' observed Mr James as he shut the front door, 'determined to kill herself.'

'Lack of will-power,' said I, sounding more prim than clever.

'Perhaps. In that case I should have added some vervain but I used the last of that a week ago for a tonic.' He glanced up at the rafters from which bunches of herbs, among them broom, loosestrife, sage, rosemary and comfrey were hanging to dry, their combined fragrance making the warm air of the room deliciously heady.

'Is vervain important?' I inquired. I was trying to learn all I could about herbs.

'Very.' Mr James, slumped in an armchair big enough to support a man of his size, had lit his pipe and was staring into the fire, his legs stretched out in front of him. I was on the settle opposite, one of the sheepdogs next to me, the other asleep at my feet. It was comforting to reflect that I would not have to leave soon to cycle back to Aberystwyth. Already the night was drawing in but though the room was quite dark, Mr James made no attempt to light the oil lamp on the table.

'Vervain's good for the nerves,' he continued, 'like most plants with blue or mauve flowers. Lavender, for instance, or violets; even catnip.'

'And heather?'

'Heather's the same. That cures depression as well.'

Next to me, warm and soft, the dog snuggled closer, his head resting on my lap.

'You should take vervain before your exams,' counselled Mr James. 'It's a funny plant; it steadies the nerves and quickens the brain both together. Only valerian and one or two others work the same way. That's why it helps with exams.'

This reminded me I had two pages of Latin verbs to revise by Monday morning. In my head I ran through a few of their principal parts. Several minutes were to pass before Mr James spoke again.

'It's a magic herb, vervain, connected with Venus, though in Roman times they used to scatter it on the altars of Jupiter.'

To scatter, I thought, *spargo, spargĕre, sparsi, sparsum*. The darkness, the scent of drying herbs and the warmth of the fire conspired to make me feel sleepy. Yet I wanted so much to stay awake and talk to Mr James now that, for once, I had a whole night in which to do it.

'Why is it a magic herb?' I asked, struggling to overcome my drowsiness. Mr James leant forward and threw a fresh log on the fire.

'The Druids, you've heard of them, thought it had magical powers, especially in love spells. They mixed it with elecampane and mistletoe berries. Vervain was one of their favourite plants.'

'You mean the real Druids?' It was as well to establish this. The only Druids I had ever seen were members of a bardic order connected with the National Eisteddfod who, beneath the disguise of their pastel-coloured robes, were teachers, bank managers and ministers of religion, none of them capable of recognising vervain.

'The real ones, yes. They had several sacred herbs – some say seven, others ten – and the strange thing is, they've all got their uses today. Mistletoe they liked most of all, and when you've learnt enough Latin you can read how they used to cut it down with a golden sickle on the sixth day of the new moon. A writer called Pliny – there were two of them, this one and his nephew – wrote all about it.'

As yet our class had not managed to progress beyond a selection of the simplest passages in Caesar's Gallic War and these were not the ones that mention the Druids. The two Plinys, elder and younger, were completely new to me. I wondered how their name was spelt.

'There used to be lots of Druids in Wales,' added Mr James, his bulky shape now dissolved completely in the shadow of his chair. 'They still fascinate people. That's why such a lot of nonsense gets written about them.'

For a long time neither of us spoke. About the nonsense he had mentioned, Mr James was perfectly right. To blame for it is the little we know about the Druids and their ways, with the result that anyone with an ounce of imagination can say anything about them without real fear of contradiction. The fantasising began in the seventeenth century and continued well into the last, ending up as part of that resurgence of occultism and Celtic nationalism which was to captivate such committed romantics as W. B. Yeats and A. E. (George Russell). [12] Even the Freemasons and the British Israelites, the latter in the steps of William Blake, lost no time in appropriating Druidism to their own cherished causes, [13] though their hereditary claim to it was arguably less valid than that of the Welsh stonemason and poet Edward Williams (Iolo Morganwg) who in 1819 introduced the National Eisteddfod to the Gorsedd or bardic circle and all the pseudo-Druidic ceremonial that nowadays goes with it. Inspiration for much of this had come from the eighteenth-century antiquary Dr William Stukeley, an amateur archaeologist who convinced many of his more gullible contemporaries that Druidism was the pristine religion of humankind, with (as John Aubrey had declared before him) Stonehenge its most important place of worship.

To some extent the eccentric Dr Stukeley was correct, if not about Stonehenge which, as even our latter-day Druids [14] seem willing to concede, was built long before the Celts had reached Britain, but about the universal basis of Druidic belief. In western Europe, particularly in Gaul and Britain, it was the Druids who represented the post-Atlantean tradition which, having sprung up in Takla Makan or somewhere close by, had been carried by 2000 BC to the remotest parts of Asia and Europe. Here we have an explanation for the many correspondences scholars have noted between, on the one hand, Druidic teachings, as described by the Stoic philosopher Posidonius in the second century BC and later quoted by Diodorus Siculus and Strabo, and, on the other, Brahminical teachings in India. Prominent among them is the doctrine of reincarnation, [15] so prevalent in Celtic society that the Roman author Valerius Maximus reported that loans could be secured in this life on an undertaking to repay them in the next. In the introduction to his *Lives and Opinions of Famous Philosophers*, Diogenes Laërtius (AD 200–250) joins several other writers who, echoing Dion Chrysostom a century earlier, speak of a primitive philosophical system whose 'riddles and dark sayings' are common to the Persian magi, the sages of Babylon and Assyria, the Gymnosophists of India and the Druids. That Druidic belief also resembled the views of Pythagoras had already been remarked upon by Diodorus but it was Clement of Alexandria and other residents of that learned city who took this up with most verve. Writing from Rome in the fourth century AD, the historian Ammianus Marcellinus summarised the case by saying that Pythagoras had studied not only with the Brahmins but also with the Galatai, meaning by this the Druidic priesthood of Gaul. [16] To both sets of mentors, we are told, he owed his views on metempsychosis.

Whether the esoteric system in which Mr James had by then begun to instruct me owed anything to the Druids, I cannot pretend to know. Sometimes he implied that it did and, imitating the Theosophists with their fondness for subterranean libraries near Shigatze in Tibet, he would mention a vault in the ancient city of Bibactris, not far from Autun in modern France, where its secrets were formerly stored. On other occasions, however, he seemed eager to impress upon me that the Druids, like the early Brahmins, never wrote their teachings down but relied exclusively on an oral tradition which it took neophytes as many as twenty years to learn. That the system Mr James taught me was Celtic and old, this much at least seems quite certain, with traces of it recognisable in the earliest fragments of Irish [17] and Welsh literature. Its symbolism, too, has much in common with that found on religious and decorative objects excavated from Celtic sites in Britain, Ireland and continental Europe. About its possible link with the Druids, however, it may be wise not to speculate.

Some prudence is also necessary with respect to its link, fondly and frequently evoked by Mr James, with Taliesin, a sixth-century Welsh poet who is allegedly buried under a moss-covered slab (in reality a Bronze Age grave) about twelve miles north of Aberystwyth. Of the verses Taliesin composed, very few remain and the authorship of these is often disputed. Certainly there are no grounds for thinking that his poetry ever exhibited the 'complete system of Druidism' claimed for it by the inventive pen of Iolo Morganwg who, after giving the National Eisteddfod its quaint Druidic trappings, went on to propagate a Druidic version of the kabbalah. Our knowledge of Taliesin's poems, such as it is, comes from a thirteenth-century anthology, *The Book of Taliesin*, and the fulsome language these contain is clearly intended to keep their author in favour with the Brythonic princes who gave him board and lodging. Nevertheless, there exists an oral tradition, unsuspected even by Iolo Morganwg, which makes Taliesin out to be not only a 'bread-and-butter' poet, but also the patron of a magico-mystical system that stems from the oldest pre-Christian past of Celtic Europe. This is the system that the Welsh national hero Owen Glendower (Owain Glyndŵr) got to know, either in Sycharth where he was born, or, later, as a young man among expatriate Welshmen in London. When, on his return to Wales, he became the leader of a rebellion against the occupying English, he was feared both for his valour and for the 'deep experiments' that his esoteric training allowed him to undertake. Shakespeare, at a safe distance of two hundred years, was able to poke fun at his occult reputation in *1 Henry IV*. There, anticipating the Fox sisters and every table-turner since, Glendower boasts:

> I can call spirits from the vasty deep.

To which Hotspur, hard-headedly English, responds drily:

> Why, so can I, or so can any man;
> But will they come when you do call for them?*

For Mr James, being Welsh, the answer would have been a wholehearted yes.

Historians may well scoff at the idea of an oral tradition unknown to them that stretches from a sixth-century poet to an elderly sheep farmer in twentieth-century Cardiganshire. Yet the endurance of oral traditions is itself beyond dispute. Indeed, the survival of Taliesin's own poetry, however sparse, over seven turbulent centuries suggests that the survival for a further seven of a tradition closely related to it is not as implausible as might at first appear. Naturally, this does nothing to confirm that the system taught by Mr James was linked to the Druids, as he liked to claim, especially as back-dating is a common weakness among occultists,[18] but as its worth was independent of its antecedents, this never worried me unduly: puddings, even occult ones, have in the end to be proved by the eating, not by checking the age of the cook.

Fundamental to Mr James's system was a mandala-like diagram composed of seven coloured circles, each representing a first principle which, though outside the phenomenal world, corresponded to one of the seven planes of being, four manifested and three not, or, more subjectively, seven states of consciousness, all of them experienced by human beings and related to the chakras of oriental tradition.[19] For the record, these states

* *1 Henry IV*, III. i. 53–5.

(through which every one of us must pass in the course of monadic evolution) are, with their Sanskrit equivalents in brackets, trance consciousness, deep sleep consciousness (sushupti), dream consciousness (svapna), waking consciousness (jagrat), psychic, super-psychic and spiritual consciousness (samadhi). In addition there are five 'creative' states of consciousness, the resulting dozen being linked to the twelve signs of the zodiac. In Welsh the basic seven circles were known as cantrefi and named after seven regional divisions (cantref means a 'hundred') of the ancient Welsh princedom of Dyfed. Subsidiary to this was their connection with the seven pole stars of Ursa Major – representing the seven holy Rishis, according to Hindu tradition – which complement the seven properties of the physical world listed by the alchemists (matter, cohesion, flux, coagulation, accumulation, constancy and division), together with their related manifestation both in the evolution and, curiously enough, the ethno-social development of humanity.

On a more practical level, the cantrefi, backed by an arsenal of related colours, sounds and images, afford the trained mind direct access to the wider realities that lie beyond sense experience. Through them information denied to the senses can be directly ascertained, a process represented mythologically by the enchantment and subjugation of the cantrefi by Llwyd, son of Cilcoed. (A parallel account may be read in the *Mabinogion*,[20] written down in the eleventh century but containing material dating from earlier, pre-Christian times.) In graphic terms the same process is summarised thus: the circle of each cantref stands for the unknown, its midpoint everywhere (to borrow from Empedocles) and its circumference nowhere. Man, the seeker after knowledge, is represented by a square, but because he is more than the sum of his physical parts, the square may be intersected to yield a cross, the arms of which can be extended to pursue the boundless into infinity. The challenge offered to us by esoteric training, therefore, is to 'square' (i.e. subjugate and enclose) the circle, meaning that the dynamic relationship between us and the universal being is geometrically expressible in terms of diameter and circumference.

More picturesque is the connection between the circles of the cantrefi and different groups of trees which, together, make up the Wood of Celyddon (Caledonia) in whose verdant shade, so the twelfth-century *Book of Carmarthen* tells us, a soldier called Myrddin found refuge after the Battle of Arfderydd in AD 575. For fifty years Myrddin stayed in the forest, the victim of a 'divine madness' that enabled him to discover the secrets of nature and acquire the gift of prophecy, emerging in subsequent literature as Merlin, the royal wizard of Arthurian romance.[21] Here, the tree symbolism is of much older vintage than the story itself and for this, at least, Mr James may have been justified in claiming a link with the Druids whose devotion to trees and sacred groves is well known. Moreover, one feature of this tradition, a calendar of sixty-two lunar months distributed over nineteen different trees (with an additional two months to reconcile it with the solar calendar) corresponds closely to (and even completes and elucidates) a fragmentary bronze calendar found at Coligny, near Bourg-en-Bresse in France. Archaeologists concede that this, at least, belongs to the Druids. The real ones, as my host in Tanrallt would have said.

Mr James had relit his pipe, adding the pungent smell of Ringer's Shag tobacco to the sweeter scents around us. Emerging from my reverie, I once more felt a twinge of pleasure at being in Tanrallt, cosseted by the warm, herb-scented darkness, though now — and this I noticed with some surprise — I no longer felt sleepy at all. My body still felt tired (an afternoon spent catching sheep, even crippled ones, is hard work, though doubtless harder on the sheep) but my mind was quickened by a new alertness, an expectancy, which, while real enough, had no apparent object. As for Mr James, he was still talking about the Druids, his loud voice sounding louder than ever in the heavy stillness of the room.

'There aren't any real Druids left,' he said sadly, 'the Romans saw to that, a chap named Suetonius Paulinus. In AD 61 he chased them on to the island of Anglesey and let his soldiers massacre the lot. It's all written down in Latin.'

The two Plinys again, I thought, only to be corrected at once: 'That part's in a book by Tacitus — *sed nunc terminus Britanniae patet.*'*

Silence again. This last sentence I recognised as Latin, but Latin of a more advanced kind than anything we had so far learnt at school. I sensed, for I could no longer make out his face, that Mr James guessed how astonished I was to hear him quoting Latin prose. I sensed also that my astonishment amused him no end.

The butchery of the Druids near the Menai Straits in AD 61 — the air rent, Suetonius records, with screams and fearsome curses — extinguished their influence in Europe, though a few of them lingered on in Ireland, among them a Druid named Coelte whom St Patrick is reported to have chatted to one afternoon. Their disappearance is a reminder of the many setbacks occult tradition would have to overcome in the course of its long history, not least among them, as we have seen, the all too human failings

---

* 'Now the very edge of Britain lies within reach'.

of those granted stewardship of it. Older by far than the world's great religions, it was already middle-aged when the foundations of the Pyramids were laid in Egypt. Yet today it is still with us, as vigorous as ever, its central doctrines virtually unchanged since Indo-Germanic tribes first bore it out into the world from its secret birth-place in the Tarim basin. So astonishing has been its durability that its supporters feel sure that more lies behind it than a persistent streak of good luck.

What occultists contend is that highly evolved members of the human race, their earthly progress over many lives sufficient to exempt them from further rebirth, have agreed to return to help the rest of us conserve our esoteric heritage. The responsibility they have taken upon themselves is to make it available, nothing more, to the few among us whose temperament or karmic disposition urges them to seek acquaintance with it. More than this, they rarely, if ever, attempt, since to impose knowledge on us, whether we want it or not, would be to compromise that free will which is our most precious human possession. Similarly, these elevated beings make no attempt to supervise, still less interfere with, our treatment of whatever knowledge we obtain, for this too would be to inhibit the moral freedom each of us enjoys: our behaviour, be it wise or foolish, depends entirely on us. This readiness to impart knowledge unconditionally is the key to understanding how someone like Mme Blavatsky could tap genuine occult sources while producing the marvels for which she was famous and whose genuineness, whatever her real psychic powers, few can nowadays accept. The pity is that among these dubious marvels were the so-called Mahatma letters, all of them – and this is not to question the value of much that they contain – allegedly composed and dispatched by senior representatives of that esoteric task-force whose job it is to keep the tradition extant.

It would, however, be rash to dismiss the idea of such a task-force simply because of the antics the Theosophical Society's Masters got up to – or, rather, did *not* get up to, since if we accept what critics have said about them, Koot Hoomi & Co. had no part in the stunts Mme Blavatsky and her confederates are so often accused of engineering on their behalf. The Masters, an unfortunate term (what are the female kind called?) suggestive of Aryan bully boys puffed up with self-importance, were in any case not the invention of Mme Blavatsky – for even as she and others were busy setting up the Theosophical Society, her friend and rival, the British-born trance medium Mrs Emma Hardinge Britten, was completing her book *Art Magic*. This book was dictated to her, she claimed, by a European adept called the Chevalier Louis or, sometimes, the Chevalier Louis

Constant, a name that points to Eliphas Lévi (Alphonse-Louis Constant) who died in 1875, the year in which the Theosophical Society was set up. (Mrs Hardinge Britten was also a robust author in her own right and a close friend of Mrs Leah Fish, later Underhill, eldest of the Fox sisters, first of the modern spirit rappers.) Within months, Mme Blavatsky, never one to be outdone, let alone out-mastered, had discovered a whole college of adepts, the Brotherhood of Luxor, its members bearing names like Tuitit Bey, Serapis Bey, Polydorus Isurenius and the more prosaically Anglo-Saxon Robert More. It is probably fair to say that both ladies were much indebted to Bulwer-Lytton,[22] who had hinted at a mysterious band of adepts in several of his immensely successful novels, a notion that recurs in another nineteenth-century work, *The Royal Masonic Cyclopaedia* (1870), by Kenneth R. H. Mackenzie. Adepts, both incarnate and discarnate, also formed part of the *credo* of the Hermetic Order of the Golden Dawn, whose leader S. L. Mathers boasted of having met three 'Secret Chiefs' one night in the Bois de Boulogne.[23] We have seen, too, that belief in the existence of an occult fraternity whose members work in secret for the health and spiritual welfare of humanity is fundamental to Rosicrucianism. Similar beliefs are widespread also in the East where universal acceptance of reincarnation and the spiritual progress it sponsors makes it easy to admit the likelihood of highly developed beings, absolved of the need to reincarnate, who nevertheless choose to return to Earth to help more tardy pilgrims like ourselves. Often such people, known in some Buddhist communities as arhats or, at the very highest level, Boddhisattvas were credited with paranormal powers, known as siddhis, and it was these that Mme Blavatsky, keen to make her Masters more believable, tried so hard to copy.

It is one thing to suppose that esoteric tradition is watched over by exalted beings resident in this world or, as may also be the case, in a province of Elysium close at hand, quite another to accept the reports of those who have had contact with them, no matter how consistent and even banal such reports tend to be: Mme Blavatsky met her Master in Ramsgate, though she later tried to dignify the occasion by transporting the scene to London's Hyde Park; Alice Bailey, founder of the Arcane School, met hers when he turned up uninvited at her grandparents' home one Sunday morning and instructed her to mend her adolescent ways; Rudolf Steiner — he was just turned twenty at the time — met his when a student at the Technische Hochschule in Vienna, while a similar experience befell Max Heindel, founder of an American Rosicrucian fellowship, in 1919 during a visit to Germany.

Despite the ordinariness of such encounters, however, there still remains a credibility gap too wide for most of us to jump. For me it was narrowed, though then but slightly, because Mr James talked about such matters while we dug ditches together, repaired fences, tidied quickthorn hedges and, yes, treated sheep for foot-rot. Paradoxically, the down-to-earth setting rendered what he had to say far more easy to believe. At any rate, as I sat with him that Saturday night in Tanrallt, my mind filled with Druids and their magic, I was willing to keep an open mind about the Masters, though not expecting (or particularly wanting) to meet one face to face.

There we were, then, the two of us seated in that dark, mellow room, the fire lighting up a small patch of hearth and no sound except for an occasional splutter in the grate or a whimper, half-groan and half-hiccup, as one of the dogs dreamt he had caught the phantom rabbit he was chasing. Outside, beyond our sheltered little world, the night lay morose and heavy on Plynlimon, its palpable darkness unrelieved by the cloud-covered moon and stars. As I thought of the mysterious, unfriendly hills pressing up against the house, I felt more glad than ever to be safe and snug indoors.

It was the dogs that first noticed something was wrong. The one at my feet suddenly dived underneath the settle while the second jumped down from my side and slunk into some obscure corner of the room. My mouth was already open to comment on their odd behaviour when there came a loud knock on the door, at which the behaviour of the dogs struck me as still odder, for they normally barked their heads off if anyone came within two hundred yards of the farm.

Now, a knock on the door of an apartment or a terraced house or any house within sight of another does not usually cause the occupants too much alarm, even if the knock comes late at night: the proximity of other houses, as well as the people inside them, provides some reassurance that, should it be needed, help will be at hand. But when in the dead of night a knock comes on the door of an isolated farmhouse, with no other habitation for miles around, then the effect, I discovered, was far more disturbing. But Mr James was unperturbed. 'Come in,' he shouted as if expecting chance callers to arrive at Tanrallt at any hour of the day or night. The next thing I heard was the click of the latch, followed by the sound of someone closing the heavy oak door behind him. Whoever it was seemed completely familiar with the lay-out of the room since he avoided the table with the missionary box, skirted the larger table in the centre of the floor and, to confirm just how at home he was, drew up a chair and sat between us in front of the fire.

'We were talking about vervain,' said Mr James without preamble, as if our visitor had rejoined us after a brief absence and needed to be reminded of the conversation. As he spoke, he got up and lit the lamp on the table behind us, its dim light enabling me to study our visitor's profile for the first time. No feature of it struck me as particularly remarkable or offered any clue to his identity. 'I was telling this young man what a wonderful plant it is. I'd show him some but there's none left in the house. One of these days I'll go to Domen Bedwyr and get more. There's always plenty on that dry patch of ground that's up there.'

I knew that Domen Bedwyr was a prehistoric site, said to be an ancient burial ground, situated high above the main road to Llangurig. Reputed to be haunted, as were others in the neighbourhood like the churchyard at Ysbyty Cynfin or the Bronze Age circle at Bryn Bras, it was generally avoided by local people, though more on account of its remoteness than any supernatural associations.

'Have you ever been to Domen Bedwyr?' asked the man without turning his head.

I guessed he was talking to me. 'Not yet,' I replied, adding, in case my questioner thought me a coward, put off by old wives' tales, 'but I hope to go there soon.'

'So you shall, very soon.'

With these words the stranger turned towards me and I saw his face more clearly. Looking at his eyes, I observed for the first time something that was not quite commonplace about him. Their colour, I noticed, was blue, which sounds commonplace enough, but in addition to being conventionally blue, they managed to convey what I can only describe as the very *idea* of blueness. Looking at them, I found myself gazing not at so many centimetres of tinted iris but at blueness itself, at a condition in which time and space no longer held any meaning. In retrospect, it all seems a bit silly – an effect, perhaps, of the warm, sweetly scented air of the room – but at the time it was as much as I could do to stop my mind getting lost in that marvellous blue expanse, and only the sound of Mr James's voice put these fanciful notions to flight.

'First things first,' he said in a matter-of-fact way, 'and for this lad that means bed.' My heart sank. Bed was the last thing I wanted. Yet I heard myself bidding good-night to Mr James and his anonymous companion while my legs carried me, seemingly of their own volition, up the narrow stairs to the small back room in which I was to sleep.

No sooner had I started to undress than the moon emerged belatedly from behind the clouds, its bleached light washing out the colours from the patchwork quilt across the bed. Next to this stood a bamboo table bearing a stub of candle and a box of matches, nothing more, but I found I could see well enough without having to light the candle.

Elated though I was by my experiences that evening, my physical tiredness must have got the better of me as soon as my head touched the pillow. Within minutes I had fallen asleep, though whether this was a natural sleep I cannot tell, since the next thing I remember is standing near the dormer window, staring at the bed in which, to my consternation, someone who looked like my double appeared to be lying. The wish to assure myself that this was not some trick of the moonlight, evidence of a healthy scepticism, resulted in my being propelled to the side of the bed— where one swift glance was enough to convince me that what I saw there was indeed the physical me (the shock of seeing my own unmirrored image is still fresh in my memory). While my body slumbered on, my conscious- ness was somehow free to roam about the room as it pleased. Slowly, the initial feeling of panic began to recede, to be replaced by one of excitement, though not for a moment, strangely enough, did I fret about the risk of not being able to find my way back into my physical body; perhaps all that Mr James had told me about astral travel, dimly understood at the time, now came back and bore fruit. All I can say is that I gradually began to enjoy myself and even to feel a faint pride in my novel situation, though, strictly speaking, it owed nothing to my efforts.

How long I stood or, rather, hovered at the side of the bed I am unable to say: though disembodied in as much as I seemed to have left the physical part of me behind, it was consoling to see that I still inhabited a body of sorts, not a very solid one, admittedly, but one with its own distinct, if strangely pellucid, appearance, which fitted me no less comfortably than the one I had seemingly vacated. Amidst these reflections I suddenly thought of Domen Bedwyr, possibly because that had been the last thing on my mind before dropping off to sleep. Again, the mere thought was instantly translated into action: gone were the walls of the room and there I was out in the open air, standing in front of a grassy hump which I guessed must be the tumulus to which the name Domen Bedwyr had been given. Around me the moon shed a pale, candid light over everything but mingled with it was another, more phosphorescent, light which seemed to emanate from the ground itself, the two drenching the scene in a limpid, hueless luminosity which gave it the insubstantial appearance of a dream landscape. Apart from that, however, everything seemed completely real; the grass, the mound in front of me, the moon, all looked the same as might be expected. Only the achromatic, lack-lustre light made a difference and for that my own out-of-the-body state might well have been to blame.

A brusque movement startled me. Standing beside me was a man whose profile, though not unfamiliar, I could not identify at once. Before long he turned towards me, at which I recognised the face of Mr James's caller.

'You know where you are?' he asked. I believe I said yes. I know I meant to. 'I told you that you'd come here soon. Not that there's much to be seen, I'm afraid.' The implied apology was unnecessary since to me the mere fact of being there at all — never mind about the scenery — lay as far beyond belief as it must now do for many who are reading this account of it. I might even have said so, had my companion not resumed speaking; from then on I simply listened.

I listened as he explained in a language as simple as it was beautiful (even our minister in chapel did not speak such mellifluous Welsh) where the occult path I had set out on is intended to lead us. It is a path, he told me, that to begin with conducts us into our innermost being, enabling us to rediscover the true self that lives deep inside us, a self whose awareness of things is not limited to the world with which our senses have hitherto made us content. Through it we are able to perceive a wider, more beautiful reality whose own selfhood, while not the same as ours, is no different from it in essence. Thanks to this we and everything outside us, the totality of manifested being, are brought into conscious and loving union with the causeless cause of that phenomenal existence which is but the creative and personal manifestation of the one, unmanifest, uncaused and self-existent God — the algebraic x, writ large!

In practical terms, then, the occult path, its borders lined with more wonders than we can possibly conceive of, is one of self-fulfilment, and thus differs from that of mysticism which may be said, at the risk of over-simplification, to pursue the same goal by way of self-denial. It is self-fulfilling because the consciousness we have of our individual 'I' (atman) *in* and *of* the world expands at the end of it to become all-embracing (Atman) and, since our 'I' is thereby enhanced, not extinguished, it represents for us the apotheosis of our own unique selfhood. From then on, as Plutarch once put it, each of us 'has no meaning in time, only in the eternal, immovable and timeless. There is nothing before, nor after, neither future nor past, neither older nor younger. Each of us, being filled with the "Now", will himself have filled up the "Ever".'[24] This elevated state, attained by dint of our efforts, cannot but hasten the day when the karmic debt requiring us to incarnate again and again is finally redeemed. In due course will follow the consummation of the entire world 'when every blade of grass is enlightened' and we, with our human stage behind us, will be

free to continue our progress, watching new worlds come and go, until at
last.the youngest of these transcends its becoming and, in company with
us, reconciles its new-found being with the non-being that is God. *Factum
est*. The Great Work is completed.

I have to confess that all this was easier to understand when told to me
in Welsh! Or perhaps the fresh air helped. Yet even then there was a limit
to the amount of theology a fourteen-year-old boy felt able to take. Somehow, I must have betrayed signs of boredom, possibly incomprehension,
for the man next to me began suddenly to smile. Embarrassed, I looked at
the ground and immediately saw there a plant which I guessed must be the
precious vervain Mr James had spoken of. Once again, a mere thought, in
this case of Tanrallt, provoked action and, before I knew what was happening, I was back inside the tiny attic bedroom. The dormer window, the
rose-bedecked wallpaper, the bamboo table and the unlit candle, I had just
enough time to take them all in before being reunited with my body, there
to resume the sleep I had briefly started, a sleep the non-thinking part of
me had presumably never abandoned.

Next morning I woke up, refreshed and happy, with the sun streaming
in through the window, eager to banish any moon-struck fancies that
might have disturbed my night's slumber. The thought that I really had
been to the top of Domen Bedwyr and really had listened there to someone
discoursing on the meaning and purpose of occultism was one I felt reluctant to dwell on. Frankly, I was less than overjoyed to be placed in the same
eccentric company as Mme Blavatsky, whose tales of meetings with the
Masters had always struck me as extravagantly far-fetched. I realised even
then how easy it would be to retell the story of my astral mountaineering
in the same facetious way people have described her first encounter with
the Master Morya on the seafront at Ramsgate, or, for that matter, Alice
Bailey's experience when Koot Hoomi, in well-tailored suit and incongru-
ous turban, called to upbraid her, a teenager like me, for her bad behaviour.
I was also uneasy because of the exaggerated statements made about the
Masters in the few occult books I had read, such as the claim by A. P.
Sinnett, recipient of many Mahatmic letters, that in addition to being
long-lived, clairvoyant and super-humanly kind, they have mental powers
amounting 'to a species of omniscience as regards mundane affairs'.[25]
(Such omniscience, whatever the species, must have stood Koot Hoomi
in good stead if, as Theosophists claim, he studied at the University of
Leipzig in the 1870s.)

The roll-call of Masters made public by those pretending to have glimpsed
it cannot but have strengthened my unease, for there alongside Buddha,

Jesus, Lâo-Tsze and Confucius were Abraham, Moses, Jakob Boehme, Cagliostro, the Comte de Saint-Germain and Mesmer – a mixed assembly to say the least.[26] Equally off-putting were statements made by, among others, Mrs Besant who, despite a steadfast commitment to their cause, received little real help from her Theosophical Masters and, as we have seen, was badly let down when Krishnamurti renounced the messianic mission which she and, so she was given to understand, they themselves had planned for him. Among other things, Mrs Besant was to claim that these saintly persons only get in touch with mortals 'who by the practice of virtue, by unselfish labour for human good, by intellectual effort turned to the service of man, by sincere devotion, piety and purity, draw ahead of the mass of their fellows, and render themselves capable of receiving spiritual assistanceship.'[27] Fortunately, it is plain that the Masters are less fastidious than Mrs Besant and her friends like to think, as we saw earlier when we glanced at the history of occult tradition: more completely human than we are, they seem quite prepared to take us as they find us, warts and all.

And it makes sense for us to treat them in the same way. Speculation about their paranormal abilities, their longevity, their compassion and their wisdom serves only to make them incredible or, at best, intimidating and completely out of reach. They may indeed be capable of performing miracles but, if so, I suspect that for most of the time they refrain from bothering. Most sensible of all, perhaps, is to suspend belief in their existence until one of them deigns to make himself known to us: if they are as enlightened as they are said to be, they will not be offended by our scepticism. I wager, too, that if one of their number should land on your doorstep, the chances are that he – or she – would be just as ordinary and unassuming as anyone else, which is why someone who is attracted to occultism would do well to shun the more flamboyant mystery-mongers who peddle their wares, often at high prices, on the occult marketplace. If you feel inclined to study esoteric doctrine, therefore, do so quietly at home, reflect on what you learn and strive to live it every day (for occultism is above all a way of life, not a means of escape from it). Even if Koot Hoomi, turbaned or not, never walks into your living-room and no blue-eyed Welshman ever transports you at night to the top of Plynlimon, this does not mean that they or others are not close at hand. Be patient and wait.

True enough, the waiting can sometimes be lonely, for the occult path is never crowded. Yet the few who walk it, did they but know, are never completely alone. In a way, they have much in common with those tiny creatures – I forget their name – that live in the sludge at the bottom of ponds. At some stage in their development these creatures are impelled to swim upwards through the muddy water until they reach the surface where, confronted by a new and glorious world of light, they turn into winged insects and fly towards the sun. Like these, every esoteric student struggles to ascend into a world the majority of his fellow pond-dwellers know nothing about, his confidence unshaken as others, blinded by the murkiness around them, mock both his efforts and the dream that sustains them. Years ago a simple Welsh farmer pointed up at the light, and another, wiser than he, helped me find my way to it.

Two months before I left home for college, Mr James died. Almost ten years were to pass before I returned one gloomy winter's afternoon to Tanrallt, the sky grey like pewter and the sombre hills as inhospitable as ever. At the entrance to the lane stood a new iron gate, unmarked and alien, while reeds and rushes, left to grow unchecked, now covered the tracks down which I had cycled so often. No excited barking greeted my approach and no sign of life could be seen as I walked to the front of the house. Its walls, I was pleased to see, were still standing (Mr James always maintained they were built to last) but, sadly, the windows were out and the roof, already sagging when I last saw it, had finally collapsed.

Exposed now to wind and rain was the small bedroom in which I had woken up after my out-of-the-body excursion to Domen Bedwyr. As I stood looking up at it, I remembered lying in bed that summer morning, forced to acknowledge that what had happened to me was not an unusually vivid dream – even the sane and sober light of day failed to persuade me of that – though I persisted in thinking, because I wanted to, that the experience might still have been a subjective, if not psychopathic, one. For a good fifteen minutes I had kept telling myself that adventures of this kind, even if true, would never have happened so close to home: in India or Nepal, perhaps, but not, certainly not, in Aberystwyth. By the time I had pushed back the bedclothes, my inclination had been to blame the whole episode on the cheese and pickle Mr James had given me for supper. But something had put paid to all that.

For as the early sunshine poured into the room, falling full on the bamboo table next to the bed, it had passed over the box of matches and the stub of candle in its china saucer, only to linger on the table top. And there, in bright sunlight, not in fickle moonlight, lay a bunch of vervain, its greyish-green leaves still wet with dew, its purple-lidded flowers only just half-open.

Lest any reader suppose that in these closing pages I have allowed myself to be carried away by the blurred recollection of what may have been a mere quirk of adolescent perception, let me assure him or her that many other experiences, just as unsettling, have since intruded on that part of my life seeking to cope with the common-sense world all around us. These, it was, more than my friendship with Mr James and everything he taught me, that were to sustain my interest in occultism over subsequent years. But such experiences do not belong to the present book. In it I have tried, instead, to describe the findings of other individuals whose curiosity about the universe led them also to tread the occult path – occult because the landscape to which it gives access lies concealed behind the appearances that everyday things disclose to our senses. Many of these findings are strange, unexpected, and, judged by what the appearances alone would seem to suggest, highly improbable. Others, even if equally strange and unexpected, are less improbable, now that science has begun at last to look behind appearances and take into account the realities they represent.

To speak in this context of 'findings' is appropriate since the occult path is one we have no choice but to walk along ourselves, if we wish to get to know the things waiting to be found there. Admittedly, occult 'teachings' exist as well – I have described several in this book – but these, while helpful, are not necessarily true to the findings on which they are based: personal bias, faulty interpretation and, as we have noted, difficulties of language may often combine to slant the picture we are offered. Neither can such teachings ever replace real experience, any more than one man's account of his climb to the top of Mont Blanc can satisfy another whose ambition it is to plant his own two feet on the summit. In short, occultism intends to educate, not just to inform, and its path, like every other, is meant to lead somewhere. In this case it leads to the discovery within us of that unique and indestructible selfhood which animates, yet transcends, the personality we own in this life – and mistake all too often for our true, eternal self.

Once we have discovered this, we are equipped to discover also the nature and purpose of the totality around us. With new eyes we can observe for the first time the many cycles by which all that exists moves slowly closer to the source of its existence. As human beings, children of the current manvantara, we are then free to collaborate in the universal process and, as far as we can, help the whole world ascend towards a final state of being where Thought and Thinker resolve into one. This ascent will take place, whether we are aware of it or not. For those among us who prefer to know where they are heading, occultism lights the way.

Notes

I *Universe, Matter and Mind*

1 See, for example, Lucretius, *De rerum natura*, ii, 216–93.
2 Sir James Jeans, *The Mysterious Universe*, Cambridge University Press, 1937, p. 122.
3 Another way of putting it, equally mysterious, is that 'the number Ni of planets with intelligent life in the Galaxy equals the rate Rs of new-star formation (about twenty per year) times the probability Pp that the new star has planets, times the probability Pb that one of the planets has the proper conditions for life to originate there, times the probability Pi that life evolved to an intelligent species, times the average life span Li of an intelligent society.'! Thornton Page, 'ETI please phone', *New Scientist*, 29 November 1984.
4 See G. Cairns-Smith, *Genetic Takeover*, Cambridge University Press, 1982.

II *The Genesis of Humankind*

1 David Pilbeam, 'The Descent of Hominoids and Hominids' in *Scientific American*, vol. 250, no. 3, March 1984. The author uses the word 'hominoid' to describe the anthropoid apes, as well as those later primate forms which palaeontologists sometimes call 'pre-hominid'. In the present volume, 'hominid' and its adjectival form 'hominoid' have generally been used to mean all human-like creatures including some ('pre-hominids') whose anatomical characteristics are often more ape-like than human.
2 Teilhard de Chardin, *The Phenomenon of Man*, Harper & Row, New York, 1961, p. 152.
3 Erich Fromm, *The Art of Loving*, Harper Bros, New York, 1956, p. 8.
4 J. B. S. Haldane, *The Inequality of Man*, Chatto & Windus, London, 1932, p. 57.
5 H. P. Blavatsky, *The Secret Doctrine*, Theosophical Publishing House, Adyar (India), 1962, vol. III, p. 270.
6 See H. P. Blavatsky, op. cit., vol. III, p. 78. This figure, sometimes known as a solar kalpa or Saurya Manvantara, as well as those that follow it, is derived from the *Puranas* and the *Mahabharata*. Non-numerate readers

may be relieved to learn that in addition to the time-scales given, the Hindu calendar divides time into more manageable segments called maha-yugas, each consisting of 12,000 divine years or, since one divine year equals 360 of our own, 4,320,000 human years. (A thousand such maha-yugas make up a planetary manvantara – the lifetime of a 'globe' – or Day of Brahma, while 72,000 of them carry us back to the solar kalpa, the lifetime of our universe, with which our chronological speculations began!) Every maha-yuga contains four yugas or ages which vary in length (see p. 192, n. 34). Numbers apart, the cosmological theories of modern science tend increasingly to conform with those of occultism. (See, for instance, F. Capra, *The Tao of Physics: an exploration of the relationship between modern physics and eastern mysticism*, Fontana, London, 1976, and M. Talbot, *Mysticism and the New Physics*, Routledge & Kegan Paul, London, 1981.)

7 Only seven of the ten kingdoms are subject to this great cycle and these are enumerated thus: (1) first elemental, (2) second elemental, (3) third elemental, (4) mineral, (5) plant, (6) animal, (7) human. In the Round that inaugurates a new planetary chain, it is the first elemental kingdom that first enters the first in the series of globes. After finishing its evolution there, it moves on to globe 2, making way for the second elemental kingdom to replace it on globe 1. In due course the first and second kingdoms move on to globes 2 and 3, respectively, thereby giving the third elemental kingdom access to globe 1. From then on, the remaining kingdoms join the sequence in turn. From the fourth globe onwards, however, those kingdoms ahead of the rest start to slow down so that their more laggardly companions (and, above all, the seventh, human, kingdom) have time to catch up. This ensures that by the close of the first Round, all kingdoms enter the seventh globe *together*, thus allowing the seven to advance simultaneously through the successive globes of subsequent Rounds. The 'sacrifice' implicit in this slowing-down by the more primitive kingdoms is one of the noblest mysteries of occult science. A similar sacrifice is also made by a small part of the life-force in each kingdom whenever the rest of its kind moves forward from one globe to the next. In this case, the part left behind on the vacated globe provides a kind of 'vestment' to its fellows when they return to 'incarnate' on that globe on the following Round.

8 Hans Liebstoeckl, *The Secret Sciences*, Rider, London, 1939, p. 41. Apparently a loose translation of a section in Steiner's *Geheimwissenschaft im Umriss*, now available as *Occult Science: an Outline*, Rudolf Steiner Press, London, 1969.

9 Rudolf Steiner, *Occult Science: an Outline*, Rudolf Steiner Press, London, 1969, p. 142. Elsewhere, Steiner described 'old' Moon as 'a kind of pulp or purée like boiled lettuce or spinach'! (See *The Apocalypse of St John*, Rudolf Steiner Press, London, 1977, p. 98.)

10 See C. W. Leadbeater, *Textbook of Theosophy*, Theosophical Publishing House, Adyar (India), 1912.

11 Teilhard de Chardin, op. cit., p. 183.

12   See Stewart C. Easton, *Man and World in the Light of Anthroposophy*,
     The Anthroposophic Press, Spring Valley, New York, 1975, p. 29.
13   Desmond Morris, *The Naked Ape*, Jonathan Cape, London, 1967, p. 19.
     To be fair, the author does admit at the end of this stimulating book that
     'in my enthusiasm I may have overstated my case' (ibid., p. 240).
14   Desmond Morris, ibid., p. 24.
15   H. P. Blavatsky, op. cit., vol. III, p. 196. See also her *Isis Unveiled*,
     Theosophical University Press, Pasadena (U.S.A.), new ed. 1974, vol. I,
     p. 154.
16   A. B. Kuhn, *Theosophy: a Modern Revival of Ancient Wisdom*, Henry
     Hold, New York, 1930, p. 209.

III   *Lost Lands and Vanished Cultures*

 1   H. P. Blavatsky, *The Secret Doctrine*, Theosophical Publishing House,
     Adyar (India), 1962, vol. III, p. 274.
 2   Ibid., p. 324. Some lovers of lost continents postulate yet another missing
     land, now resting on the Pacific sea-bed, called Mu. Its most ardent
     champion was James Churchward, who claimed that during colonial
     service in India he was shown engraved tablets recounting the history of
     Mu and giving details of its eventual destruction. In the 1930s he wrote
     extensively on this topic, though earlier references to Mu are allegedly
     made in old Mayan texts, notably the so-called Troano Codex, as inter-
     preted by Father Brasseur de Bourbourg. The theme was treated by Dr
     Auguste le Plongeon in his *Queen Moo and the Egyptian Sphinx* (1896).
 3   Richard E. Leakey and R. Lewin, *Origins*, Macdonald & Jane's, London,
     1977, p. 8. See also the account of still older remains, this time from the
     Afar region of Ethiopia, in D. Johanson's *Lucy: the Beginnings of
     Humanity*, Granada, St Albans, 1981.
 4   Madame's speculations on these will be found in volumes I and II of
     The Secret Doctrine (Adyar edition). She stressed that these races occu-
     pied only quasi-physical bodies, referring somewhat unflatteringly to the
     early Lemurians as 'pudding bags'. The hermaphroditism which she
     attributes to these early races is consistent with ancient belief. The onset
     of sexual division is solemnly treated in the *Sushruta Samhita*, an Indian
     medical treatise of the fourth century BC.
 5   Thus in the *Aitreya Brahmana* we learn that Prajapati, 'Lord of Creation',
     formed the world from his sweat, while in Zoroastrianism it is the sweat of
     Ormudz (Ahura–Mazda) that engendered the first human beings.
     Mythology all over the world attributes the birth of many demigods and
     heroes to the same sudorific process.
 6   Genesis 6:4.
 7   See C. N. Dougherty, *Valley of Giants: the latest discoveries in paleonto-
     logy*, Cleburn (Texas), 1971. Also of interest is F. Wiedenreich's *Apes,
     Giants and Men*, Chicago, 1946, and, on the subject generally, R.
     Norvill's *Giants*, Aquarian Press, Wellingborough, 1979.

8 *Timaeus*, vi, 136. The main part of this dialogue – the Atlantis story is only a kind of introduction – is an exposition of Pythagorean cosmology, explaining how God created the universe out of two substances, the one spiritual, the other material, their different combinations giving rise to the world (and the world soul), the stars and the lesser gods, through whose efforts, based on geometrical formulae, all living things were formed. Also discussed is the origin of our sensations and the spiritual constitution of man. *Critias*, a later work, still unfinished at the time of Plato's death (347 BC), describes, among other things, the martial and colonial achievements of the Atlanteans.

9 For a comprehensive bibliography, see L. S. de Camp's *Lost Continents: the Atlantis Theme in History and Literature*, Dover, New York, 1970.

10 D. H. and M. P. Tarling, *Continental Drift*, Penguin, Harmondsworth, 1972, p. 42. To explain the gaps visible when present continents are reassembled to form the original Pangaea, a few scientists suggest that the Earth's surface 200 million years ago was up to 20 per cent smaller than today. (Not only do we live in an expanding universe, but on an expanding planet as well!)

11 Fred Hoyle, *Ten Faces of the Universe*, Heinemann, London, 1977, p. 137.

12 Space does not permit us to consider claims that land subsidence on this scale may have extra-terrestrial causes, as maintained by Velikovsky (*Worlds in Collision*, Gollancz, London, 1950) or, in the case of Atlantis, by Otto Muck (*The Secret of Atlantis*, Collins, London, 1978). While many scientists accept that a wayward asteroid may have struck the earth 65 million years ago (perhaps killing off the dinosaurs), few would concede that anything, save the odd meteorite, has collided with it since. Equally dubious are similar claims which, drawing on the eccentric speculations of Hans Hoerbiger, suggest that the flood which drowned Atlantis came about when the gravitational force of our Earth 'captured' the Moon 20,000 years ago, forcing it to become its satellite. See H. S. Bellamy, *The Myth of Atlantis*, Faber & Faber, London, 1948.

13 See *The Times*, 29 January 1971. More elusive were the 'proofs' of Atlantis promised by Paul Schliemann, grandson of Heinrich Schliemann, the discoverer of Troy. He never produced them!

14 This lecture, by the geologist Paul Termier, was later printed in the *Annual Report* (1915) of the Smithsonian Institution.

15 Nowhere is this described with more pathos than in Lewis Spence's *Problem of Atlantis*, New York University Books, new ed. 1968: 'More than one acute observer of animal life has made allusion to the strange and fatal habit of the lemmings of Norway. The lemming, a small rodent, occasionally receives a migratory instinct which sends it southward in great numbers. Most of these animals leave the Norwegian coast, and swim out far into the Atlantic. On reaching the spot to which the migratory instinct unerringly calls them, they circle around for some considerable time, as if in search of land, but failing in their quest, gradually sink into the depths. Similarly it is well known that large flocks of birds annually fly to a part of the Atlantic where no land is now visible,

and after fluttering around in dismay for some considerable time, fall exhausted into the water.'

16 Otto Muck, op. cit., pp. 88 *et seq.*

17 G. Clark and S. Piggott, *Prehistoric Societies*, Hutchinson, London, 1965, p. 97.

18 See Frank Waters, *Book of the Hopi*, Viking Press, New York, 1963 and Penguin, New York/London, 1977; J. F. Blumrich, *Kasskara und die Sieben Welten*, Econ Verlag, Vienna and Düsseldorf, 1979. For the Hopis, Lemuria is called Kasskara ('Land of the Sun') and Atlantis Talá-watíchqua ('Land in the East').

19 cf. 'the route of early migration may well have crossed territory submerged since the Ice Age by the rise in ocean-levels that followed the melting of the glaciers and in this way may have escaped detection.' G. Clark and S. Piggott, op. cit., p. 101. Quite!

20 Ibid., p. 330.

21 See I. Lissner, *The Silent Past*, Jonathan Cape, London, 1963. Whatever the truth of the occultists' account, the oldest human remains so far found in Nigeria (at Uturo in Ima county) date only from the early Stone Age, though in neighbouring Chad hominoid bones of far greater antiquity have been unearthed.

22 See 'In the Dark and in the Dumps', *The Times*, London, 28 January 1983. The Moon's influence on the rhythms of nature has been known since the earliest times but it has only recently been shown that lunar phases also determine the rate at which certain chemicals dissolve.

23 Statistical data have now been assembled to show how the disposition of the planets relates to human behaviour, a relationship postulated by Jung ('The Interpretation of Nature and the Psyche' in *Collected Works*, Routledge & Kegan Paul, London, 1971). Important research into the relationship between the planets and choice of profession has been undertaken recently by Françoise and Michel Gauquelin (see, in particular, his *Astrology and Science*, Peter Davies, London, 1969). The German astronomer Dr W. Hartmann has also argued persuasively (*Die Lösung des uralten Rätsels um Mensch und Stern*) in favour of a relationship between the planets and us, a theme dealt with by Prof. H. J. Eysenck and D. K. B. Nias in their book *Astrology: science or superstition?* (Temple Smith, London, 1983, and Penguin, Harmondsworth, 1984).

24 See G. Wachsmuth, *Werdegang der Menschheit*, Philosophisch-Anthroposophischer Verlag, Dornach (Switzerland), new ed., 1973.

25 For the record – and there is no need to treat this as fact – the seven Atlantean sub-races, with their special characteristics in brackets, were (1) Rmoahels [Lemurian throwbacks, well versed in magic]; (2) Tlavetli [ambitious, self-seeking and given to ancestor-worship]; (3) Toltecs [sociable and pious]; (4) Primary Turanians [lustful, obstinate – but logical thinkers!]; (5) Primary Semites [cautious, subservient to conscience]; (6) Akkadians [innovatory, clever and with a sense of fair play]; (7) Mongols [credulous, secretive, reputed to have secret powers]. Much of this kind of speculation, avidly seized upon by occultists, derives from

the writings of W. Scott-Elliot who, taking his cue from Mme Blavatsky, wrote such fantasies as *The Story of Atlantis and Lost Lemuria* and *The Lunar Pitris* (reissued by the Theosophical Publishing House, London, 1972). For occultists at the turn of the century, Atlantis was what flying saucers are for many of their counterparts today.

26 According to Puranic scripture, every kalpa or Day of Brahma is governed successively by fourteen manus, the reign of each of them being called a manvantara. In our present kalpa six manvantaras, the first of them ruled by Svayambhuva, have already elapsed. The current post-Atlantean manvantara is still ruled by Vaivasvata. For its own part, occultism teaches that a manu may incarnate several times during his reign: the heroic leader who guided the first Atlantean refugees to their central Asian homeland is, for instance, treated as the first incarnation of Vaivasvata. Occultism tends also to apply the term manu to any great leader, as, for example, in the case of Rama and Narada, the first of whom represents for pious Hindus (especially as Rama Chandra) an incarnation of Vishnu and, as such, should properly be called an avatara. The second is likewise not a man but a divine Rishi – there are seven in every manvantara – who is one of the acknowledged sons of Brahma. The elevation by the *Puranas* of these legendary heroes to semi-divine status testifies to the esteem in which they once were held.

27 For a scholarly account of ancient monuments and prehistoric astronomy, see Prof. Alexander Thom's *Megalithic Sites in Britain* and his *Megalithic Lunar Observatories* (both Oxford University Press, 1967 and 1971 respectively); D. Heggie, *Megalithic Science*, Thames & Hudson, London, 1981. More information, mixed with geomancy and UFOs, will be found in John Michell's *View Over Atlantis*, Sphere Books, London, 1975. Also worth reading is E. C. Krupp's *In Search of Lost Astronauts*, Chatto & Windus, London, 1979.

28 H. P. Blavatsky, op. cit. vol. III, p. 61. Basing herself on the *Puranas*, Mme Blavatsky claims that the first astronomer was Asuramaya. In Hinduism he is a contemporary of Narada, the Rishi with the honorific title 'Son of Brahma' who was held to have acted as messenger of the gods. Credited also with the invention of the vina (originally meaning a harp, the word was later applied to a kind of lute), Narada is claimed by occultists to have inspired Euclid, the Greek mathematician (300 BC) – on this, see Dion Fortune's *Applied Magic*, Aquarian Press, London, 1962, pp. 85–6.

29 E. G. E. L. Bulwer-Lytton (1803–73), the author of popular works like *Pelham, The Caxtons* and *The Last Days of Pompeii*, also wrote imaginative fantasies like the Rosicrucian-inspired *Zanoni, A Strange Story* and *The Haunted and the Haunters*. He was a keen student of magic and acquainted with the French magus, Eliphas Lévi, whom he entertained in London. With Lévi's assistance, Lytton is believed to have set up his own esoteric order which, according to the credulous Montague Summers (*History of Witchcraft and Demonology*, Routledge & Kegan Paul, London, 1963) still flourished in Cambridge after the Second World War.

30 See T. C. Lethbridge, *Gogmagog: the Buried Gods*, Routledge & Kegan Paul, London, 1957; Guy Underwood, *The Pattern of the Past*, Abacus, London, 1972, and J. Havelock Fidler, *Ley Lines*, Turnstile Press, Wellingborough, 1983. Archaeologists, when they deign to consider the theory at all, tend to treat it with lofty professional disdain. On this point, and for a sensible treatment of the subject generally, see *Ley Lines in Question* by Tom Williamson and Liz Bellamy (World's Work, London, 1984).

31 First reported in the *Journal* of the Société des Africanistes ('Un système soudanais de Sirius', XXI, Paris, 1951), the matter is dealt with at greater length in the book *The Sirius Mystery* by Robert Temple, Sidgwick & Jackson, London, 1976). Centuries later, post-Atlantean settlers along the Nile were to turn Sirius into the 'Star of Egypt', sacred to the mother-goddess Isis. It is not to be excluded that knowledge of Sirius B reached the Dogons from Egypt although this does not mean that Atlantean refugees may not have brought it to Egypt in the first place!

32 See E. von Dänicken, *According to the Evidence*, Souvenir Press, London, 1977, chapter III.

33 *Li-Yun*, XII, II, v. 13.

34 Kali-yuga is the fourth and, therefore, final yuga in the present maha-yuga (see page 187, n. 6), its predecessors being krita, treta, and dvapara. (In each group of four yugas, the sequence represents a progressive decline from an initial Golden Age.) Most authorities attribute 1,728,000 years to the first yuga (krita) and, in order 1,296,000/864,000/ 432,000 to the remaining three. The different numbers sometimes found is due to the expression of these same figures in terms of divine years ($\div 360$). Kali-yuga ended its first phase in 1897–8, an event said to coincide with a renewed interest in occultism throughout the Western world.

35 cf. Dion Fortune, op. cit., pp. 85–6. Modern scholarship tends to posit a later date for these Aryan incursions, seemingly basing itself on the tradition – nothing more – that the great war described in the *Mahabharata* took place around 1400 BC. The advanced civilisation of these proto-Dravidian tribes is evident from references in the *Rigveda* and the *Atharveda Samhita*.

36 Another theory claims that the alphabet derives from marks used by Mediterranean people to identify ownership, among them brand marks on animals. The runic script peculiar to northern Europe is unrelated to these developments and may have been a form of sacred 'writing' developed in the mystery centres of Atlantis. The carved inscriptions found on Easter Island and among Australian Aborigines are likewise unrelated, having been invented by the descendants of Lemurian survivors who never migrated to Atlantis. Some interesting reflections on the origins of language will be found in Alfred Kalir's *Sign and Design: the psychogenetic source of the alphabet*, James Clark, London, 1961.

IV   *Ancient Wisdom and the Esoteric Tradition*

1   H. P. Blavatsky, *Isis Unveiled*, Theosophical University Press, Pasadena, 1974, vol. II, p. 99.
2   See, for instance, Ian Suttie, *The Origins of Love and Hate*, Penguin, Harmondsworth, 1963.
3   See E. Schuré, *The Great Initiates*, Harper & Row, San Francisco, new facs. ed., 1974. In his book *Alchemy Rediscovered and Restored* (Rider, London, 1940) Archibald Cockren draws attention to a tradition that places Hermes in the Egypt of Sesoris II, a Pharaoh of the 12th Dynasty (*c.* 1900 BC).
4   Himself the divine Word or Logos, Hermes/Tehuti went about at the beginning of time giving names to all created things. On his role as both god and pre-Adamic man, see C. G. Jung, 'Psychology and Alchemy', in *Collected Works*, Routledge & Kegan Paul, London, 1971, vol. XII, pp. 349–50.
5   A recent biography is *Pythagoras: a life*, by Peter Gorman, Routledge & Kegan Paul, London, 1979.
6   These Archons were Ia, Astaphios, Adonai, Ailoaios, Horaios, Sabaoth and Ialdabaoth. Gnostic priests used to whisper their names into the ear of those who were dying so that they could be sure of remembering to address them correctly. Gnosticism enjoyed a revival in late nineteenth-century France when a certain Jules Doinel founded the Universal Gnostic Church.
7   See J. M. Rist, *Plotinus*, Cambridge University Press, 1967. For a modern translation of his work, see *The Enneads*, translated by Stephen Mackenna, Faber & Faber, London, 4th ed., 1969.
8   One of the most prolific translators of both Averroës and the great Aristotle himself was the occult philosopher Michael Scot (1175–1232) who, after completing his studies in Oxford and Paris, joined a group of scholars at the Court of Frederick II. There, in addition to his translations, he wrote several books dealing with the secret sciences (notably *Super Actorem sphaerae* and *de Sole et de Luna*), all of them popular in the fifteenth and sixteenth centuries. Known as the 'Wizard of the North', Scot inspired many legends, among them one that tells how he met his death. According to this, Scot had once predicted that he would be killed by a stone weighing not more than two ounces. In order to protect himself he always went about with a helmet on his head. One morning in church, just as the respectful magus raised his helmet at the elevation of the Host, down fell the fatal stone. Sir Walter Scott has more to say about him in a note to his *Lay of the Last Minstrel* where the opening of his tomb is described. Scot is also mentioned by Boccaccio and figures as one of the damned in Dante's *Inferno* (Canto XX, 115–17).
9   Available in English as *Hermetica*, ed. W. Scott, first published by the Clarendon Press, Oxford, in 1924 and now republished at Boulder, Colorado, by Hermes House, 1981. An interesting survey – and selection – of these writings can be found in *Pagan and Christian in an Age of Anxiety* by E. R. Dodds, Cambridge University Press, 1965. Meanwhile,

the collected letters of Marsilio Ficino are in the course of being published: *Letters of Marsilio Ficino*, Shepheard Walwyn, London, vol. 1, 1974; vol. 2, 1976; and vol. 3, 1981.

10 See J. Lindsay, *The Origins of Alchemy in Graeco-Roman Egypt*, Robert Muller, London, 1970.

11 For details of Dr Dee's life, see Richard Deacon, *John Dee, scientist, geographer, astrologer and secret agent to Elizabeth I*, Frederick Muller, London, 1968; P. J. French, *John Dee, The World of an Elizabethan Magus*, Routledge & Kegan Paul, London, 1972. An insight into the magical world of this period is given in Frances Yates's *Occult Philosophy in the Elizabethan Age*, Routledge & Kegan Paul, London, 1979.

12 Available in English as *The Most Holy Trinosophia*, Philosophical Research Society, Los Angeles, 1963.

13 Claims of this nature, many of them based on the memoirs, published in 1821, of Mme d'Adhémar, former lady-in-waiting to Marie-Antoinette, are critically examined in the chapter devoted to the count in Prof. E. M. Butler's *Myth of the Magus* (Macmillan, London, 1948). The occultists' response to the sceptics is to argue that there were *two* individuals who passed for the enigmatic count, the one a French officer and courtier, the other a high initiate, son of Franz-Leopold, Prince Racoczi of Transylvania. Saint-Germain became something of a hero for nineteenth-century occultists. Mme Blavatsky had a particularly soft spot for him.

14 On Fulcanelli himself and contemporary alchemical research, see: Fulcanelli, *Les Demeures philosophales*, 1971; J. Sadoul, *Alchemists and Gold*, 1972; Lapidus, *In Pursuit of Gold*, 1976; and K. R. Johnson, *The Fulcanelli Phenomenon*, 1981 (all published by Neville Spearman in Sussex or Jersey). More recently, Jung's preoccupation with alchemy as an indication of man's search for wholeness has attracted attention. His treatment of the subject, e.g. in the 'Psychology of Transmutation', 'Spiritual Symbolism' and the 'Mysterium Conjunctionis', offers stimulating reading: see *Collected Works*, Routledge & Kegan Paul, London, 1971, vols 12, 13, 14. On alchemy itself, see J. Lindsay, op. cit., and F. Sherwood Taylor, *The Alchemists: the Founding of Modern Chemistry*, Heinemann, London, 1952.

15 Eliphas Lévi, *Transcendental Magic*, translated by A. E. Waite, Rider, London, 1968, p. 19.

16 See B. J. T. Dobbs, *The Foundations of Newton's Alchemy*, Cambridge University Press, 1975.

17 His real name was Giuseppe Balsamo (1743–95) but he changed it to Count Alessandro di Cagliostro during his early travels to Greece and Egypt. In Rhodes, he is said to have studied occultism under a philosopher called Althotas. With his wife Lorenza Feliciani he journeyed through Europe and grew rich on the sale of love philtres, rejuvenating potions and alchemical compounds. But times were not always good: Cagliostro was imprisoned in London's Fleet prison, the Paris Bastille and, on a visit to Rome in 1789, was arrested and later sentenced to

death for heresy. The sentence was commuted to life imprisonment but, after enduring great hardship, he died in the fortress of San Leo at the age of fifty-two. In Warsaw and in Paris, Cagliostro had established Masonic lodges to which women were admitted. He was also famous for his prophetic gifts and implicated in the scandal of the Queen's Necklace, thereby earning himself a place in the novel of that name by Alexandre Dumas. At least one biographer sympathetic to him has denied that Cagliostro and Giuseppe Balsamo were the same person, claiming also that the 'mistrust that mystery and magic always inspire make Cagliostro an easy target for calumny ... For over 100 years his character has dangled on the gibbet of infamy ... remembered in history, not so much for anything he did, as for what was done to him.' (W. K. H. Trowbridge, *Cagliostro, the Splendour and Misery of a Master of Magic*, Chapman & Hall, London, 1910.)

18 Son of an actor, Giovanni Jacopo Casanova (1725–98) gave up his work as violinist at a theatre in Venice in order to travel around Europe. He became interested in occultism and was received into a Masonic order in Lyons in 1750, finally joining the Egyptian Order founded by his compatriot Cagliostro. In 1755 he returned to Venice, where he was sentenced by the Inquisition to five years' imprisonment. On 31 October 1756 he effected the dramatic escape he was later to describe in his famous *Histoire de ma fuite* (1786). He fled to Paris and lived well on his reputation for magic, even attempting to change the sex of one of his clients, Mme D'Urfé, by magical means. Afterwards he retired to Bohemia where he was appointed librarian and archivist. There he wrote his celebrated *Mémoires* which afford a fascinating glimpse of the *beau monde* that came to an end with the Revolution.

19 'Discours préliminaire' to the *Encyclopédie* by d'Alembert. In his article 'Encyclopédie' Diderot wrote that the mere transmission of knowledge was not enough, but 'il faut aussi changer la façon de penser.'

20 This is not to say that speculative masonry dates only from then. Its possible link with Rosicrucianism (see page 95) suggests that its heritage is far older. The Corpus Symbolicum of Masonry, based on the construction of King Solomon's temple in the 480th year after the Israelites' flight out of Egypt, contains much that is genuinely ancient. The central legend of the Craft which describes how Hiram Abiff, master architect and builder, was sent to Jerusalem by King Hiram of Tyre and there cruelly murdered is itself based on the rites of Osiris in ancient Egypt. There may even be a semantic connection between the name Hiram and the legendary Hermes.

21 Giambattista della Porta (1550–1615), who claimed to have started his magical apprenticeship at the age of fifteen. He was the author of a *Magica Naturalis* in no fewer than twenty volumes. The rest of those named will by now be old friends.

22 Among them, *The Restitution of the Hebrew Tongue* and *A Catechism of Kabbalistic Principles*. Much of his subject matter was obtained through the clairvoyant faculties of his wife. His two-volume *Histoire philoso-*

phique du genre humain, recently reissued (Editions Traditionnelles, Paris, 1974), is an interesting curiosity.

23 This (titled in French *Dogme et Rituel de la Haute Magie*) and his other important book, *The History of Magic*, are often republished in England by Rider. My own copies are dated 1968 and 1967 respectively.

24 There was nothing new about all this. Writing in AD 197, the Christian apologist Tertullian talks of assorted spiritualistic manifestations: '*phantasmata edunt defunctorum informant animas … Somnia emittunt mensae per daemones divinare consuerunt*' (*Apologeticus*, 13). Almost one hundred years before the Foxes (in 1762) the Cock Lane ghost had been the talk of London. Even Dr Johnson went to listen to its importunate rapping.

25 These rituals have become well known following their publication by Dr Israel Regardie and others. See I. Regardie, *The Golden Dawn: an encyclopedia of practical occultism*, Llewellyn Press, St Paul, Minnesota, 1970. Of interest still is Mathers' *Kabbalah Unveiled*, Routledge & Kegan Paul, London, new ed., 1981, based on Knorr von Rosenroth's compendium, *Kabbala Denudata* (1677).

26 *The Confessions of Aleister Crowley*, edited by John Symonds and Kenneth Grant, Jonathan Cape, London, 1969. John Symonds is also the author of both a biography of Crowley (*The Great Beast*, Rider, London, 1951) and a study of his magical system (*The Magic of Aleister Crowley*, Frederick Muller, London, 1958), both of which have been reissued in a combined paperback volume by Mayflower Books, St Albans (1973).

27 Dion Fortune, *Psychic Self-Defence: a study in occult pathology and criminality*, Aquarian Press, London, 1963. Other books include *Practical Occultism in Daily Life, Esoteric Orders and their Work, The Training and Work of an Initiate, Sane Occultism, Aspects of Occultism, The Cosmic Doctrine* and, most valuable perhaps, *The Mystical Qabalah*, Ernest Benn, London, new ed., 1979. New editions are regularly appearing, all (except the last) published by Aquarian Press, now at Wellingborough (and in the U.S.A. by Weiser of New York).

28 Howard Murphet, *When Daylight Comes*, Theosophical Publishing House, Wheaton, Illinois, 1975, p. 56. A more recent biography, thoroughly researched, elegantly written, critical but not too unkind, is by Marion Meade: *Mme Blavatsky, the Woman Behind the Myth*, Putnam, New York, 1980.

29 See Count Sergei Yulevich Witte, *The Memoirs of Count Witte*, Heinemann, London, 1921; reissued by Fertig, New York, 1967. By then Mme Blavatsky had only just turned forty, though Witte, a cousin of hers, was much younger.

30 It is said of Hodgson that 'from his own letters and those of others he emerges as a fairly obnoxious human being, extremely intelligent but also belligerent, insensitive and vituperative … in full cry he was as subtle as an air raid and twice as unpleasant.' This is not the judgment of an aggrieved Theosophist but of Professor Eysenck and Carl Sargent in their book *Explaining the Unexplained* (Weidenfeld & Nicolson, London, 1982,

p. 169). It should be noted that Hodgson claimed to have gone to Adyar to begin his investigation with a bias in favour of Mme Blavatsky and her Mahatmas.

31 'Report on Phenomena connected with Theosophy', *Proceedings of the Society for Psychical Research*, London, December 1885, III, p. 207.

32 V. S. Solovyoff, *A Modern Priestess of Isis*, Longman, Green & Co., London, 1895, p. 155. This outburst, made at Würzburg in 1885, allegedly continued, 'I should have achieved simply nothing, and would long ago have pegged out for hunger ... If only you knew how many lions and eagles in every quarter of the globe have turned into asses at my whistle, and obediently wagged their great ears in time, as I have piped the tune.' Against it must be set Madame's own protestations of innocence, as when she wrote to one of her favourite disciples, 'had I been guilty *only once* – of a deliberate, purposely concocted fraud, especially when those deceived were my best, my *truest* friends – no "love" for such a one as I! At best pity or eternal contempt. Pity, if proved that I was an irresponsible lunatic, a hallucinated *medium*, made to trick by my "guides" whom I was representing as *Mahatmas*: contempt – *if* a conscious fraud – but then where would be the *Masters*?' Letter to Patience Sinnett, quoted in *The Letters of H. P. Blavatsky to A. P. Sinnett*, Unwin, London, 1925, p. 103.

33 Largest of contemporary Theosophical groups is the Theosophical Society (Adyar), with almost 40,000 members. Next comes the Theosophical Society (Pasadena), born of a rivalry following Mme Blavatsky's death between Col. Olcott and Mrs Besant, on the one hand, and W. Q. Judge, the Society's leader in America, on the other. In 1895 the American branch seceded from the parent organisation. A third group, the United Lodge of Theosophists, has about 2,000 'associates' and is primarily dedicated to the study of Mme Blavatsky's writings. Other offshoots of the Theosophical movement, particularly in the U.S.A., have been the 'I am' group, the Church Universal and Triumphant of Elizabeth Clare Prophet, and countless Rosicrucian groups. Worthy also of mention is the Arcane School, founded by Alice M. Bailey (1880–1949), an ex-Theosophist who claimed that as a girl of fifteen she was visited by someone, wearing a European suit and silk turban, who she later discovered was the Master Koot Hoomi. Her copious writings are said to have been supervised (but not, alas, simplified) by a Mahatma whom she simply calls the Tibetan. Jung was to dismiss him as a product of Mrs Bailey's subconscious mind, though she retorted by asking 'how my personified higher self can send me parcels all the way from India, for that is what He has done'.

34 Presented in the East as the Lord Maitreya, a Bodhisattva (the name is that of the next Buddha due on Earth), and in the West as a second Christ, the lad was even provided, thanks to Leadbeater's clairvoyance, with a biography stretching back to 21,000 BC. In 1912 Krishnamurti's father tried to recover him from the Theosophists who had by now established an Order of the Star in his honour. In 1929 he disbanded the Order and

rejected the Messianic role foisted on him. Since then he has taught – in books and lectures – a way of individual development. Wisely, he claims to have no recollection of his adventures with the Theosophists.

35 For a recent life of Steiner in English, see Stewart C. Easton's *Rudolf Steiner: herald of a new epoch*, The Anthroposophic Press, Spring Valley, New York, 1980. Also worth reading is Steiner's unfinished autobiography *Mein Lebensgang*, newly translated by Rita Stebbing as *Rudolf Steiner, an Autobiography*, Rudolf Steiner Publications, Blauvelt, New York, 1977. For a recent, balanced biography, written by a non-Anthroposophist but available only in German, see G. Wehr's *Rudolf Steiner*, Aurum Verlag, Freiburg, 1982.

36 R. Steiner, *Anthroposophical Leading Thoughts*, Rudolf Steiner Press, London, 1973, p. 13. A comprehensive exposition of Anthroposophy, its theory and practice, will be found in Stewart C. Easton's *Man and World in the Light of Anthroposophy*.

37 These mysteries are not always identical to those, whatever their merit, taught by any and every organisation nowadays calling itself Rosicrucian. Most celebrated of these, perhaps, is the Ancient Mystical Order of the Rosy Cross (AMORC), founded in 1915 by Harvey Spencer Lewis, whose son Ralph was to succeed him as 'Imperator' in 1939. (A second American group, the Rosicrucian Fellowship, founded by one R. Swinburne Clymer, likewise claims to be the true repository of Rosicrucian secrets.) With headquarters in San Jose, California, AMORC offers courses in the 'Mastery of Life', with lessons supplemented by the founder's books on Atlantis, reincarnation and old Egypt. A European rival to AMORC is the Lectorium Rosicrucianum, founded in 1928 by a Dutchman known as Jan van Rijkenborgh. It is an offshoot of yet another Rosicrucian group established twenty years earlier in America by Max Heindel, a German-born occultist who is accused of having stolen lots of Rudolf Steiner's ideas during a year spent with him in Berlin. Immediate source of many teachings of these varied groups is Mme Blavatsky's *Secret Doctrine*, once described by Manly P. Hall as 'unquestionably the magnum opus of the literature of the modern world' (*The Phoenix*, Philosophical Research Society, Los Angeles, 1975, p. 124).

38 Much of the credit for the folk lore goes to Charles Leland who in 1899 had published details of an Italian tradition in a book called *Aradia or the Gospel of the Witches*. The anthropology was provided by Dr Margaret Murray: *The Witch Cult in Western Europe*, Clarendon Press, Oxford, 1921; *The God of the Witches*, Sampson Low, London, 1931; Faber & Faber, London, 1952. Both elements plus the sexual bonus were combined in the work of G. B. Gardner, notably in his *Modern Witchcraft*, Rider, London, 1954, and his more interesting *Witchcraft Today*, Rider, London, 1957.

39 K. Preisendanz, *Papyri Graecae Magicae*, Leipzig, 1928–31, vol. I, p. 91. Author's translation.

V   *The Attainment of Occult Knowledge*

1   'Presidential Address', *Proceedings of the Society for Psychical Research*, London, vol. 5, 1888, p. 271. The speaker, with proper caution, added, 'Observe that we did not affirm that these negative conclusions were scientifically erroneous. To have said that would have been to fall into the very error we were trying to avoid. We only said that they had been arrived at prematurely.'

2   According to the well-known psychical researcher Dr S. G. Soal (SPR *Journal*, XXXV, p. 257): 'There is no sense in talking about distance between two minds, and we must not consider brains as focal points in space at which Mind produces *physical* manifestations in its interaction with Matter.' Since his death, Soal's research methods have been called into question. (See 'The Soal-Goldney Experiments with Basil Shackleton: new evidence of data manipulation', *Proceedings of the Society for Psychical Research*, vol. 56, May 1978, pp. 250–77.) Telekinesis involves the movement of objects at a distance, without physical contact, an effect also known as psychokinesis or PK.

3   Similarly, the processes earlier described can also be re-stated in Indian terms, as, for instance, is commonly done in Theosophy, with the impact of sense impressions attributable to the vibrations of prana or vitality, and the feelings they produce, to kama or Desire. The 'soul' and sense-orientated activities of the astral body – here called the kama-rupa – are predominantly kama-manas by nature, rather than the higher form of manas or, nobler still, buddhi-manas. (Buddhi is the intuitive faculty by which wisdom – bodhi – is attained.)

4   Being, as opposed to becoming, lacks the three conditions which, according to Buddhism, characterise the phenomenal world: anicca (impermanence), dukkha (imperfection or suffering) and anatta (the non-absolute). All conditional existence (samsara) is in a state of becoming rather than being (nirvana) and consists of five skandhas or elements, though in some objects some of these may only be latent. Individually, the five, with their Pali spelling in brackets, are rupa: form; vedana: sensation; sanjna [sanna]: perception; samskara [sankhara]: mental impressions and tendencies; vijnana [vinnana]: consciousness and discernment. The doctrine of sakkayaditthi maintains that an individuality or ego [atta] is present in one or all of the five skandhas, being the first of ten fetters that bind us to the wheel of life. This 'false' ego, however, is impermanent since it exists in samsara and has therefore to be subject to the three conditions, one of them impermanence, that govern all manifested existence.

5   Revived at the beginning of this century by Nyanaponika, this, the seventh way on the eightfold path, encourages pupils to let their attention dwell on their physical, feeling, conscious and spiritual selves, all the time observing the experience from the outside. The Pali word Satipathana (Sanskrit: Smrityupasthana) means literally, 'The application of attention'.

6   Still one of the best sources of information on kundalini is *The Serpent*

Power by Arthur Avalon (Sir J. G. Woodroffe Wilson, 1865–1936), Ganesh & Co., Madras, 1918, containing a translation of the *Satchakra Nirupana*. Further details on exercises involving the chakras, especially under the appearance of lotus flowers, will be found in Rudolf Steiner's *Knowledge of Higher Worlds and its Attainment*, The Anthroposophic Press, Spring Valley, New York, reprinted 1977.

7   There exists a special relationship between the fiery kundalini and a minor eight-spoked chakra situated under the heart. This supernumerary chakra (there is also a ninth, known as soma, just above the eyebrows, as well as several others in the same region) is itself the emitter of a subtle type of radiation whose source is the etheric body. When meditating on kundalini, close attention is also paid to its mid-point, the fourth chakra (anahata), located at the heart, though beginners are nowadays urged to concentrate on its next-but-one neighbour, ajna. Mme Blavatsky, in her *Theosophical Glossary* (ed. G. R. S. Mead, Theosophical Publishing Co., London, 1982) prudently advises readers against experimenting heedlessly with these forces. She is, of course, right: playing with fire, be it in the grate or at the bottom of one's spine, can be dangerous and those who are careless risk ending up with burnt fingers, or worse . . . Direst warnings of what happens to those who court kundalini appear in many occult books: 'Such men become satyrs, masters of depravity', thunders A. E. Powell in *The Astral Body* (Theosophical Publishing House, London, 1926, p. 39). The *Hatha-Yoga-Pradipika* simply states: 'It gives liberation to yogis, bondage to fools.'

8   For the record, it should be added that according to *The Secret Doctrine* (vol. III, pp. 295–6), the earliest members of the third root race had a third eye at the back of their heads, enabling them to see behind as well as in front. They were also, *mirabile dictu*, not only hermaphroditic but also equipped with four arms! (To blame for much of the wilder speculation about human origins indulged in by Mme Blavatsky and others was a misapplication of popular Darwinism. This, rather than occult tradition, led them to give to human beings an evolutionary history more correctly attributable to the physical forms from which our species finally evolved.) Zoologists nowadays accept that a rudimentary third eye, still identifiable in certain reptiles, is the remnant of a pineal gland which slowly retreated into the cranial chamber of our mammalian ancestors.

9   The ten sefiroth and, in parentheses, the corresponding bodily parts are the following: Kether (head); Hokmah (left side of face); Binah (right side of face); Hesed (left arm); Geburah (right arm); Tifareth (heart and chest); Netsah (loins and hips); Hod (legs); Yesod (sex organs); Malkuth (feet). In meditation, special attention is paid to the royal sphere of Tifareth, ruled by the Sun, and located in the anahata chakra. The internal organs also have their sefirothic counterparts, not all of them corresponding with the list just given. In their case these are: Kether (brain); Hokmah (lungs); Binah (heart); Hesed (stomach); Geburah (liver); Tifareth (gall bladder); Netsah (spleen); Hod (kidneys); Yesod and Malkuth (respectively the male and female reproductive organs).

10   An idea of what such geometry involves, particularly in relation to etheric forces, can be gleaned from O. Whicher's *Projective Geometry*, Anthroposophic Press, London, 1972, and G. Adams's *Physical and Etheric Spaces*, Rudolf Steiner Press, London, 1965. Geometrical figures, said to derive from Pythagoras, also played a part in the mathematical speculation of the neo-Platonists and kabbalists. See also: Dr R. Allendy, *Le Symbolisme des Nombres*, Chacornac, Paris, 1932, and Papus, *La Science des Nombres*, same publisher, 1934. Meditative exercises in geometry are described in H. Keller von Asten's *Encounters with the Infinite: geometrical exercises through active contemplation*, Walter Keller Press, Dornach, 1971, while hints on how to think in four-dimensional terms – ending up with a 'hyper-reality' containing as many dimensions as the sum of the perceptions of those living in it – are given in Rudy Rucker's stimulating book, *The Fourth Dimension: Toward a Geometry of Higher Reality*, Hutchinson, London, 1985. Somewhat different was the attempt by Ramón Lull, the thirteenth-century Spanish visionary, to show in his *Ars Magna* that geometrical figures could be used as a means of discovering metaphysical truths. The young Leibniz (*Dissertio de arte combinatoria*, Leipzig, 1666) saw Lull's work as a kind of universal algebra that summed up all moral and spiritual truths.

11   See 'Other Dimensions of Space: Sci-fi or reality', *The Economist*, 2–8 July 1983, p. 85. For a more detailed account, see Paul Davies's *Superforce: the Search for a Grand Unified Theory*, Heinemann, London, 1985.

12   The terminology reminds us that emigrants from Takla Makan initially carried this knowledge to India (it would later reappear with special force in the *Avatamsaka Sutra* of Mahayana Buddhism). With subsequent migrations it arrived in Persia and there its influence is discernible in the tendency to contrast the time that is timeless (Zurvan Akarana) with space-bound time (Zurvan dareghochvadhata). So ancient is the conviction that time is an abstraction without meaning for the inner self that it has long been part of our folk consciousness, assuming narrative form in stories like that of Rip van Winkle and others who fall asleep or else wander into fairy lands where one day equals a year or more in the 'outside' world.

VI *A Many-sided Nature*

1   Several hundred of these near-death experiences have been assembled by Dr Raymond A. Moody, author of the book *Life after Life: the investigation of a phenomenon – the survival of bodily death* (Bantam Books, New York, 1975) and its sequel, *Reflections on Life after Life* (same publisher, 1978). Similar studies by Maurice Rawlings (*Beyond Death's Door*, Sheldon, London, 1979) and his fellow-cardiologist, Michael Sabom (*Recollections of Death*, Harper & Row, London, 1982) bear out Moody's findings, all of them consistent with esoteric tradition.

2   David Conway, *Magic: an Occult Primer*, Jonathan Cape, London, 1972, p. 224.

3   See Sir Oliver Lodge, *Raymond or Life After Death*, Methuen, London, 1916. The book, marking the conversion to Spiritualism of a world-famous scientist, caused a sensation, and brought comfort to thousands whose sons and husbands had died in the First World War. Critical reception of these revelations from 'Summerland' was unseasonably frosty: 'Raymond Lodge tells his father that the houses in the Beyond are made "from sort of emanations from the earth"; that his white robe is "made from decayed worsted on your side"; that he has his "little doggie" with him; that cigars made "out of essences and ethers and gases" are provided for smokers, and "whisky-sodas" for drinkers! Faugh!' (Edmund Clodd, *Strand Magazine*, July 1917, p. 54.) On the possible nature of such a post-mortem world, individually subjective but telepathically responsive to the ideas of others dwelling in it, see Professor H. H. Price's lecture, 'Survival and the Idea of Another World' in *Proceedings of the Society for Psychical Research*, vol. 50, 1953.

4   Dr Raymond A. Moody, *Reflections on Life after Life*, pp. 38–9.

5   H. P. Blavatsky, *The Secret Doctrine*, vol. II, p. 182. Plato and his successors had long taught that to discover the true nature of the elements, attention had to be paid to the incorporeal principles at work behind them – what the East calls their simultaneous manifestation on the loka (noumenal) and tala (phenomenal) planes. The *Bhagavad-Gita* (VII, 30, VIII, 4) talks of their simple or material aspect (adhibhuta) and their spiritual or subjective life (adhidaiva). Misunderstanding can best be avoided if one remembers that when occult tradition talks about 'elements' – Tanmatras in Sanskrit – it usually means the elementary potential, not its actual manifestation, a distinction Science is happy enough to recognise when dealing with force-fields. (In matters like these, physics and occultism are exploring the same hidden reality, part of what Paracelsus called the Mysterium Magnum or Great Mystery.) In Eastern tradition the four elements – tejas (fire), vayu (air), apas (water) and prithivi (earth) – fall under the government of the four Lokapalas (Guardians of the Earth): Agni, Pavana, Indra and Kshiti. In the kabbalistic system the same elements are ruled by the four Archangels: Michael (fire), Raphaël (air), Gabriel (water) and Uriel (earth). The same archangels, believed to be the protectors of humankind, also rule the four cardinal points (respectively, South, West, East and North), their oriental equivalents, the Chatur Maharajahs, being Virudhaka (S), Virupaksha (W), Dhritarasrtra (E) and Vaishvanara (N). The elemental hosts subordinate to these four were, respectively, the Kumbhardas, Yakshas, Gandharvas and Nagas. Meanwhile, according to the *Laws of Manu*, even the intermediate compass points have their Maharajic rulers: Agni (SE), Surya (SW), Pavana (NW) and Soma or Chandra (NE). After all this, it should be noted that occultism further teaches that the simple elements in fact number *seven*: the fifth is the quintessence (possibly, ether) supposed by Aristotle, the other two are as yet beyond human perception.

6   Rudolf Steiner went so far as to state that 'human existence should really

be a perpetual releasing of the elemental spirits enchanted in minerals, plants and animals.' (Second lecture in a cycle given in Vienna, September–October 1923, reproduced in *Anthroposophy and the Human Gemüt*, Anthroposophic Press, New York, 1946, p. 22.) The air elementals (sylphs) are held to look to angelic beings for the same favour, while those of fire – the aristocrats of the elemental world – rely on the goodwill of certain solar entities, the Agnishvatta Pitris, whose concern is with cosmic evolution and, microcosmically, with the development of human intelligence.

7   Entities of this kind are not to be confused with the homunculi which alchemists were said to manufacture and which provoked much discussion among theologians who could not decide whether such 'test-tube' people had an immortal soul or not. Quite a different character again was the golem which Jewish kabbalists were credited with making. Their usual method was to mould a human figure out of clay and place on it pieces of paper bearing holy names. The assembled company would then recite passages from the book of Genesis, interspersed with more names of power and magical gestures. After the chief kabbalist had breathed into its nostrils the clay figure was said to glow eerily, shudder and open its eyes. Such creatures were particularly common in sixteenth-century Prague where many kabbalists, among them the celebrated Rabbi Löw ben Bezaleel (1513–1609), used to work. One melancholic golem which lived in the attic of the Altneu Synagogue and did menial work was viewed and interrogated by Rudolf II, whose interest in alchemy has already been noted. The last recorded golem was in nineteenth-century Russia.

8   Alexandra David-Neel, *With Mystics and Magicians in Tibet*, Penguin, London, 1936, pp. 283–4, reissued by the same publisher, as *Magic and Mystery in Tibet*, 1971.

9   The great yogi, Shri Aurobindo (1872–1950), preached that in its manifestation (Ishvara), the Absolute evolves through all levels of being and returns, via, among others, the mineral, plant, animal and human kingdoms, to its spiritual source. Earlier, Mme Blavatsky had bluntly declared that no being can 'be born suddenly on the plane of life as a full-blown angel' but must first evolve through all the levels of existence. Being, she writes, 'is an endless cycle within the One Absolute Eternity, wherein move numberless inner cycles, finite and conditioned' (H. P. Blavatsky, op. cit., vol. I, p. 268). For occultists, the evolution of all earthly things has three aspects, often called *uphadis*. These relate to the progress through nature of (i) *the monad or spiritual element*; (ii) *the mind or intellect* which, in the human phase, will enable the monad to gain awareness of itself as an individual ego; and (iii) *the physical body* whose propitious development, notably the cerebral organisation, facilitates the first two in our present stage of evolution.

10 The story of Wenna's misfortune, reminiscent of many European folk-tales, suggests that these, too, might have a basis in fact. Their conventional fairy-tale imagery should not delude us into thinking that the experiences they describe were any less real to those who underwent

them, than Wenna's was to her. The same might be said of the numerous accounts, some well-attested, of people who disappear or appear from, so it would seem, 'nowhere'. The most well-known modern foundling is Kaspar Hauser, a sixteen-year-old boy who appeared in the streets of Nuremberg on 26 May 1828, and died of stab wounds in December 1833. Claims formerly made that he was the illegitimate son of Karl Ludwig Friedrich, Grand Duke of Baden (1786–1818) or even of Napoleon, the Grand Duke's father-in-law, are now discounted by scholars, though nobody is any closer – despite over 10,000 books, learned papers and articles – to showing where he came from. Rudolf Steiner and others read great occult significance in Kaspar Hauser's brief life.

11 A similar case, already noted above on p. 104, is that of Netta Fornario who, as Dion Fortune writes (*Psychic Self-Defence*, Aquarian Press, London, 1963, p. 100), 'was especially interested in the Green Ray elemental contacts; too much interested for my peace of mind'. Miss Fornario was found dead on Iona, having, the same author tells us, 'been on an astral journey from which she never returned'. Equally mysterious was the death in 1939 of Harry Dean on Bredon Hill, a prehistoric religious site in Gloucestershire. (See Colin Wilson, *Enigmas and Mysteries*, Aldus, London, 1976, chapter IV.)

12 See, in particular, the lectures collected in *Life between Death and Rebirth*, Anthroposophic Press, New York, 1968. It is no coincidence that Dr Raymond Moody's subjects have reported how, when clinically 'dead', they seemed to possess, as one of them put it, 'knowledge of all that had started from the very beginning, that would go on without end – that for a second I knew all the secrets of all ages, all the meaning of the universe, the stars, the moon – of everything' (op. cit., p. 10).

13 With typical vigour, Mme Blavatsky, herself no atheist, sums it up thus: 'For when one unacquainted with the noble doctrine looks around him and observes the inequalities of birth and future, of intellect and capacities; when one sees honour paid to fools and profligates, on whom fortune has heaped her favours by mere privilege and birth, and their nearest neighbour, with all his intellect and noble virtues – far more deserving in every way – perishing for want and for lack of sympathy, when one sees all this and has to turn away, helpless to relieve the undeserved suffering, one's ears ringing and heart aching with the cries of pain around him – that blessed knowledge of karma alone prevents him from cursing life and men, as well as their supposed Creator. Of all the terrible blasphemies . . . none is greater than that (almost always) false humility which makes the presumably "pious" Christian assent, in the face of every evil and undeserved blow, that "such is the will of God".' (Op. cit., vol. III, pp. 304–5.) Self-operating karma, as implied here, is closer to Jainism than orthodox Hinduism, which tends to see the hand of God behind its every operation.

14 Not all of those whose virtues exempt them from further incarnations linger in a state of perpetual bliss. Some, out of pity for their less perfect brothers and sisters, choose instead to return to Earth, where they guide, teach and inspire more laggardly pilgrims. These altruistic beings are

called Bodhisattvas, a name meaning 'vessels of wisdom' and borrowed from northern Buddhism where one of the most revered Bodhisattvas is Avalokiteshvara ('the visible Lord'), a term collectively applicable also to the spiritual order made up of Dhyani-Buddhas. Lord Avalokita, tutelar god of Nepal, is the patron saint of Tibet where he is known as Chenresi and popularly believed to incarnate in successive Dalai Lamas. The self-sacrifice of the Bodhisattvas is a reminder of the sacrifice, too often overlooked by us, which the rest of nature – stones, plants and animals – makes on our behalf when it delays its own evolution – as, for example, in the first Round of each planetary chain (see p. 187, n. 7) – in order to keep pace with our own. (Related, yet surpassing all this, is the self-sacrifice regularly made by those spiritual beings whose hierarchical position is several stages above that of the life-stream currently undergoing the 'human' condition. Here we draw close to one of the most sublime and secret teachings of occult philosophy.)

15 Hebrews 9:27. The first quotation comes from the Nicene Creed: '*et exspecto resurrectionem mortuorum et vitam venturi saeculi*'.

16 Reissued by Sphere, London, 1981.

17 Recorded in de Rochas's book *Les Vies successives*, these cases were critically assessed by Professor Gustave Geley in his book *Reincarnation*, London, 1924. For a more up-to-date review of such experiments recourse may be had to Ian Wilson's *Mind out of Time*, Gollancz, London, 1981. Mesmer (1734–1815), the father of modern hypnotism – he called it somnambulism – had already said that in hypnotic trance, 'Man by his inner sense, is in touch with the whole of nature and is always capable of feeling the concatenation of cause and effect. Everything in the universe is present; past and future are only different relations of the separate parts.' A related phenomenon is psychometry where the entranced sensitive can, by touching a particular object, 'relive' its history. An interesting account of research in this field, entitled 'Past Events' Seership' is given by Dr Walter Franklin Prince in the American Society for Psychical Research's *Proceedings*, vol. XVI, part 6.

18 One of these cases, known as *The Three Faces of Eve*, became the subject of a successful book by C. H. Thigpen and H. M. Cleckley (Secker & Warburg, London, 1957) and, later, an equally successful film. Another famous example, this time linked with reincarnation, was that known as the Bridey Murphy case. Bridget (Bridey) Kathleen Murphy, allegedly born in Cork in 1798, was the previous identity claimed by a subject hypnotised by a Colorado businessman, Morey Bernstein. His entranced subject, a lady named Virginia Tighe, gave an extremely detailed account of her past life in Cork and in Belfast, where her husband, Sean Joseph McCarthy, had lectured in law. In 1956 there appeared the best-selling book, *The Search for Bridey Murphy*, which was again turned into a film. A thorough analysis of the case by Professor C. J. Ducasse concludes that while the information given by the soi-disante Bridey was paranormally obtained, it fell short of being proof of reincarnation (see 'How the Case of the Search for Bridey Murphy Stands Today', American Society for Psychical

Research *Journal*, vol. IV, p. 22). For completeness, mention should be made of the claim (which first appeared in a Chicago newspaper) that Mrs Tighe, the latter-day Bridey, had merely served up unconscious memories of a real Bridey Murphy who had lived across the street from her in her childhood.

19 The story was told in Flournoy's book *Des Indes à la planète Mars, Etude sur un Cas de Somnambulisme*, Paris and Geneva, 1900, reissued in translation (New York University Press, 1963) as *From India to the Planet Mars: a study of a case of somnambulism with Glossolalia.*

20 See Ranhuat Banshi Dhar, 'Study of Spontaneous Cases', *Indian Journal of Parapsychology*, vol. I, pp. 76–80, June 1959.

21 Dr I. Stevenson, *Twenty Cases Suggestive of Reincarnation*, Virginia University Press, 1974.

22 Recently compiled, too, is a word-association test alleged to excite the subliminal memory of the 'I'. It is, its inventors claim, too soon to say if it works. The theory, a trifle optimistic, is that by presenting us with a key word from a language we may formerly have spoken, we shall remember the incarnation in which we once used it. The test is largely based on Indo-Germanic root words – this, you will recall, was the original language of Takla Makan – but includes later words derived from other language families, classified as, for instance, Hamitic, Finno-Ugric, Sino-Tibetan, but not forgetting other, more Westerly groups like Mayan and even Red Indian languages such as Algonquian and Siouxan. Not included in the test, I have noticed, is the Enochian tongue which the angels are said to have used when addressing Dr Dee and Edmund Kelley (see p. 92), though some occult philologists are currently studying this closely. The Enochian language, said Aleister Crowley, was 'very much more sonorous, stately and impressive than even Greek or Sanskrit . . . though in places difficult to understand'! (*The Confessions of Aleister Crowley*, edited by John Symonds and Kenneth Grant, Jonathan Cape, London, 1969.)

23 A scientist's approach to the development of the embryo, its subtle bodies and its 'I' will be found in Dr Frits Wilmar's book, *Vorgeburtliche Menschenwerdung*, Mellinger Verlag, Stuttgart, 1983.

VII *First Steps Along the Path*

1 By all accounts this trait he shared with Mme Blavatsky. Mabel Collins (1851–1927), a writer of fatuous occult romances, peeved at Madame's impatience with her mystical pretensions, is reported to have passed the following shrewish judgment on her former guru: '. . . she was a big woman; she had . . . a larger waist, a more voracious appetite, a more confirmed passion for tobacco . . . a greater disrespect for *les convenances*, a worse temper, a greater command of bad language, and a greater contempt for the intelligence of her fellow human beings than I had ever

supposed possible to be contained in one person' (quoted by J. N. Maskelyne in his *Fraud of Modern 'Theosophy' Exposed*, G. Routledge & Sons Ltd, London, 1913, pp. 62-3). One doctrinal difference between Blavatsky and Collins was the latter's contention that the Masters lived only in the human soul, being representative of our higher self. Earlier Miss Collins (who in happier days had briefly shared her Upper Norwood home with the irascible Mme Blavatsky) had claimed that her book *Light on the Path* was dictated by the Master Hilarion. It is certainly a remarkable and valuable work.

2   The first complete edition of Goethe's scientific works was edited by Rudolf Steiner who called him 'the Copernicus of the organic world'. Goethe's researches covered optics (where he elaborated his own theory of colour) and animal and plant morphology. He announced the existence of the intermaxillary bone in the jaw before it was discovered anatomically, while his speculation on plant forms led him to see clairvoyantly the prototype or *Urpflanze* from which all earthly plants have sprung. Discussing this with a sceptical, but not unsympathetic, Schiller, Goethe assured his friend that this archetypal plant form had a real, though non-physical, existence, and was not a mere product of the imagination. On this subject, see G. Adams and O. Whicher, *The Plant between Sun and Earth*, Rudolf Steiner Press, London, 1976. On the Goethean way of thinking referred to later in the text, see Ernst Lehrs' *Man or Matter*, Faber & Faber, London, 2nd ed., 1958.

3   Second lecture in a cycle given in Vienna in 1923 and reproduced in *Anthroposophy and the Human Gemüt*, Anthroposophic Press, New York, 1946, pp. 21-2.

4   In the past, speculation on micro-macrocosmic relationships has degenerated into assertions (even Paracelsus came close to making them) that human 'eyes were the equivalent of the two great lights in the sky, the Sun and Moon . . . bones of rocks, hair of vegetation, pulse of tides, flesh of soil and earth, warts and boils of mountains, and veins of rivers' (J. Grant, *A Dictionary of Discarded Ideas*, Corgi, London, 1983, p. 56). The same tendencies are discernible in the *Rig-Veda*, though their purpose there is to stress the essential unity of the self (atman) and the cosmos, as the visible manifestation of Brahman.

5   Generally speaking, occultists are careful not to lose sight of the external world, knowing that the life of the universe and that of the human spirit are so united that the investigation of either must perforce take in the other. One of the aims of esoteric training is to cultivate an awareness that embraces simultaneously the world outside us and the world within, a reconciliation of object and subject known in alchemy as the marriage of the Moon and Sun: it is the fruitful coition of our intellectual activity, by nature cold and lunar, and, its solar counterpart, our *feelings* towards the external world. It is also one of the secrets of true yoga (see p. 125). The danger now facing science, increasingly concerned with abstractions, hypotheses and mathematical formulae, is that by withdrawing completely into an intellectual and morally neutral 'interiority', it will become

as cold and unproductive as a moonlit landscape in mid-winter. Already, nuclear and chemical weaponry, widespread vivisection, genetic engineering and environmental pollution are morbid symptoms of the scientific age we live in. It is interesting to note that the discovery by modern physicists that they, as observers, *participate* in the micro-processes they observe, serves only to confirm that the involvement cultivated by occult scientists is more 'natural' than the detached, empirical approach currently favoured.

6 It would probably be rash to identify Mr James's 'non-matter' with the anti-matter of physics. Interestingly, some occultists suggest that the galaxies of anti-matter acknowledged by science belong to a parallel universe, in reality a complementary aspect of our own, currently in a state of contraction. Others declare them to be prior or later, though in reality contemporaneous, manifestations of the universe, each one representing a different act in the drama of cosmic evolution.

7   All nature is but art unknown to thee
       All chance, direction which thou canst not see;
       All discord, harmony not understood,
       All partial evil, universal good;
       And, spite of pride, in erring reason's spite,
       One truth is clear, Whatever is, is right.
              Alexander Pope, *An Essay on Man*

8 These words come from an essay entitled 'The Pattern and the Law', the writer's contribution to a celebratory volume entitled *H. P. Blavatsky and the Secret Doctrine*, ed. Virginia Hanson, Theosophical Publishing House, London, 1971, p. 28.

9 Cancer therapy owes much to Rudolf Steiner's 'Goethean' reflections on mistletoe, a semi-parasitic plant (traditionally a symbol of Air) whose growth pattern betrays its affinity with etheric forces. From it Anthroposophical doctors have produced Iscador, a medicament that lessens the impact of such forces and so thwarts the neo-plastic ambitions of cancer-prone cells. Iscador is now widely used in hospitals and clinics, though non-Anthroposophical doctors have presumably invented a more congenial, less 'occult', explanation to account for its success. It is also used in Anthroposophical clinics (such as the Lukas Clinic at Arlesheim in Switzerland) to *prevent* cancer, following a diagnostic test in which the patient's etheric pre-disposition to the disease is determined by studying crystallised blood samples. Mr James's cancer therapy also included mistletoe and a repertoire of other herbs, some (garlic, horse-radish, ivy, cleavers, etc.) aimed at treating the original site, others (periwinkle, rock rose, etc.) at preventing metastasis, and still others (parsley, red clover, etc.) at restoring the entire organism, but in particular the etheric body, to a state of alertness to future attack. A near meatless diet, beetroot juice, brewer's yeast and an increased intake of foods rich in potassium were also part of the supportive treatment, as was the practice of meditation and auto-suggestion.

10 Most celebrated defender of the doctrine was Giambattista della Porta (see

p. 195, n. 21), author of two influential books on herbs, the *Phytognomica* and *Villa*. It was he who extended the doctrine to the actual site in which wild plants commonly flourished. On this basis, the willow tree, which grows best in damp places, was assumed to be good for treating rheumatism, a condition aggravated (if not caused) by a damp atmosphere. Decoctions of willow bark were thus prescribed for the easing of rheumatic pain – and worked so well that curious scientists discovered in willow bark a high concentration of a glucoside to which they gave the name of salicin (Latin *salix* = willow): from this was derived salicylic acid (HO_6H_4COOH) which became the progenitor of aspirin (acetylsalicylic acid), still the most reliable analgesic for easing rheumatic pain. Coincidences of this kind are numerous.

11 *Journal of George Fox*, edited by N. Penney, Cambridge University Press, vol. I, 1911, chapter II.

12 The growth of the Druid myth is entertainingly recounted in A. L. Owen's book *The Famous Druids*, Oxford University Press, 1962.

13 In his essay *The Origin of Freemasonry* (1804) Tom Paine had argued that the Druids were the founding fathers of the Craft. A *völkisch* offshoot of Freemasonry, the Druidenorden, still flourishes in Germany. Among the the wilder speculations of enthusiasts like the Anglesey cleric the Rev. Henry Rowlands (*Mona Antiqua*, 1725), is that Noah's Ark came to rest on the summit of Snowdon, not on Mount Ararat, and that the Druids were descendants of Noah.

14 Principally these are the British Circle of the Universal Bond and, since 1963, its schismatic offshoot, the Order of Bards, Ovates and Druids. There are also continental groups, mainly in France and Germany.

15 Human sacrifice is likewise imputed to both. Roman commentators on the Druids, none of them totally impartial, professed to be shocked by such barbarism, the worst case of it being the mass incineration of criminals (and innocents as well, if numbers fell short) inside gigantic wickerwork figures. Too often was it forgotten that in Rome human sacrifice had been proscribed only in 98 BC and that public entertainment there was still every bit as cruel.

16 T. G. E. Powell, in his book *The Celts* (Thames & Hudson, London, 1958), also draws attention (p. 153) to the 'common heritage' shared by Celtic and Aryan/Indian mythology.

17 Of special interest here is K. H. Jackson's *Oldest Irish Traditions: a window on the Iron Age*, Cambridge University Press, 1964.

18 Mme Blavatsky's *Stanzas of Dzyan*, alleged to be the source book for her *Secret Doctrine*, was said to be derived from the oldest book in the world. Other occult writers had ascribed their works to, among others, Adam, Abel, Noah, Moses, Elijah and, of course, Hermes Trismegistus. Solomon's legendary wisdom made him a special favourite of magicians (and, later, Freemasons) with so many grimoires or magical textbooks attributed to him that Roger Bacon, the thirteenth-century friar and alchemist (see p. 91), felt driven to protest.

19 The seven are also related to the septenary composition of man. Earlier,

we saw that man functions through four vehicles, his physical, etheric and astral bodies, plus, of course, his all-important ego or 'I'. We saw, too, that a three-fold division was also possible by distributing the activity of these vehicles over the trinity of body, soul and spirit, a trinity accepted by the Church until AD 869 when the Eighth Ecumenical Council reduced the human being to body and soul only. By combining vehicles and functions we arrive at a seven-fold constitution, often enumerated as physical body, etheric body, life-force (prana), astral body, mind (manas), intuitive or spiritual awareness (buddhi) and spirit being or selfhood (atman).

20 The well-known translation by Lady Charlotte Guest has now been superseded by more recent ones, among them those of Geoffrey Gantz (Penguin, Harmondsworth, 1976) and Gwyn Jones and Thomas Jones (Dent, London, 1978).

21 According to Nennius, ninth-century author of a fanciful *History of the Britons*, the historical Myrddin, like Taliesin, was a courtly poet in the old British kingdom of Rheged, situated in what is now Cumberland. However, it is a young lad named Emrys (Latin: Ambrosius) whom Nennius casts in the role of Court magician, in this case serving a fourth-century chieftain called Vortigern (Gwrtheyrn). Three hundred years later, Geoffrey of Monmouth, writing his *History of the Kings of Britain*, would substitute Myrddin for Emrys and, in doing so, change his name to Merlin. The battle of Arfderydd, at which Myrddin is said to have fought before fleeing to Celyddon, may have occurred around AD 570 near Carlisle, though Nennius speaks of an actual battle of Celyddon, probably our modern Renfrewshire.

22 Some commentators have even suggested that Bulwer-Lytton, glimpsed by Mme Blavatsky on the promenade at Ramsgate, was 'the Master of my dreams' mentioned in her diary entry for that day. Madame was always to insist that the person so described was the Master Morya, on mission from his native India. (In private life he was said to be a Rajput prince.)

23 In the hierarchy of the Golden Dawn, adepts belonged to an Inner Order known as the R.R.A.C. (Ordo Roseae Rubeae et Aureae Crucis). Above this, however, was the A.A. (Astrum Argenteum) – not to be confused with Aleister Crowley's order of that name – whose members were the Secret Chiefs or Masters.

24 In Indian philosophy, liberation of this sort, achieved in one's lifetime, is known as jivanmukti, while our ultimate and eternal release is videha-mukti, with its universal equivalent called karma-mukti. The *Chandogya Upanishad*, source (6.8, 6) of the grand statement 'That, thou art' (Tat tvam asi), puts it like this (11.14, 3 and 4): 'The "I" within me is smaller than a grain of rice, smaller than a mustard seed or the kernel of a millet grain. The "I" within me is greater than the earth, greater than the sky, greater than a galaxy, greater than the universe . . . The "I" within me is one with Brahman.' For its part, the *Bhagavad-Gita* (VIII, 61) declares that God 'dwells in the heart of all beings', the jewel within the lotus (Om mani padme hum).

25 A. P. Sinnett, *The Occult World*, Theosophical Publishing Society, London, 1913, p. 15. Sometime editor of the *Pioneer*, a respected paper in nineteenth-century India, and author of an influential book called *Esoteric Buddhism*, Theosophical Publishing House, London, reprinted 1972. In this book he implies that the adepts when concerned with mundane affairs are just as fallible as the rest of us (p. 13). Sinnett was an early convert to Theosophy, as was his wife, Patience.

26 Also of their number are, of course, Koot Hoomi (said to have been Pythagoras in a previous life), Morya, Djual Kuhl, and a Greek adept named Hilarion. More details – and more Masters – can be found in Mrs Bailey's curious book, *Initiation: Human and Solar*, England/New York, Lucis, new ed. 1973. Mercifully, at fourteen I still knew nothing of the claim that the entire company of Masters assembles once a year in a remote Himalayan valley, to celebrate the festival of Wezak, night of the May full moon and anniversary of Siddartha Gautama's Enlightenment or accession to Buddhahood. Neither had I heard of the view, propagated by a group in California, that the Masters are in reality expatriate Venusians. It seems, moreover, that on the Pacific coast, mere marriage to an amanuensis of the Masters can ensure posthumous promotion to their ranks. This was the happy fate of one Mark Prophet who, after his death, was proclaimed to be the Master Lanello by his widow Elizabeth, co-founder of a Malibu-based organisation (see p. 197, n. 33), variously called the Summit Lighthouse and the Church Universal and Triumphant.

27 Annie Besant, *An Outline of Theosophical Teachings*, Theosophical Publishing House, Adyar (India), 1872, p. 325. Poor Mrs Besant was cruelly deceived when a letter from Koot Hoomi reached her after Mme Blavatsky's death, at a time when leadership of the Society was up for grabs, a letter which later turned out to be the work of W. Q. Judge, one of the would-be grabbers. Worth reading is the biography, in two volumes, by A. H. Nethercot: *The First Five Lives of Annie Besant*, Hart-Davis, London, 1960, and *The Last Four Lives of Annie Besant*, Hart-Davis, London, 1963.

Bibliography

Below are some of the books relevant to subjects dealt with in the present volume, including several referred to in the text. Many are being regularly reprinted so the year shown is not necessarily that of the most recent edition or of first publication: often, it is simply that of whatever edition I happen to possess.

The number of books available that treat occult topics is impressively high, their quality frequently less so. For that reason some discernment is required if one is to separate the good from the bad, the sound from the downright foolish. Discernment comes with experience. In the absence of experience, keep an open mind and a proper sense of the ridiculous.

I   Ancient Wisdom: Sources and Teachings (Chapters I and II)

The oldest source of the esoteric teachings described in this book is probably Hindu scripture where, as in the sacred texts of other religions, these teachings appear in their *exoteric* form. Many excellent anthologies are available to the student and can be read for spiritual as well as intellectual gain. Also relevant is the literature of Buddhism and as likewise so much of this is available in translation no specific references need be given here. Worthy of particular mention, however, are the following books, among them one or two dealing with Western philosophical development, their inclusion intended as a reminder that students of occultism should not limit themselves to oriental thought alone.

Bhagavad-Gita. In addition to Sir Edwin Arnold's poetic rendering (*The Song Celestial or Bhagavad-Gita*) which has become something of a classic, there exist many excellent translations, above all that of S. Radhakrishnan (*Bhagavadgita*, Allen & Unwin, London, 1954, and now Blackie, Bombay, 1974). A more recent translation, with commentary, of the first six chapters of the *Gita* has been made by Maharishi Mahesh Yogi and published by Penguin (*On the Bhagavad-Gita*, Harmondsworth. 1976).

DASGUPTA, S. N. *Hindu Mysticism*, M. Barnarsidass, Delhi, 1976.

ELIADE, MIRCEA. *Yoga, Immortality and Freedom*, Bollingen, Princeton, 1969.

—— *From·Primitives to Zen: a thematic source book of the history of religions*, Collins, London, 1967.

HIRIYANNA, M. *The Essentials of Indian Philosophy*, Allen & Unwin, London, 1956.

HUMPHREYS, CHRISTMAS. *Buddhism*, Penguin, Harmondsworth, 1983.

RADHAKRISHNAN, S. *Indian Philosophy*, Allen & Unwin, London, 2 vols, 1953.

—— *The Principal Upanishads*, Allen & Unwin, London, 1957.

RAHULA, WALPOLA. *What the Buddha Taught*, Gordon Fraser, London, 1978.

ROBINSON, RICHARD and JOHNSON, W. L. *The Buddhist Religion*, Dickinson, London, 1982.

RUSSELL, BERTRAND. *The History of Western Philosophy*, Allen & Unwin, London, 1969.

WILKINS, W. J. *Hindu Mythology*, Rupa & Co., Calcutta, 1982.

ZAEHNER, R. C. *Hinduism*, Oxford University Press, 1966.

—— (ed.) *The Concise Encyclopaedia of Living Faiths*, Hutchinson, London, 1977.

For a more esoteric account of the ancient wisdom, recourse may be had to the following works:

BAILEY, ALICE A. *Initiation: Human and Solar, The Consciousness of the Atom, Discipleship in the New Age, Esoteric Astrology, Treatise on Cosmic Fire*, etc., all Lucis Press, London, various reprintings. Not as readable as Mme Blavatsky (even at her most long-winded!) and more Christ-centred, Mrs Bailey needs to be read more than once before her meaning — and it often repays close attention — becomes clear. Skip the more far-fetched bits, especially those concerning the Masters.

BLAVATSKY, H. P. *The Secret Doctrine: the synthesis of science, religion and philosophy*. First published in 1888, various editions are currently available. References previously made in the text refer to the standard six-volume edition published at Adyar (India) by the Theosophical Publishing House. Other editions, including a two-volume facsimile of the first, are also available (e.g. from the Theosophical University Press in Pasadena), as is the one-volume *Abridgement of the Secret Doctrine* by E. W. Preston and C. Humphreys (Theosophical Publishing House, Adyar, 1964). A helpful study guide to the main work is G. A. Barborka's *Divine Plan* (Theosophical Publishing House, Adyar, 1961, new ed., 1980), as well as his *Peopling of the Earth* (Theosophical Publishing House, Adyar, 1975).

—— *Isis Unveiled: a Master-key to the Mysteries of Ancient and Modern Science and Theology*, first published in 1877 (J. W. Bouton, New York), now available (many reprintings) from the Theosophical Publishing House and its chief rival, the Theosophical University Press, Pasadena.

—— *Complete Writings*, Theosophical Publishing House, vols I–VII, Wheaton (Illinois); vols VIII–X, Adyar; vols XI–XIII, Wheaton (Illinois).

FORTUNE, DION. *The Cosmic Doctrine*, Aquarian Press, Wellingborough, 1976. Sparsely written and difficult (unlike the author's other works), this book needs to be read several times before it surrenders its message.

PURUCKER, G. de. *Fundamentals of the Esoteric Philosophy*, Theosophical University Press, Pasadena, 1972.

SINNETT, ALFRED PERCY. *Esoteric Buddhism*, Wizard's Bookshelf, Minneapolis, 1973.

STEINER, RUDOLF. *Occult Science: an Outline*, translated by G. and M. Adams, Rudolf Steiner Press, London, 1969.

—— *Theosophy*, Rudolf Steiner Press, London, 1973. The few books written, by Steiner suffer because of the difficulty translators have in rendering his abstruse German into English. His hundreds of lectures, the majority now printed in English, have the additional handicap of being meant for listeners, not readers. Still, his presentation is often more orderly than that of Mme Blavatsky.

—— *An Esoteric Cosmology* (eighteen lectures given in Paris in 1906), Rudolf Steiner Press, London, 1972.

—— *Fundamentals of Esotericism* (thirty-one lectures given in Berlin in 1905), Rudolf Steiner Press, London, 1983.

—— *The Apocalypse of St John* (twelve lectures given at Nuremberg in 1908), Rudolf Steiner Press, London, 1977. This book provides a good example of Steiner's restatement of the ancient wisdom in Western, Christ-centred terms. These may appeal to some readers.

—— *The Inner Realities of Evolution*, Rudolf Steiner Press, London, 1953.

—— *The Spiritual Beings in the Heavenly Bodies and in the Kingdoms of Nature*, Rudolf Steiner Publishing Co., London, 1951.

Much of the ancient wisdom is concerned with the origins and nature of the universe and humankind. To appreciate its relevance to modern scientific speculation, reference should be made to the following books, the older among them a little out-dated by now but nevertheless still worth reading. Some are sympathetic to the view that evolution, like the human being, is more than its outward appearance, others are not.

AYER, A. J. *The Problem of Knowledge*, Penguin, Harmondsworth, 1961.

BOHM, D. *Wholeness and the Implicate Order*, Routledge & Kegan Paul, London, 1980.

BONDI and others. *Rival Theories in Cosmology*, Oxford University Press, 1960.

BRAINE, LORD. *Science and Man*, Faber & Faber, London, 1966.

BROAD, C. W. *The Mind and its Place in Nature*, Routledge & Kegan Paul, London, 1962.

CAIRNS-SMITH, G. *Genetic Takeover*, Cambridge University Press, 1983.

CAMPBELL, JOSEPH (ed.). *Spirit and Nature*, vol. I of the Bollingen Series xxx (Eranos Yearbooks), Princeton University Press, 1977.

CAPRA, F. *The Tao of Physics: an exploration of the relationship between modern physics and eastern mysticism*, Fontana, London, 1976.

CHARDIN, TEILHARD de. *The Phenomenon of Man*, Harper & Row, New York, 1961.

—— *The Divine Milieu*, Harper Torchbooks, New York, 1960.

COLLINGWOOD, R. G. *The Idea of Nature*, Oxford University Press, 1945.

DAVIES, PAUL. *The Runaway Universe*, Dent, London, 1978.

ECCLES, SIR JOHN. *The Neuro-physiological Basis of Mind*, Oxford University Press, 1953.

EISLEY, LOREN. *The Unexpected Universe*, Dent, London, 1978.

HARDY, SIR ALEISTER. *The Living Stream: a restatement of evolution and its relationship to the spirit of man*, Collins, London, 1965.

—— *The Divine Flame*, Collins, London, 1966.

——, with HARVIE, R. and KOESTLER, A. *The Challenge of Chance*, Hutchinson, London, 1973.

HOYLE, FRED. *Ten Faces of the Universe*, Heinemann, London, 1977.

JEANS, SIR JAMES. *The Mysterious Universe*, Cambridge University Press, 1937.

KING, URSULA. *Towards a New Mysticism: Teilhard de Chardin and Eastern Religions*, Seabury Press, New York, 1980; Collins, London, 1980.

KNOX, RICHARD A. *Foundations of Astronomy: from Big Bang to Black Holes*, David & Charles, Newton Abbot, 1979.

KOESTLER, ARTHUR. *The Sleepwalkers*, Hutchinson, London, 1959.

LEHRS, ERNST. *Man or Matter*, Faber & Faber, London, 1958.

LOVEJOY, A. O. *The Great Chain of Being*, Harvard University Press, 1936.

NARLIKAR, J. *The Structure of the Universe*, Oxford University Press, 1977.

ORNSTEIN, ROBERT E. *The Psychology of Consciousness*, Penguin, Harmondsworth, 1975.

RYLE, GILBERT. *The Concept of Mind*, Penguin, Harmondsworth, 1964.

SAGAN, CARL. *The Dragons of Eden: Speculation on the Evolution of Human Intelligence*, Random House, New York, 1977.

SHALLIS, MICHAEL. *On Time*, Penguin, Harmondsworth, 1983.

STEINER, RUDOLF. *The Philosophy of Freedom: the Basis for a Modern World*

Conception, translated by Michael Wilson, Rudolf Steiner Press, London, 1979.

TALBOT, M. *Mysticism and the New Physics*, Routledge & Kegan Paul, London, 1981.

THORPE, W. H. *Biology and the Nature of Man*, Oxford University Press, 1960.

WACHSMUTH, GUENTHER. *The Etheric Formative Forces in Cosmos, Earth and Man*, translated by O. D. Wannamaker, Anthroposophic Publishing Co., London, 1933.

—— *Erde und Mensch* and *Die Entwicklung der Erde*, Dornach, Philosophisch-Anthroposophisch Verlag, new ed., 1965.

WATSON, LYALL. *Supernature: a Natural History of the Supernatural*, Hodder & Stoughton, London, 1973.

—— *Lifetide: a biology of the Unconscious*, Hodder & Stoughton, London, 1979.

II *Ancient World (Chapter III)*

In addition to its cosmological theory and its teachings about the origins of man, occult literature has much to say, too much at times, about the societies that pre-dated those that are known to historians. The following books, some by occultists, some not, are but a few of those relevant to the topic.

ARDREY, ROBERT. *African Genesis*, Collins, London, 1961.

BELLAMY, H. S. *The Myth of Atlantis*, Faber & Faber, London, 1948.

BERLITZ, CHARLES. *Atlantis: the eighth continent*, G. P. Putnam, New York, 1984.

BLUMRICH, J. F. *Kasskara und die Sieben Welten*, Econ Verlag, Vienna, 1979.

BRAGHINE, COL. A. *The Shadow of Atlantis*, Aquarian Press, Wellingborough, 1980.

BRAMWELL, JAMES. *Lost Atlantis*, Newcastle Publishing Co., Hollywood (U.S.A.), 1974.

CAMP, L. S. de. *Lost Continents: the Atlantis Theme in History and Literature*, Dover, New York, 1970.

CLARK, G. and PIGGOTT, S. *Prehistoric Societies*, Hutchinson, London, 1965.

DONNELLY, IGNATIUS. *Atlantis, the Antediluvian World*, Sidgwick & Jackson, London, new ed., 1970.

DOUGHERTY, C. N. *Valley of Giants: the latest discoveries in paleontology*, Cleburn (Texas), 1971.

FIDLER, J. HAVELOCK. *Ley Lines*, Turnstile Press, Wellingborough, 1983.

GALANOPOULOS, A. G. and BACON, E. *Atlantis, the Truth behind the Legend*, Nelson, London, 1969.

HEGGIE, D. *Megalithic Science*, Thames & Hudson, London, 1981.

HITCHING, FRANCIS. *Earth Magic*, Cassell, London, 1976.

KRUPP, E. C. *In Search of Lost Astronauts*, Chatto & Windus, London, 1979.

LEAKEY, RICHARD E. and LEWIN, R. *Origins*, Macdonald & Jane's, London, 1977.

LETHBRIDGE, T. C. *Gogmagog: the Buried Gods*, Routledge & Kegan Paul, London, 1957.

LISSNER, I. *The Silent Past*, Jonathan Cape, London, 1963.

LUCE, J. V. *The End of Atlantis*, Thames & Hudson, London, 1969.

MICHELL, JOHN. *View over Atlantis*, Sphere, London, 1975.

MORRIS, DESMOND. *The Naked Ape*, Jonathan Cape, London, 1967.

MUCK, OTTO. *The Secret of Atlantis*, Collins, London, 1978.

NORVILL, R. *Giants*, Aquarian Press, Wellingborough, 1979.

PURUCKER, G. de. *Man in Evolution*, Theosophical University Press, Pasadena, rev. ed., 1976.

RAMAGE, EDWIN (ed.). *Atlantis, Fact or Fiction?*, Indiana University Press, Bloomington, 1978.

RENFREW, COLIN. *Before Civilization: the Radiocarbon Revolution and Prehistoric Europe*, Jonathan Cape, London, 1973.

ROBERT, ANTHONY. *Atlantean Tradition in Ancient Britain*, Rider, London, 1977.

SCOTT-ELLIOT, W. *The Story of Atlantis and Lost Lemuria*, Theosophical Publishing House, London, 1972.

SPENCE, LEWIS. *The Problem of Atlantis*, University Books, New York, 1968.

STEINER, RUDOLF. *Cosmic Memory*. Rudolf Steiner Publications, Englewood (N.J.), 1959.

STEMMAN, ROY. *Atlantis and the Lost Lands*, Aldus, London, 1976.

THOM, ALEXANDER. *Megalithic Sites in Britain*, Oxford University Press, 1967.

—— *Megalithic Lunar Observatories*, Oxford University Press, 1971.

UNDERWOOD, GUY. *The Pattern of the Past*, Abacus, London, 1972.

VELIKOVSKY, I. *Worlds in Collision*, Victor Gollancz, London, 1950.

VITALIANO, D. R. *Legends of the Earth: their Geological Origins*, Indiana University Press, Bloomington, 1973.

WACHSMUTH, GUENTHER. *The Evolution of Mankind*, Philosophic-Anthroposophic Press, Dornach (Switzerland), 1961.

WATERS, FRANK. *Book of the Hopi*, Penguin, Harmondsworth, 1977.

WILLIAMSON, TOM and BELLAMY, LIZ. *Ley Lines in Question*, World's Work, London, 1984.

III   Esoteric Tradition (Chapter IV)

The following is a representative selection, nothing more, of books dealing with esoteric tradition or particular aspects of it. An attempt has been made to arrange the titles under various headings though a great deal of overlap is inevitable.

1 Ancient Mysteries

A welcome event in publishing has been the reappearance of papers originally issued (in German) as part of the Eranos series of yearbooks. Edited by Joseph Campbell and published in Princeton by the University Press ('Papers from the Eranos Yearbooks', Bollingen Series xxx). Volume 1 (*Spirit and Nature*) has already been mentioned. Also of special interest are: vol. 2, *The Mysteries* (1978); vol. 5, *Man and Transformation* (1979); vol. 6, *The Mystic Vision* (1980). Further reading is offered by the following books:

ALLCROFT, A. H. *The Circle and the Cross*, Macmillan, London, 1927.

BUDGE, SIR E. A. WALLIS. *The Book of the Dead*, Routledge & Kegan Paul, London, 1974.

CAMPBELL, JOSEPH. *The Masks of God: Primitive Mythology; Occidental Mythology; Oriental Mythology*, vols 1–3, Souvenir Press, London, 1973–4.

CHADWICK, HENRY. *The Early Church*, Penguin, Harmondsworth, 1967.

CHAMBERS, J. (trans.). *The Divine Pymander and Other Writings of Hermes Trismegistus*, Weiser, New York, 1975.

DODDS, E. R. *Selected Passages illustrating Neo-Platonism*, London, 1923.

—— *Proclus and the Elements of Theology*, Clarendon Press, Oxford, 1933.

—— *The Greeks and the Irrational*, University of California Press, Berkeley, 1951.

—— *Pagan and Christian in an Age of Anxiety*, Cambridge University Press, 1965.

FESTUGIÈRE, A. J. *Epicurus and his Gods*, translated by C. W. Chilton, Oxford University Press, 1955.

—— *Corpus Hermeticum*, les Belles Lettres, Paris, 1972 (vol. 1 contains 'The Pymander').

—— *La Révélation d'Hermès Trismégiste*, J. Gabalda, Paris, 4 vols, 1950–4; new ed., les Belles Lettres, Paris, 3 vols, 1983.

GORMAN, PETER. *Pythagoras: a life*, Routledge & Kegan Paul, London, 1979.

GRAVES, ROBERT. *The White Goddess*, Faber & Faber, London, 1952.

HALL, MANLY P. *An Encyclopaedic Outline of Masonic, Hermetic, Quabbalistic and Rosicrucian Symbolical Philosophy*, Philosophical Research Society, Los Angeles, 1977.

HUXLEY, ALDOUS. *The Perennial Philosophy*, Chatto & Windus, London, 1946.

IAMBLICHUS. *On the Mysteries of the Egyptians, Chaldeans and Assyrians*, translated by Thomas Taylor, Stuart & Watkins, London, 1968.

JACOBI, J. (ed.). *Paracelsus: Selected Writings*, Routledge & Kegan Paul, London, 1951.

JUNG, C. G. *The Archetypes and the Collective Unconscious*, Routledge & Kegan Paul, London, 1971.

—— *Man and his Symbols*, Aldus Books, London, 1974.

KING, C. W. *The Gnostics and their Remains*, Wizard's Bookshelf, Minneapolis, 1973.

MCINTOSH, CHRISTOPHER. *The Astrologers and their Creed, an historical outline*, Hutchinson, London, 1969.

PAGELS, E. *The Gnostic Gospels*, Weidenfeld & Nicolson, London, 1980.

PLOTINUS. *The Enneads*, translated by Stephen Mackenna, Faber & Faber, London, 1969.

PURUCKER, GOTTFRIED de. *The Esoteric Tradition*, Theosophical University Press, Pasadena, 1973.

RIST, J. M. *Plotinus*, Cambridge University Press, 1967.

SCHURÉ, EDOUARD. *The Great Initiates*, Harper & Row, San Francisco, facs. edition, 1974.

—— *From Sphinx to Christ*, Rudolf Steiner Publications, Blauvelt (N.Y.), 1970.

—— *From Sphinx to Christ*, Harper & Row, New York, 1983.

SCOTT, W. (ed.). *Hermetica*, Hermes House, Boulder (Colorado), 1981.

STEINER, RUDOLF. *Mystery Knowledge and Mystery Centres* (fourteen lectures given at Dornach in 1923), Rudolf Steiner Press, London, various printings.

—— *The Occult Movement in the 19th Century and its Relation to Modern Culture*, Rudolf Steiner Press, London, 1973.

—— *Egyptian Myths and Mysteries*, Anthroposophic Press, New York, 1971.

WILSON, COLIN. *The Occult*, Hodder & Stoughton, London, 1971.

YATES, FRANCES A. *Giordano Bruno and the Hermetic Tradition*, Routledge & Kegan Paul, London, 1966.

2 Alchemy

BURLAND, C. A. *The Art of the Alchemists*, Macmillan, London, 1967.

COCKREN, ARCHIBALD. *Alchemy Rediscovered and Restored*, Rider, London, 1940.

COLQUHOUN, I. *The Goose of Hermogenes*, Peter Owen, London, 1961.

DEACON, RICHARD. *John Dee, scientist, geographer, astrologer and secret agent to Elizabeth 1st*, Frederick Muller, London, 1968.

DOBBS, B. J. T. *The Foundations of Newton's Alchemy*, Cambridge University Press, 1975.

ELIADE, MIRCEA. *The Forge and the Crucible*, Rider, London, 1962.

FELL SMITH, CHARLOTTE. *John Dee*, Constable, London, 1909.

FRENCH, P. J. *John Dee, The World of an Elizabethan Magus*, Routledge & Kegan Paul, London, 1972.

FULCANELLI (JEAN-JULIEN CHAMPAGNE). *Les Demeures Philosophales*, Neville Spearman, Suffolk, 1971.

HOPKINS, A. J. *Alchemy, Child of Greek Philosophy*, Columbia University Press, New York, 1934.

HUTIN, SERGE. *Histoire de l'Alchimie*, Marabout, Verviers, 1971.

JOHNSON, K. R. *The Fulcanelli Phenomenon*, Neville Spearman, Jersey, 1981.

JOLLIVET-CASTELOT, F. *Comment on devient alchimiste*, Chamuel, Paris, 1897.

—— *La Science alchimique*, Chaçornac, Paris, 1904.

JUNG, C. G. 'Psychology of Transmutation', 'Spiritual Symbolism', 'Mysterium Conjunctionis', etc. in *Collected Works*, Routledge & Kegan Paul, London, 1971.

LAPIDUS. *In Pursuit of Gold*, Neville Spearman, Suffolk, 1976.

SADOUL, J. *Alchemists and Gold*, Neville Spearman, Suffolk, 1972.

TAYLOR, F. SHERWOOD. *The Alchemists: the Founding of Modern Chemistry*, Heinemann, London, 1952.

WAITE, A. E. *The Secret Tradition in Alchemy*, Rider, London, 1929.

—— *Alchemical Writings*, Stuart & Watkins, London, 1970.

—— *Alchemists Through The Ages*, Rudolf Steiner Publications, Blauvelt (N.Y.), 1970.

YATES, FRANCES A. *Occult Philosophy in the Elizabethan Age*, Routledge & Kegan Paul, London, 1979.

3 Kabbalah

BUTLER, W. E. *Magic and the Quabbalah*, Aquarian Press, London, 1968.

FORTUNE, DION. *The Mystical Qabalah*, Ernest Benn, London, 1979.

GRIMBERG, M. *Lumière du Zohar*, Maisonneuve, Paris, 1973.

KNIGHT, GARETH. *A Practical Guide to Occult Symbolism*, Helios, Toddington, 1964.

LÉVI, ELIPHAS. *Mysteries of the Kabbalah*, Aquarian Press, Wellingborough, 1981.

MATHERS, S. L. *The Kabbalah Unveiled*, Routledge & Kegan Paul, London, 1981.

PAPUS. *The Quabalah*, Thorsons, Wellingborough, 1977.

REGARDIE, ISRAEL. *The Tree of Life*, Aquarian Press, Wellingborough, 1975.

SCHOLEM, GERSHON G. *Kabbalah*, Keter, Jerusalem, 1974.

—— *Major Trends in Jewish Mysticism*, Schocken Books, New York, 1954.

WAITE, A. E. *The Holy Kabbalah*, University Books, New York, n.d.

4 Rosicrucianism

ALLEN, P. M. (ed.). *A Christian Rosenkreutz Anthology*, Rudolf Steiner Publications, Blàuvelt (N.Y.), 1968.

ARNOLD, PAUL. *Histoire des Rose-Croix et les Origines de la Francmaçonnerie*, Mercure de France, Paris, 1955.

HEINDEL, MAX. *Rosicrucian Philosophy in Questions and Answers*, L. N. Fowler, London, 1910.

—— *The Rosicrucian Cosmo-Conception*, L. N. Fowler, London, 1937.

JENNINGS, H. *The Rosicrucians*, Chatto & Windus, London, 1879.

MCINTOSH, CHRISTOPHER. *The Rosy Cross Unveiled*, Aquarian Press, Wellingborough, 1980.

STEINER, RUDOLF. *Rosicrucian Esotericism*, The Anthroposophic Press, Spring Valley (N.Y.), 1978.

—— *Rosicrucian and Modern Initiation*, Rudolf Steiner Press, London, 1965.

WAITE, A. E. *The Brotherhood of the Rosy Cross*, Rider, London, 1924; University Books, New Jersey, 1973.

YATES, FRANCES A. *The Rosicrucian Enlightenment*, Routledge & Kegan Paul, London, 1972.

YEATS, W. B. *The Real History of the Rosicrucians*, Rider, London, 1924; Rudolf Steiner Publications, Blauvelt (N.Y.), 1970.

5 Magic

ALLIETTE, JEAN-FRANÇOIS. *Etteilla ou manière de se créer avec un jeu de cartes*, Lesclupart, Paris, 1770.

BARRETT, FRANCIS. *The Magus or Celestial Intelligencer*, Lockington, Allen and Co., London, 1801.

BILLY, ANDRÉ. *Stanislas de Guaita*, Mercure de France, Paris, 1971.

BUDGE, SIR E. A. WALLIS. *Egyptian Magic*, Routledge & Kegan Paul, London, 1975.

BUTLER, W. E. *Magic: its Power, Ritual and Purpose*, Aquarian Press, London, 1961.

—— *The Magician: his Training and Work*, Aquarian Press, London, 1963.

—— *Apprenticed to Magic*, Aquarian Press, London, 1965.

CAMWELL, CHARLES. *Aleister Crowley*, University Books, New York, 1962.

CAVENDISH, RICHARD. *The Black Arts*, Routledge & Kegan Paul, London, 1967.

CHACORNAC, PAUL. *Eliphas Lévi, rénovateur de l'occultisme en France*, Chacornac, Paris, 1926.

—— *Le Comte de Saint-Germain*, Chacornac, Paris, 1947.

CONWAY, DAVID. *Magic: An Occult Primer*, Jonathan Cape, London, 1972.

CROWLEY, ALEISTER. *Magick in Theory and Practice*, Routledge & Kegan Paul, London, 1973.

—— *Confessions*, ed. J. Symonds and K. Grant, Jonathan Cape, London, 1969.

—— *The Book of Thoth*, Weiser, New York, 1969.

—— *Magick without Tears*, ed. I. Regardie, Llewellyn, St Paul (Minnesota), 1973.

CROWTHER, ARNOLD and PATRICIA. *The Witches Speak*, Weiser, New York, 1976.

DAVID-NEEL, ALEXANDRA. *With Mystics and Magicians in Tibet*, Penguin, London, 1936; reissued as *Magic and Mystery in Tibet*, Souvenir Press, London, 1967.

ELIADE, MIRCEA. *Shamanism*, Routledge & Kegan Paul, London, 1964.

ENCAUSSE, DR PHILIPPE. *Sciences Occultes ou vingt-cinq années d'occultisme occidental: Papus sa vie, son oeuvre*, Editions Ocia, Paris, 1949.

FORTUNE, DION. *Applied Magic*, Aquarian Press, London, 1962 (now Wellingborough and often reprinted).

—— *Psychic Self-Defence: a study in occult pathology and criminality*, Aquarian Press, London, 1963.

—— *Sane Occultism*, Aquarian Press, London, 1972.

—— *The Training and Work of an Initiate*, Aquarian Press, London, 1978.

—— *Esoteric Orders and their Work*, Aquarian Press, Wellingborough, 1982.

GARDNER, GERALD. *Modern Witchcraft*, Rider, London, 1954.

—— *Witchcraft Today*, Rider, London, 1957.

GILBERT, R. A. *The Golden Dawn, Twilight of the Magicians*, Aquarian Press, Wellingborough, 1981.

GRANT, KENNETH. *The Magical Revival*, Muller, London, 1972.

GUAITA, STANISLAS de. *Le Temple de Satan*, Librairie du Merveilleux, Paris, n.d.

—— *La Clef de la Magie noire*, Georges Carré, Paris, 1897.

HOWE, ELLIC. *The Magicians of the Golden Dawn: a documentary history of a magical order*, Routledge & Kegan Paul, London, 1973.

KING, FRANCIS. *Ritual Magic in England*, Neville Spearman, Suffolk, 1970.

LELAND, CHARLES. *Aradia or the Gospel of the Witches*, London, 1899.

LÉVI, ELIPHAS. *Transcendental Magic*, translated A. E. Waite, Rider, London, 1968.

—— *The Key to the Mysteries*, Rider, London, 1969.

—— *The History of Magic*, Rider, London, 1969.

MCINTOSH, CHRISTOPHER. *Eliphas Lévi and the French Magical Revival*, Weiser, New York, 1974.

MACKENZIE, KENNETH. *The Royal Masonic Cyclopaedia*, Hogg, London, 1877.

MATHERS, S. L. (ed.). *The Key of Solomon the King*, Routledge & Kegan Paul, London, 1972.

MURRAY, MARGARET. *The Witch Cult in Western Europe*, Clarendon Press, Oxford, 1921.

—— *The God of the Witches*, Sampson Low, London, 1931; reissued by Faber & Faber, London, 1952.

PAPUS. *Le Tarot des Bohémiens*, Georges Carré, Paris, 1889; a translation, *The Tarot of the Bohemians*, was published by the Wilshire Book Co., Hollywood (California), 1978.

—— *Traité méthodique de science occulte*, Georges Carré, Paris, 1891.

—— *La Science des Mages*, Chamuel, Paris, 1892.

—— *Traité méthodique de magie pratique*, Georges Carré, Paris, 1893.

—— *Qu'est-ce que l'occultisme*, Lemayrie, Paris, 1929.

REGARDIE, ISRAEL. *The Golden Dawn: an encyclopedia of practical occultism*, Llewellyn Press, St Paul (Minnesota), 1970.

—— *A Garden of Pomegranates*, Llewellyn, St Paul (Minnesota), 1978.

SAINT-GERMAIN, COMTE de. *The Most Holy Trinosophia*, Philosophical Research Society, Los Angeles, 1963.

SYMONDS, JOHN. *The Great Beast*, Frederick Muller, London, 1951.

—— *The Magic of Aleister Crowley*, Frederick Muller, London, 1958.

THOMAS, KEITH. *Religion and the Decline of Magic*, Weidenfeld & Nicolson, London, 1971.

TORRENS, R. *The Secret Rituals of the Golden Dawn*, Aquarian Press, Wellingborough, 1972.

TROWBRIDGE, W. K. H. *Cagliostro, the Splendour and Misery of a Master of Magic*, Chapman & Hall, London, 1910.

VAN RIJKENBERK. *Martines de Pasqually, sa vie, son oeuvre, son ordre*, Félix Alcan, Paris, 1935.

WILSON, COLIN. *The Occult*, Hodder & Stoughton, London, 1971.

—— *Mysteries*, Hodder & Stoughton, London, 1978.

WIRTH, OSWALD. *Stanislas de Guaita, Souvenirs de son Secrétaire*, Editions du Symbolisme, Paris, 1935.

YATES, FRANCES A. *Giordano Bruno and the Hermetic Tradition*, Routledge & Kegan Paul, London, 1964.

6 Theosophy

ANON. *The Theosophical Movement, 1875–1950*, The Cunningham Press, Los Angeles, 1951.

BAILEY, ALICE A. *The Externalisation of the Hierarchy*, Lucis Press, London, 1975. For Mrs Bailey's relations with Theosophy, see page 197, n. 33.

—— *The Unfinished Autobiography*, Lucis Publishing Co., New York, 1959.

BAIRD, ALEXANDER T. *Richard Hodgson, the story of a Psychical Researcher*, Psychic Press, London, 1949.

BARBORKA, GEOFFREY A. *H. P. Blavatsky, Tibet and Tulku*, Theosophical Publishing House, Adyar (India), 1966.

—— *The Mahatmas and their letters*, Theosophical Publishing House, Wheaton (Illinois), 1973.

BESANT, ANNIE. *Annie Besant, an Autobiography*, Althemus, Philadelphia, 1893.

BLAVATSKY, H. P. *The Key to Theosophy*, Theosophical University Press, Pasadena, 1972.

—— *Theosophical Glossary*, ed. G. R. S. Mead, Theosophical Publishing House, London, 1982.

CAMPBELL, BRUCE F. *Ancient Wisdom Revived: A History of the Theosophical Movement*, University of California Press, Berkeley, 1980.

EEK, SVEN and de ZIRKOFF, BORIS (eds). *William Quan Judge*, Theosophical Publishing House, Wheaton (Illinois), 1971.

HANSEN, VIRGINIA (ed.). *H. P. Blavatsky ana the Secret Doctrine: commentaries on her Contribution to World Thought*, Theosophical Publishing House, Wheaton (Illinois), 1971.

HODGSON, RICHARD. 'Report of the Committee appointed to Investigate Phenomena connected with the Theosophical Society', *Proceedings*, Society for Psychical Research, London, 1885. This is the notorious report which Mme Blavatsky insisted Annie Besant should read before deciding whether to join the Theosophists. The controversy over it has been revived more recently by one of Mme Blavatsky's defenders, Adlai E. Waterman, in his *Obituary: the 'Hodgson Report' on Mme Blavatsky*, Theosophical Publishing House, Adyar (India), 1963, and by Robert Thouless' review of the book in the *Journal* of the Society for Psychical Research, No. 44 (Sept. 1968), pp. 341–9.

JINARĀJADĀSA, C. *Did Mme Blavatsky Forge the Mahatma Letters?*, Theosophical Publishing House, Adyar (India), 1935.

—— *Letters from the Masters of Wisdom*, Theosophical Publishing House, Adyar (India), 1948.

JUDGE, W. Q. *The Ocean of Theosophy*, The Theosophical Co., Los Angeles, . 1937.

LINTON, GEORGE E. *Readers' Guide to the Mahatma Letters*, Theosophical Publishing House, Wheaton (Illinois), 1972.

MASKELYNE, J. N. *The Fraud of Modern 'Theosophy' Exposed*, G. Routledge & Sons, London, 1913.

MEADE, MARION. *Mme Blavatsky, the Woman Behind the Myth*, Putnam, New York, 1980.

MURPHET, HOWARD. *Hammer on the Mountain: a life of Henry Steel Olcott (1832–1907)*, Theosophical Publishing House, Wheaton (Illinois), 1972.

—— *When Daylight Comes; a Biography of Helena Petrovna Blavatsky*, Theosophical Publishing House, Wheaton (Illinois), 1975.

NETHERCOT, ARTHUR H. *The First Five Lives of Annie Besant*, Hart-Davis, London, 1960.

—— *The Last Four Lives of Annie Besant*, Hart-Davis, London, 1963.

OLCOTT, H. S. *Old Diary Leaves; the History of the Theosophical Society*, Theosophical Publishing House, Adyar (India), 6 vols, 1972–5.

RUDHYAR, DANE. *Occult Preparations for a New Age*, Theosophical Publishing House, Wheaton (Illinois), 1975.

RYAN, CHARLES J. *H. P. Blavatsky and the Theosophical Movement*, Theosophical University Press, Point Loma (Calif.), 1937.

SINNETT, A. P. *The Occult World*, Theosophical Publishing Society, London, 1913.

SOLOVYOFF, V. S. *A Modern Priestess of Isis*, Longman, Green & Co., London, 1895.

SYMONDS, JOHN. *Mme Blavatsky, Medium and Magician*, Odhams, London, 1950.

WACHTMEISTER, COUNTESS. *Reminiscences of H. P. Blavatsky and The Secret Doctrine*, Theosophical Publishing House, Wheaton (Illinois), 1976.

WITTE, S. Y. de. *The Memories of Count Witte*, Heinemann, London, 1921; new ed., Fertig, New York, 1967.

ZIRKOFF, BORIS de. *Rebirth of the Occult Tradition*, Theosophical Publishing House, Wheaton (Illinois), 1977.

7 Anthroposophy

AHERN, GEOFFREY. *The Sun at Midnight: Rudolf Steiner and the Western Esoteric Tradition*, Aquarian Press, Wellingborough, 1984.

EASTON, STEWART C. *Man and World in the Light of Anthroposophy*, The Anthroposophic Press, Spring Valley (N.Y.), 1975.

—— *Rudolf Steiner, Herald of a New Epoch*, the Anthroposophic Press, Spring Valley (N.Y.), 1980.

HARWOOD, CECIL (ed.). *The Faithful Thinker*, Hodder & Stoughton, London, 1961.

LIEBSTOECKL, HANS. *The Secret Sciences*, Rider, London, 1939.

NESFIELD-COOKSON, BERNARD. *Rudolf Steiner's Vision of Love*, Aquarian Press, Wellingborough, 1983.

RIHOUËT-CROZE, S. *Qui était Rudolf Steiner: une épopée du 20e siècle*, Triades, Paris, 1973.

RITTELMAYER, F. W. *Rudolf Steiner Enters My Life*, Christian Community Press, London, 1963.

SHEPHERD, A. P. *A Scientist of the Invisible*, Hodder & Stoughton, London, 1954.

STEINER, RUDOLF. *An Autobiography*, translated by Rita Stebbing, Rudolf Steiner Publications, Blauvelt (N.Y.), 1977.

—— *Anthroposophical Leading Thoughts*, Rudolf Steiner Press, London, 1973.

WACHSMUTH, GUENTHER. *The Life and Work of Rudolf Steiner from the Turn of the Century to his Death*, Whittier Books, New York, 1955.

WEHR, G. *Rudolf Steiner*, Aurum Verlag, Freiburg, 1982 (in German).

IV   *Occultism in Practice (Chapters V, VI and VII)*

ADAMS, G. *Physical and Etheric Spaces*, Rudolf Steiner Press, London, 1976.

ADAMS, G. and WHICHER, O. *The Plant Between Sun and Earth*, Rudolf Steiner Press, London, 1976.

ALLENDY, R. *Le Symbolisme des Nombres*, Chacornac, Paris, 1932.

AVALON, ARTHUR. *The Serpent Power*, Ganesh & Co., Madras, 1918.

BAILEY, ALICE A. *Light of the Soul*, Lucis Publishing Co., New York, 1965 (a translation of the *Yoga Sutras* of Patanjali).

BARRETT, SIR WILLIAM. *Deathbed Visions*, Methuen, London, 1926.

BEGG, PAUL. *Into Thin Air: People who Disappear*, David & Charles, Newton Abbot, 1979.

BLAVATSKY, H. P. *The Voice of the Silence, being chosen Fragments from the Book of Golden Precepts*, Theosophical University Press, Pasadena, 1971.

BOTT, VICTOR. *Anthroposophical Medicine*, Rudolf Steiner Press, London, 1971.

BROAD, C. D. *Religion, Philosophy and Psychical Research*, Routledge & Kegan Paul, London, 1953.

BRUNTON, PAUL. *The Hidden Teaching Behind Yoga*, Rider, London, 1969.

BUDGE, SIR E. A. WALLIS *The Egyptian Book of the Dead*, Routledge & Kegan Paul, London, 1969.

BULWER-LYTTON, E. G. E. L. *Zanoni*, Rudolf Steiner Press, London, 1971.

COLLINS, MABEL. *Light on the Path*, Theosophical Publishing House, London, and Theosophical University Press, Pasadena, many reprints.

CONWAY, DAVID. *The Magic of Herbs*, Jonathan Cape, London, 1972.

CROOKALL, R. *Out-of-the-body Experiences*, University Books, New York, 1970.

—— *The Techniques of Astral Projection*, Aquarian Press, London, 1964.

—— *More Astral Projections*, Aquarian Press, London, 1964.

EVANS-WENTZ, W. Y. *The Tibetan Book of the Dead*, Oxford University Press, 1960.

FLOURNOY, THÉODORE. *From India to the Planet Mars: a Study of A Case of Somnambulism with Glossolalia*, University Books, New Hyde Park (N.Y.), 1963.

GAUQUELIN, M. *Astrology and Science*, Peter Davies, London, 1969.

GRANT, JOAN. *The Winged Pharaoh*, Sphere, London, 1981.

—— *Lord of the Horizon*, Corgi, London, 1976.

GRANT, JOHN (ed.). *The Book of Time*, Westbridge, Newton Abbot, 1980.

GREEN, C. E. *Lucid Dreams*, Institute of Psychophysical Research, Oxford, 1968.

—— *Out of the Body Experiences*, Institute of Psychophysical Research, Oxford, 1968.

HALL, TREVOR H. *New Light on Old Ghosts*, Duckworth, London, 1965.

HARGRAVE, J. *The Life and Soul of Paracelsus*, Victor Gollancz, London, 1951.

HEAD, JOSEPH and CRANSTON, S. L. (ed.). *Reincarnation in World Thought*, Julian Press, New York, 1967.

HEYWOOD, ROSALIND. *The Infinite Hive*, Chatto & Windus, London, 1963.

HODSON, G. *Devas and Men*, Theosophical Publishing House, Adyar (India), 1972.

HUMPHREYS, CHRISTMAS. *Concentration and Meditation*, Watkins, London, 1953.

IYENGAR, B. K. S. *Light on Yoga*, Allen & Unwin, London, 1982.

JUNG, C. G. *Psychology and the Occult*, Princeton University Press, 1977.

KANDINSKY, W. *Concerning the Spiritual in Art*, Wittenborn, New York, 1947.

KOEPF, PETTERSON and SCHAUMANN. *Bio-dynamic Agriculture*, Anthroposophic Press, Spring Valley (N.Y.), 1976.

KOESTLER, ARTHUR. *The Roots of Coincidence*, Hutchinson, London, 1972.

LEADBEATER, C. W. *The Chakras*, Theosophical Publishing House, Wheaton (Illinois), often reprinted.

LODGE, SIR OLIVER. *Raymond or Life after Death*, Methuen, London, 1916.

MOODY, RAYMOND A., JR. *Life after Life: the investigation of a phenomenon: the survival of bodily death*, Bantam, New York, 1975.

—— *Reflections on Life after Life*, Bantam, New York, 1978.

MULDOON, S. and CARRINGTON, W. *The Phenomenon of Astral Projection*, Rider, London, 1969.

—— *The Projection of the Astral Body*, Rider, London, 1969.

NICHOLSON, R. A. *Studies in Islamic Mysticism*, Cambridge University Press, 1921.

NYANAPONIKA THERA. *The Heart of Buddhist Meditation*, Rider, London, 1969.

OSIS, KARLIS. *Deathbed Observations*, Parapsychology Foundation, New York, 1961.

PAPUS. *La Science des Nombres*, Chacornac, Paris, 1934.

PEARSALL, RONALD. *The Table Rappers*, Michael Joseph, London, 1972.

POWELL, A. E. *The Astral Body*, Theosophical Publishing House, London, 1926.

PRICE, H. H. 'Parapsychology and Human Nature', *Journal of Parapsychology*, vol. XXIII (1959), pp. 180–95.

—— 'Survival and the Idea of Another World', *Proceedings*, Society for Psychical Research (1953), pp. 3–25.

PRIESTLEY, J. B. *Man and Time*, Aldus/Allen, London, 1964.

SCHILLER, PAUL EUGEN. *Rudolf Steiner and Initiation*, Anthroposophic Press, Spring Valley (N.Y.), 1981.

SMYTHIES, J.-B. (ed.). *Science and ESP*, Routledge & Kegan Paul, London, 1967.

STEINER, RUDOLF. *Spiritual Science and Medicine*, Rudolf Steiner Publishing Co., London, 1948.

—— *Life Between Death and Rebirth*, Anthroposophic Press, New York, 1968.

—— *The Social Future*, Anthroposophic Press, New York, 1973.

—— *Eurythmy as Visible Speech*, Rudolf Steiner Press, London, 1977.

—— *Knowledge of Higher Worlds and its Attainment*, Anthroposophic Press, Spring Valley (N.Y.), 1977. .

—— *Evolution of Conciousness*, Rudolf Steiner Press, London, 1979.

VITHOULKAS, GEORGE. *The Science of Homoeopathy*, Grove Press, New York, 1980.

WACHSMUTH, GUENTHER. *Reincarnation*, translated by O. Wannamaker, Philosophic-Anthroposophic Press, Dornach, new ed., no date.

WEEKS, NORAH. *The Medical Discoveries of Dr Edward Bach, Physician*, C. W. Daniel, Rochester, 1940.

WHICHER, O. *Projective Geometry*, Anthroposophic Press, London, 1971.

WILMAR, FRITS. *Vorgeburtliche Menschenentwicklung*, Mellinger Verlag, Stuttgart, 1979.

WILSON, COLIN. *The Occult*, Hodder & Stoughton, London, 1971.

—— *Enigmas and Mysteries*, Aldus, London, 1976.

—— (ed.). *Men of Mystery*, Star Books, London, 1977.

—— *Mysteries*, Hodder & Stoughton, London, 1978.

WILSON, IAN. *Mind Out Of Time*, Victor Gollancz, London, 1981.

WOLFF, OTTO. *Anthroposophically orientated Medicine and its Remedies*, Weleda, Arlesheim, 1977.

Among the books already listed on this and previous pages are many that are hostile to occultism. They are included — and wholeheartedly recommended — because no occultist worth his salt can afford to overlook the opposition's case. And, as the few remaining books below make plain, salt is what every esoteric student needs — not only by the pinch but often by the handful!

EVANS, BERGEN. *The Natural History of Nonsense*, Michael Joseph, London, 1947.

EVANS, CHRISTOPHER. *Cults of Unreason*, Harrap, London, 1975.

GARDNER, MARTIN. *Fads and Fallacies in the Name of Science*, Dover, New York, 1957; now expanded and reissued as *Science, Good, Bad and Bogus*, Oxford University Press, 1983.

GRANT, JOHN. *A Directory of Discarded Ideas*, Corgi, London, 1983.

SLADEK, JOHN. *The New Apocrypha: a Guide to Strange Sciences and Occult Beliefs*, Hart-Davis, McGibbon, St Albans, 1974.

Index and Glossary